Marita Rainsborough
Foucault Today

Philosophy

Marita Rainsborough teaches as an associate professor (PD) at the Institute for Philosophy and Art History at Leuphana Universität Lüneburg and at the Institute for Romance Studies at Christian-Albrechts-Universität zu Kiel. She is also an associate member of the Centre for Philosophy of the University of Lisbon (CFUL) and co-editor of the journal 'Estudos Kantianos'. She was visiting professor at several universities in Brazil, for example at the Federal University of Minas Gerais (UFMG), the Federal University of Bahia (UFBA) and the University of Campinas (UNICAMP).

Marita Rainsborough

Foucault Today

New Perspectives in Philosophy and Cultural Studies

Translated from German by Alison Fry and Dominic Rainsborough

Bibliographic information published by the Deutsche Nationalbibliothek

The Deutsche Nationalbibliothek lists this publication in the Deutsche Nationalbibliografie; detailed bibliographic data are available in the Internet at https://dnb.dnb.de

2025 © transcript Verlag, Bielefeld

Hermannstraße 26 | D-33602 Bielefeld | live@transcript-verlag.de

Cover design: Kordula Röckenhaus

https://doi.org/10.14361/9783839476246
Print-ISBN: 978-3-8376-7624-2 | PDF-ISBN: 978-3-8394-7624-6
ISSN of series: 2702-900X | eISSN of series: 2702-9018

Contents

1. Introduction

1.1   On the topicality of Foucault's philosophical concept

Revisiting Foucault makes it possible, on the one hand, to review Foucault's philosophy as a whole, to shed light on the roots of his philosophising and to highlight the focal points of his thinking, and, on the other hand, to examine the contemporary relevance of his theorems in new directions of thought. Is Foucault outdated[1] and should his work be considered as being among the philosophical classics which only have historical significance and no longer contribute to the current dialogue in the humanities and socio-political analysis? Foucault's ambition has always been to use his archaeological and genealogical procedures as well as the analysis of the topics he selected to play a part in detaching humans from existing structures of knowledge and power as well as to change humans and society. His philosophy must be understood as a real life-oriented theory with political implications. Can his emancipatory impetus of an experimental critique still be maintained in this form today or do we need new types of critical-emancipatory thought and action in the global context amidst emerging social challenges, such as those demanded by the new realism?[2] What is the significance of his conclusions in the 21st century? The objec-

---

1   This thesis is particularly represented by Barad's new materialism, *Agential Realism*, in which she combines constructivism and realism, a form of new materialist ontology. Cf. Barad, Karen: *Meeting the Universe Halfway: Quantum Physics and the Entanglement of Matter and Meaning*. Durham, London (Duke University Press), 2007. Although she refers to Foucault, she considers him outdated, especially with regard to his 'ideational' constructivism and his concepts of biopower and biopolitics. Postcolonial and decolonial theorists such as Mbembe, Bhabha and Mignolo accuse Foucault of Eurocentrism and vehemently criticise his theory of power. They also consider him outdated. See Section 2.3 of this book in this regard.

2   For example, Bruno Latour – who criticizes Foucault's constructivism – calls for a new form of critique. Cf. Latour, Bruno: "Why Has Critique Run Out of Steam? From Matters

tive of this book, which incorporates all elements of his philosophy, is to provide a comprehensive analysis of his thinking, in particular on the basis of his
Kantian influences and with reference to Bloch, which are often not sufficiently
taken into account or emphasised in the reception of Foucault but are of particular relevance with regard to the assessment of his socio-political significance
today. This should, in particular, lead to a better understanding of the surprising emphasis on the role of the subject in Foucault's concept of emancipation
with its theorems of critique and freedom and his interest in the phenomena of
hope and the future. This book focuses on the emancipatory moments of Foucault's philosophy, which revolve around concepts such as freedom, autonomy
and critique. In this context, there is a lack of studies on Foucault's reception of
Kant, which is particularly significant with regard to the critique of knowledge
and the topicality of philosophy and its social relevance, and which also require
the joint understanding of critique[3] and parrhesia as a form of critique and/or,
conversely, of critique as a variant of parrhesia and its critical rethinking.[4]

The question of topicality thus arises in two respects – as topicality in and
of Foucault's philosophy. In this context, we encounter topicality in the sense
of Foucault's interpretation of Kant as the claim of philosophy to be able to do
justice to contemporary society in analytical terms and to be relevant for it – as
'ontology of the present', 'ontology of present reality', 'ontology of modernity'
and 'ontology of ourselves',[5] which has been elaborated in *Kritik und Geschichte –
Foucault ein Erbe Kants?* by Andrea Hemminger, the most important work to date

---

of Fact to Matters of Concern Application". In: *Critical Inquiry – Special issue on the Future
of Critique*, 30(2), 2004, pp. 225–248. Latour provides a "somewhat dismal portrayal of
the critical landscape" and states "The Zeus of Critique rules absolutely, to be sure, but
over a desert." (Latour 2004: 239, 241) He wants to alter this destructive critique, writing "[T]his return to the realist attitude, that I'd like to offer as the next task for the
critically minded." (Latour 2004: 232) He continues "Can we devise another powerful
descriptive tool that deals this time with matters of concern and whose import then
will no longer be to debunk but to protect and to care [...]?" (Latour 2003: 232) Further
he states "The critic is not the one who debunks, but the one who assembles." (Latour
2004: 246) Latour argues that this form of criticism must be developed.

3   Cf. Foucault, Michel: *The Government of Self and Others. Lectures at the Collège de France
1982–1983*. Burchell, Graham; Davidson, Arnold (Eds.), London (Palgrave Macmillan),
2010a, p. 20.

4   In recent years research has shifted regarding the approach to these topics, particularly due to the publication of Foucault's lectures. Cf. Gehring, Petra; Gelhard, Andreas
(Eds.): *Parrhesia: Foucault und der Mut zur Wahrheit*. Zürich (diaphanes), 2012.

5   Cf. Foucault 2010a: 21.

on the relationship between Foucault and Kant.[6] Foucault assumes the position of a diagnostician and an "anatomist who performs an autopsy".[7] Foucault also describes this as a hunt for the blind spot

> "Also, to try to surround, to draw, to point out that blind spot through which we speak and see, to grasp what makes it possible for us to see into the distance, to define the proximity around us that orients the general field of our gaze and our knowledge. To grasp that invisibility, that invisible of the too visible, that distancing of what is too close, that unknown familiarity is for me the important operation of my language and my speech."[8]

The more recent works on Foucault's reception of Kant, for example by Jens Kertscher[9] and Markus Gabriel,[10] following the complete publication of Foucault's lectures, emphasise the relationship between critique and parrhesia, thus bridging Foucault's epistemological aspects and his ethics which employ technologies of self-formation. This book aims to contribute to this discussion. In addition, it will analyse critical examinations of Foucault in contemporary philosophy, for example by Judith Butler and Byung-Chul Han, and in the post-colonial and decolonial theories of Achille Mbembe, Homi K. Bhabha, and Walter Mignolo. These authors and their works serve as selected examples of the

---

6   Hemminger, Andrea: *Kritik und Geschichte – Foucault ein Erbe Kants?* Berlin (Philo Verlagsgesellschaft), 2003. As another example of an appreciation of Foucault's Kant reception in literature, refer to Raffnsøe, Sverre; Gudmand-Høyer, Marius; Thaning, Morten S.: *Foucault: Studienhandbuch.* Munich (Fink), 2011.

7   Foucault, Michel: *Speech Begins after Death. In Conversation with Claude Bonnefoy.* Artières, Philippe (Ed.), Minneapolis, London (University of Minnesota Press), 2013, p. 40. Foucault says "I'm neither one nor the other, I'm a doctor, let's say I'm a diagnostician. I want to make a diagnosis and my work consists in revealing, through the incision of writing, something that might be the truth of what is dead." (Foucault 2013: 45) Foucault considers this a similarity to Nietzsche "For Nietzsche, philosophy was above all else a diagnosis, it had to do with man to the extent that he was sick. For him, it was both a diagnosis and a kind of violent therapy for the diseases of culture." (Foucault 2013: 47)

8   Foucault 2013: 71.

9   Kertscher, Jens: "Vorurteilslosigkeit oder Wahrhaftigkeit: Kant und Foucault über Aufklärung". In: Gehring, Petra; Gelhard, Andreas (Eds.): *Parrhesia: Foucault und der Mut zur Wahrheit.* Zürich (diaphanes), 2012, pp. 143–159.

10   Gabriel, Markus: "Analytik der Wahrheit und Ontologie der Gegenwart? Der späte Foucault über Freiheit, Wahrheit und Kontingenz". In: Gehring, Petra; Gelhard, Andreas (Eds.): *Parrhesia: Foucault und der Mut zur Wahrheit.* Zürich (diaphanes), 2012, pp. 33–47.

current critical reception of Foucault's work in this theoretical area. Apart from a rejection of Foucault, it often also entails a continuation of his theorems. This book focuses on the subject between knowledge, power, ethics and aesthetics in history and politics – and thus the subject between autonomy and heteronomy. In addition to his interest in what has become historical and providing a diagnosis of what is current, in particular as a result of the historicising process, Foucault has a strong interest in shaping human future. A particular focus of the afore-mentioned critical analysis is on investigating feasibility as a dimension of Foucault's work.

The starting point of Foucault's philosophising is his investigation of the heteronomous moments of the subject constitution in knowledge and power complexes. He is primarily concerned with analysing knowledge-structuring epistemes or rules of discourses in discourse formations and their power-theoretical implications for individual areas of the synchronous and diachronic dimensions. The analyses of *Madness and Civilization; Mental Illness and Psychology; The Birth of the Clinic; Discipline and Punish; I, Pierre Riviere, Having Slaughtered my Mother, my Sister and my Brother* and *Herculine Barbin*, among others, reveal that Foucault has a general interest in discourse-analytical questions related to shifts in power.[11] He carries out a concrete archaeological and genealogical analysis of various subject orders in order to rethink philosophy and test its suitability as a concrete project of social analysis and critique – including a temporary provocative rejection of philosophy. The new mode of work originates from Foucault's underlying interest in a social analysis which is closely related to individual phenomena which determine the formation of subjects and potentially reveal possibilities for change. From the outset, his work has shown a clear predisposition to examine the subject's possibilities to break out of existing constraints, to change prevailing formations and to confront these

---

11   Cf. Foucault, Michel: *Mental Illness and Psychology*. Dreyfus, Hubert L.; Sheridan, Alan (Eds.), Berkeley (University of California Press), 1987b; Foucault, Michel: *Madness and Civilization. A History of Insanity in the Age of Reason*. New York, Toronto (Vintage Books), 1988b; Foucault, Michel: *I, Pierre Riviére, Having Slaughtered my Mother, my Sister, and my Brother: A Case of Parricide in the 19th Century*. Lincoln (University of Nebraska Press), 1982; Foucault, Michel: *Death and the Labyrinth. The World of Raymond Roussel*. London, New York (Continuum), 2004; Foucault, Michel: *Discipline and Punish: the Birth of the Prison*. New York (Vintage Books), 1995; Foucault, Michel: *Herculine Barbin. Being the Recently Discovered Memoirs of a Nineteenth Century French Hermaphrodite*. New York (Vintage Books), 2010b; Foucault, Michel: *The Birth of the Clinic. An Archaeology of Medical Perception*. London, New York (Routledge), 2003b.

problem complexes. Foucault's preoccupation with the topics of madness and literature indicates his need for other forms of thinking and feeling, and the experiences of corporeality in the sense of a 'counter-discourse' and transgression. His so-called *subject-theoretical turn* is located precisely in this context as a continued processing of a problem complex, for which he has not yet found a satisfactory theoretical solution, by means of specification, expansion and/or displacement. In addition, he is also concerned with clarifying the references and connections between the separate areas of his philosophy. The social change which Foucault anticipates and the associated alteration of individual ways of life are inconceivable without the active assistance of the individual. Consequently, this topic becomes an increasing focal point of his thinking, as also reflected in Foucault's interest in the topics of resistance and revolution. Baudrillard wrote an early farewell to Foucault's philosophy in *Oublier Foucault* (1977).[12] However, it is generally evident that Foucault's thinking can only be described as being highly successful. Around the world disciplines as diverse as economics, disability studies, security studies, criminal science, literary studies, psychology, sociology and political science, to name but a few, reference Foucault's work. This connection is still evident today, with Foucault continuing to be regarded as one of the most important sources of inspiration for the humanities and social sciences. However, there is also a growing number of critical voices which consider Foucault's thinking to be of only limited use and possibly even outdated. Postcolonial and decolonial theories, for example, accuse Foucault of having a Eurocentric viewpoint, while the main focus of criticism in new realism theories is his constructivism. He also comes in for criticism in the power theory of Byung-Chul Han, which is primarily based on Hegel's ideas. The political/governmental and power-theoretical focus of Foucault's reception does not, however, include the postcolonial and decolonial critique of Foucault. An analysis of these critical receptions has yet to be carried out; a research gap which this book intends to close. In this context, the following questions arise: Does Foucault's theory enable a social analysis which goes beyond Europe, does it do justice to global change or is new thinking required beyond Foucault?

Secondary literature on Foucault is extensive and diverse. On the one hand, the emphasis on the discourse-analytical and power-theoretical side of his work is evident, ranging from a focus on the heteronomy of the subject,

---

12   Baudrillard, Jean: *Oublier Foucault*. Paris (Édition Galilée), Réédition de 2004 [1977].

supporting Foucault's thesis of the 'death of the subject',[13] which overstates the individual's subjection to governmental and institutional settings, through to the notion of an 'act without perpetrator'.[14] On the other hand, this literature emphasises the aesthetic formation of the individual against the backdrop of the social insignificance of individual hedonism.[15] This is most commonly associated with the allegation of self-centredness and solipsism in Foucault. However, this is an obvious misinterpretation of his work, as pointed out in particular by Fransisco Ortega when analysing the topic of friendship in Foucault's work.[16] Parrhesia, which in certain forms is associated with friendship, also presupposes a relationship with the other in a distinctive way.

> "In other words: one cannot attend to oneself, take care of oneself, without a relationship to another person. And the role of this other is precisely to tell the truth, to tell the whole truth, or at any rate to tell all the truth that is necessary, and to tell it in a certain form which is precisely parrēsia, which once again is translated as free-spokenness (franc-parler)."[17]

---

13   "We should not be particularly upset about the end of humanity; it is simply a special case or, if you will, one of the visible forms of a far more general process of death. By this I do not mean the death of God but rather the death of the subject; the subject as the origin and foundation of knowledge, freedom, language and history." In: Foucault, Michel: "Die Geburt einer Welt". In: Foucault, Michel: *Dits et Écrits: Schriften: Schriften in vier Bänden: Dits et Écrits: Band I: 1954–1969.* Defert, Daniel; Ewald, François (Eds.), Frankfurt a.M. (Suhrkamp), 2001c, p. 1002. (Own translation) Also refer to: Nagl-Docekal, Herta; Vetter, Helmuth (Eds.): *Tod des Subjekts?* Vienna, Munich (Oldenbourg), 1987.

14   Benhabib, Seyla: *Selbst im Kontext: Kommunikative Ethik im Spannungsfeld von Feminismus, Kommunitarismus und Postmoderne.* Frankfurt a.M. (Suhrkamp), 1995, p. 27. A transformation of this view into a concept of the subject's freedom can be observed in the work of Philipp Sarasin when he asserts Foucault's proximity to Sartre's concept of will and freedom. In my view, this is an overinterpretation of Foucault's concept of freedom. Cf. Sarasin, Philipp: *Foucault zur Einführung.* Hamburg (Junius), 2016a.

15   Suárez Müller describes Foucault's hedonism as socially critical hedonism. Cf. Suárez Müller, Fernando: *Skepsis und Geschichte: Das Werk Michel Foucaults im Lichte des absoluten Idealismus.* Würzburg (Königshausen & Neumann), 2004, p. 199. I agree with this interpretation of Foucault's hedonism.

16   Ortega, Francisco: *Michel Foucault: Rekonstruktion der Freundschaft.* Munich (Fink), 1997. Ortega demonstrates the significance of the other for Foucault's ethical concept.

17   Foucault 2010a: 43.

Contemporary research has still not sufficiently considered the relational sub-ject-theoretical references in the context of Foucault's ethics of care of the self, especially with regard to the dimensions of emotion and aesthetics. This book also aims to contribute to the analysis of these aspects, in particular by asking what role affectivity plays in the context of a diagnosis of the present based on a genealogical analysis of historical formation as regards questions of subjec-tivity, power and knowledge and possibilities to shape the future.

Critical reception of Foucault usually fails to create a coherent synopsis of the individual elements of his philosophy as these are often regarded as disjointed, fragmentary pieces which manifest frequent theoretical changes and thereby cause his philosophy to appear as a repeatedly revised sequence of philosophical insights.[18] The focus of this book is to present the general orientation of Foucault's philosophy in order to reveal the intertwining of its individual elements.[19] According to Foucault, the analysis of phenomena such as madness, crime and sexuality should be included in "the general project".[20]

> "[T]he general project, which is [...] to analyze them according to the correla-tion of the three axes which constitute these experiences: the formation of forms of knowledge (savoirs), the normativity of behavior, and the constitu-tion of the subject's modes of being."[21]

However, this should not be misunderstood as the author's assessment that Foucault's philosophy is based on an elaborate plan and has a systemic char-acter. Instead, the author suggests that Foucault's thinking remains continu-ously related to the desire to solve certain theoretical/practical problems of so-cio-political relevance linked to the relationship between subject, knowledge and power. These problems do not necessarily have to be elaborated fully from the outset, but instead can develop on the basis of previous works and their results or of open questions which emerge from these works – in the sense

---

18 Philipp Sarasin's analysis is an example of this. He describes the subject-theoretical el-ement of Foucault's philosophy as a turning point. (Cf. Sarasin 2016a) Petra Gehring, on the other hand, represents a hypothesis of coherence which is exemplified by the ex-ample of the theorem of freedom. The author shares this viewpoint. Cf. Gehring, Petra: "Foucault's Scenes of Freedom". In: Gehring, Petra; Gelhard, Andreas (Eds.): *Parrhesia: Foucault und der Mut zur Wahrheit*. Zurich (diaphanes), 2012, pp. 13–31.

19 A similar approach can be found in Raffnsøe/Gudmand-Høyer/Thaning 2011.

20 Foucault 2010a: 41.

21 Ibid.

of philosophy as work in progress. The outcome is a consistent theme in Foucault's thinking, which creates a specific form of coherence. It is not associated with a system, but instead with themes and problems dealt with at various levels and areas, combined with shifts, specifications and extensions, forming the contextual framework and enabling the derivation of an orientation and objective. This can be described as an emancipatory concern understood in a specific sense. It is not only connected to an increase in knowledge, but also incorporates emotionality and corporeality in a critical impetus in a practical dimension. This dimension presupposes a reflection of becoming and the possibilities of changing the subject on the basis of an archaeological and genealogical analysis of knowledge and power formations. Foucault's concern to connect individual threads of his work to one another becomes apparent time and again, in particular in the context of his theorems *Parrhesia*, *Governmentality* and *Practices of the Self*, which create continuity and context against the backdrop of transitions.

> "The first theoretical displacement to be made was this transition, this shift from the development of bodies of knowledge to the analysis of forms of veridiction. The second theoretical displacement to be carried out consists in freeing oneself from any would-be general Theory of Power (with all the capital letters), or from explanations in terms of Domination in general, when analyzing the normativity of behavior, and in trying instead to bring out the history and analysis of procedures and technologies of governmentality. Finally, the third displacement consists, I think, in passing from a theory of the subject, on the basis of which one would try to bring out the different modes of being of subjectivity in their historicity, to the analysis of the modalities and techniques of the relation to self, or again to the history of this pragmatics of the subject in its different forms [...]."[22]

---

22   Foucault 2010a: 41–42. And he further states "I have, if you like, devoted myself mostly to studying each of these three axes in turn: that of the formation of forms of knowledge and practices of veridiction; that of the normativity of behavior and the technology of power; and finally that of the constitution of the subject's modes of being on the basis of practices of self." (Foucault 2010a: 42)

Pointing out the 'correlation' between the areas[23] is an attempt to bring together disparate, scattered analyses.

"You can see that with parrēsia we have a notion which is situated at the meeting point of the obligation to speak the truth, procedures and techniques of governmentality, and the constitution of the relationship to self."[24] Foucault says "It is a spidery kind of notion"[25] and must be located on the border between individual leadership and the political domain.[26] It thus also interweaves the theories of knowledge and of the subject with the theory of power, as is the case regarding the concepts of governmentality and self-technology, thereby creating a link between theory and practice in the philosophical conception. These theorems are striking because of their capacity to intertwine various theoretical elements. The emphasis on politics and power, especially with regards to discipline, pastoral power and biopolitics, governmentality and economics,[27] in addition to the aspect of parrhesia is particularly noticeable in the debate in secondary literature regarding Foucault's contemporary relevance, whereby the existing connection between the aforementioned focus areas is not sufficiently considered. It can be observed that problems have shifted and been refined, expanded and specified. This topic will be explored in detail in this book, in particular regarding the subject between limit and transgression.

---

23 "And, [...] in posing the question of the government of self and others, I would like to try to see how truth-telling (dire-vrai), the obligation and possibility of telling the truth in procedures of government can show how the individual is constituted as subject in the relationship to self and the relationship to others." (Ibid.)

24 Foucault 2010a: 45. And "Truth-telling by the other, as an essential component of how he governs us, is one of the essential conditions for us to be able to form the right kind of relationship to ourselves that will give us virtue and happiness." (Ibid.)

25 Ibid.

26 Cf. Foucault 2010a: 46.

27 Cf. Faubian, James D. (Ed.): *Foucault Now: Current Perspectives in Foucault Studies*. Cambridge (polity), 2014; Bröckling, Ulrich; Krasmann, Susanne; Lemke, Thomas (Eds.): *Governmentality: Current Issues and Future Challenges*. London, New York (Routledge), 2010; Binkley, Sam; Capetillo, Jorge (Eds.): *A Foucault for the 21st Century: Governmentality, Biopolitics and Discipline in a New Millennium*. Newcastle (Cambridge Scholars Publishing), 2009; Pickett, Brent: *On the Use and Abuse of Foucault for Politics*. London, Boulder, New York (Lexington Books), 2006.

1.2   The subject between heteronomy and autonomy in Foucault's works

According to Foucault, the constitution of an autonomous subject cannot be understood without external factors, therefore autonomy and heteronomy are not mutually exclusive in an oppositional sense, but must be thought of as interwoven, detached and juxtaposed with partial moments. This view is based on the idea that the constitution of the subject and its possibility of self-constitution can occur simultaneously and is reflected in Foucault's concept of power as a game or struggle for power relations in his micro- and macro-physics of power. Archaeological and genealogical procedures examine the subject between heteronomy and autonomy in relation to knowledge, power and ethics/aesthetics. Foucault's reception of Kant was instrumental in the development of his concepts of autonomy and heteronomy, which modified Kant's understanding of these terms. For Kant, autonomy must primarily be understood as the "supreme principle of morality",[28] as self-legislation[29] in the sense of an unconditional moral obligation.[30] The principle of autonomy

---

28   Kant, GMS, AA 04: 440; KrV A 14/B 28. In: Kant, Immanuel: *Practical Philosophy (The Cambridge Edition of the Works of Immanuel Kant)*. Translator and Editor Gregor, Mary J., Cambridge et al. (Cambridge University Press), 1996, p. 89. And: Kant, Immanuel: *Critique of Pure Reason*. Guyer, Paul; Wood, Allen W. (Eds.), Cambridge (Cambridge University Press), 1998, p. 151. Kant's works are cited in this book according to the abbreviations used in the philosophical journal *Kant-Studien*. The following German editions are used: Kant, Immanuel: *Gesammelte Schriften*. Vol. 1–22 edited by the Preußische Akademie der Wissenschaften; vol. 23 Deutsche Akademie der Wissenschaften zu Berlin; vol. 24–27 Akademie der Wissenschaften zu Göttingen. Berlin (De Gruyter), 1900 et seq. Whenever available, English translations are taken from *Cambridge Edition of the Works of Immanuel Kant*. For foreign-language texts, too, the sigles of the original are given according to the Kantstudien index. See: https://www.kant-gesellschaft.de /gallery/KANT_Hinweise%20f%C3%BCr%20Autoren_2023.pdf (Retrieved: 8 January 2025)

29   Cf. Kant, GMS, AA 04: 431; Kant, Vorl, AA 29: 629.

30   In his published writings, Kant uses the term *autonomy*, which is oriented towards political sovereignty and originally stems from political philosophy, in the *Groundwork of the Metaphysics of Morals* (GMS) for the first time. Kant refers autonomy primarily to the will of rational beings and speaks of "the autonomy of reason itself" (Kant, KpV, AA 05: 125–126; cf. Kant, GMS, AA 04: 443–445), which in the GMS no longer needs a commitment guaranteed by God. "Autonomy of the will is the characteristic of the will by which it is a law to itself (independently of any characteristic of the objects of willing). The principle of autonomy is thus: not to choose in any other way than that the maxims of

is therefore "to choose only in such a way that the maxims of your choice are also included as universal law in the same volition".[31] Free will can act independently of interests, inclinations and external causes. Autonomy and freedom are thereby closely linked

> "*Autonomy* of the will is the sole principle of all moral laws and of duties in keeping with them [...]. Thus the moral law expresses nothing other than the autonomy of pure practical reason, that is, freedom, and this is itself the formal condition of all maxims, under which alone they can accord with the supreme practical law."[32]

The ability to act autonomously as a capability of the will and to follow the categorical imperative corresponds to Kant's positive concept of freedom.[33] In his work, the term autonomy simultaneously describes a capability and a principle and concerns the concepts of knowledge, judgement and action. It is used both descriptively and normatively in his moral philosophy. According to Kant, the ability to self-legislate, which is conferred on man with the categorical imperative, both constitutes human dignity and also safeguards it at the same time.[34]

Kant expands the concept of autonomy developed in his moral philosophy as self-legislation; humans as beings of reason in general; and universal con-

---

one's choice are also comprised as universal law in the same willing." (Kant, GMS, AA 04: 440) Moral autonomy is also decisive for the relationship between morality and law and must be regarded as a common basic norm; it represents both the primary source and the limitation of law. See: Kant, Immanuel: *Groundwork of the Metaphysics of Morals (A German-English Edition).* Gregor, Mary J.; Timmermann, Jens (Eds.), Cambridge (Cambridge University Press), 2011.

31   Kant, GMS, AA 04: 440.

32   Kant, KpV, AA 05: 33.

33   "[W]hat else, then, can freedom of the will be, but autonomy, i.e. the property of the will of being a law to itself?" (Kant, GMS, AA 04: 446) This refers to the individual's possibility of free moral action, which goes hand in hand with the recognition of the categorical imperative. In this context, Kant's categorical imperative as a formula of autonomy is of significance. (Cf. Kant, GMS, 04: 429)

34   Kant observes "Autonomy is thus the ground of the dignity of a human and of every rational nature." (Kant, GMS, AA 04: 436) Kant describes dignity in different ways. On the one hand, it is based on the human ability to act morally and, on the other, it presupposes action according to the categorical imperative. Furthermore, Kant refers to human dignity in general as belonging to the human species. Kant's motivational basis is the feeling of respect for the law, which is close to reason. The categorical imperative thus has a self-motivating effect in autonomous action.

ditions of moral action in his essay "What is Enlightenment". Here autonomy can be understood as an independent judgement; a right to self-determination, self-control and/or action according to principles in the social or political context. With regard to the terms autonomy and freedom, Foucault primarily refers to Kant's shorter writings, most of which are of a historical philosophical nature.[35] Correspondingly, Kant's theorems of *Enlightenment, Critique, Public Sphere*, and *Revolution* serve as reference points in the socio-political context. According to Foucault, Kant strives to establish a "[...] relationship of autonomy with ourselves which enables us to make use of our reason and our morality"[36] within the scope of the process of Enlightenment. Foucault is concerned with self-determination[37] in the sense of independence from forms of governance which promote the heteronomy of the subject. For Foucault, the heteronomy of the subject[38] consists in the oppressive mechanisms of control

---

35   Foucault primarily refers to the two texts 'What is Enlightenment' and 'The Contest of Faculties'.

36   Foucault 2010a: 33.

37   In contrast to Foucault, Kant's self-determination means, on the one hand, the subject's free choice of maxims and actions and, on the other, the subject's determination by a purpose. Overall he uses the term self-determination sparingly. He also associates self-determination with the self-constitution and self-affection of the subject. (Cf. Kant, GMS, AA 04: 427; Anth, AA 07: 251; OP, AA 22: 82, 87) This means, in a relative sense, the independence of action from certain factual impulses, which provides an opportunity for choice. "[F]reedom of the power of choice has the characteristic, entirely peculiar to it, that it cannot be determined to action through any incentive *except so far as the human being has incorporated it into his maxim* (has made it into a universal rule for himself, according to which he wills to conduct himself); only in this way can an incentive, whatever it may be, coexist with the absolute spontaneity of the power of choice (of freedom)". (Kant, RGV, AA 06: 23–24) In the absolute sense self-determination as adequacy of reason refers to the determination of recognition, judgement and action using a priori principles of reason in moral terms. In anthropology, the power as the subject's capacity to act is exercised by influencing oneself through imagination. In the *Opus Postumum* a tendency towards the definition of terms in the sense of a self-constitution can be discerned. (Cf. Kant, OP, AA 22: 82) In this context further references of Foucault to Kant can be identified and are frequently the focus of this book, revealing deeper structures in Foucault's philosophising.

38   Kant understands 'heteronomy', the opposing term to 'autonomy', as the dependence of a human faculty on an external law. (Cf. Kant, GMS, AA 04: 444; KpV, AA 05: 33) The term can primarily be found in Kant's practical philosophy. Heteronomy prevails when the will is determined not by a priori moral law but by striving for happiness, an action based on hypothetical imperatives. Dependence on an object to be created cannot constitute a moral obligation. Kant also adopts the term heteronomy from political phi-

to which they are exposed and which determine their thought and action, but do not fundamentally define them. Foucault's understanding of autonomy establishes the ability of human beings to form themselves as ethics or aesthetics of the self and is firmly rooted in a discursive and power-theoretical context. Suárez Müller criticises the hidden normative character of Foucault's theorems

> "It seems to me that explicit clues for the latent criteria of Foucault's social critique can be found in his ethics. Foucault emphasizes human autonomy and freedom in his ethics, but since this ethics does not present a normative justification, he does not present this autonomy and freedom as generally valid normative criteria."[39]

He continues "Something similar happens in his cultural critique: here autonomy and freedom are also not explicitly recognized as criteria, even though they are repeatedly used as such."[40] Indeed, these theorems prove to be the root and foundation of his Enlightenment thinking. The focus of his understanding of Kant is thus on Enlightenment and critique in socio-political contexts, not Kant's ethical universalism and his concept of reason. The terms autonomy and heteronomy are completely shifted from deontological ethics to the concepts of individual self-design and social transformation, going hand in hand with Foucault's specific concepts of power and ethics/aesthetics. Like Kant, Foucault thus anchors autonomy and freedom in ethics but understands them in an aesthetic twist which does not permit any universal principle. In Foucault's work,

---

losophy. In this context he describes a limited political autonomy which is the result of laws imposed from outside and thus a lack of legislative sovereignty. He transfers this thought to moral philosophy. "If it is *in anything other* than the fitness of its maxims for its own universal legislation, hence if – as it goes beyond itself – it is in a characteristic of any of its objects that the will seeks the law that is to determine it, the outcome is always heteronomy." (Kant, GMS, AA 04: 441) In this case, the will is not directly self-determining, but is motivated by the anticipation of the effect of actions: "[T]he will does not give the law to itself, but an alien impulse gives it to it, by means of a nature of the subject that is attuned to its receptivity." (Kant, GMS, AA 04: 444) Morality should not be based on lust or displeasure and preconceived values. "If the concept of the good is not to be derived from an antecedent practical law but, instead, is to serve as its basis, it can be only the concept of something whose existence promises pleasure and thus determines the causality of the subject, that is, the faculty of desire, to produce it." (Kant, KpV, AA 05: 58)

39   Suárez Müller 2004: 90. (Own translation)
40   Ibid. (Own translation)

freedom and autonomy are ultimately based on power theory; he argues that they are logically rooted in the concept of power. The power-logical derivation provides these concepts with a new form of universal validity in subject-theoretical terms.

1.3   Research approach and structuring of the book

This book strives to re-read Foucault's philosophy on the basis of comprehensive analysis and by comparing certain aspects of his theory, such as *body, affectivity, power,* and *resistance,* with his key critics – especially regarding the facets of topicality and the future. Overall, the approach is based on a hermeneutic and comparative procedure. In the first chapter of the book, the goal is to identify the subject between limit and transgression in the context of Foucault's conception of history and in light of his preoccupation with Kant and Hegel, as a heterotopic model of a pragmatic ad-hoc orientation, in which human hope (referring to Bloch) finds its justification. This clearly highlights Foucault's socio-political objectives. Foucault stands out in his specific interpretation of Kant, according to which Kant must be understood primarily as a philosopher who is concerned with the topicality of his thinking in relation to the socio-political processes of his time. It becomes clear that Foucault's socio-political ambition was to use his philosophy to provide an analysis of the social phenomena of his day and to suggest solutions which enabled the subject to be *de-subjectified* and *de-subjugated.* To shed light on this, the metaphors limit and transgression (chapter 2.1.1), the conception of *a prioritisation* (chapter 2.1.2) and, among other things, the relationship between freedom, nature and history (chapter 2.1.3) in Foucault's and Kant's works will be compared to *new realism.* Further, chapter 2.1.4 focuses on Foucault's concept of history based on a comparative analysis with Hegel and Kant. Chapter 2.1.5 deals with Ernst Bloch's and Kant's philosophical concepts regarding the aspect of hope. What is the relationship between subject and history? What conception of the future becomes visible in Foucault's works in this context? These questions are also the focus of chapter 2.1.6's analysis of the aspects of critique, violence and progress in the works of Kant, Foucault and Mbembe, with a special focus on the postcolonial and global contexts, in particular with reference to Africa.

The second chapter of the main section (2.2.1) discusses Foucault's concept of the subject in comparison to Hegel's anthropological perspective – also in his aesthetics – and aims to elaborate the specific orientation of Foucault's philosophy with regard to the question of the subject in the context of ethics and aesthetics. How can Michel Foucault's theorem of the empty form of salvation be understood in this context? This question is explored with reference to the aspect of human happiness in chapter 2.2.2. In chapter 2.2.3 it will be demonstrated that Foucault uses the ethics or aesthetics of the self to examine the conceptual space of the subject, which, considering self-formation through technologies of the self, simultaneously contains the hope of liberation from the determination of the subject through discourse formations and power strategies and thus the possible autonomy of the subject in the context of its subjugation to rule. This is also connected to the foundation of the subject's capacity to act and their potential for transformative thinking, feeling and acting as well as for shaping human future. Chapter 2.2.4 further develops this topic, examining the neoliberal form of government as the key contemporary method of governmentality, which is also related to the constitution of a specific subject mode, and posing the question of the constitutionality of affects and the body; the possibility of their transformative formation through the application of technologies of the self in emancipatory intention; and their role in the process of the subjugation of the subject. Following this, Foucault's affectivity is compared to Judith Butler's preoccupation with the subject and Butler's critique of Foucault in general is examined (refer to chapter 2.2.5). The final chapters of the second section of the book explore the specific role of affectivity in Foucault's works and the resulting implications.

The analysis of Foucault's concept of power in the third section of the book and the investigation of human potential for resistive action illustrate the scope for change in individual and societal spheres. Foucault's concept of power and resistance is examined in chapter 2.3.1. In this context, the question is posed whether Foucault's concept of power still provides an adequate analytical instrument for power phenomena in the global context in comparison to Han's theory of power, which must be regarded as one of the most significant theories on the subject today, and to the insights of postcolonial and decolonial theorists such as Mignolo, Bhabha and Mbembe (see 2.3.2 and 2.3.3). What consequences does this have when considering the subject between power and ethics/aesthetics from today's perspective? In this context, the author explores the accusation that Foucault's philosophy is Eurocentric. Is it true that his concepts are no longer a viable instrument to adequately grasp global socio-political changes and the associated subject constitutions between autonomy and heteronomy? Does his philosophy still provide useful theorems, categories and criteria for analysis and evaluation when investigating current problems in the global context? Does it provide the means to deal with the future in theoretical and practical ways?

2. Foucault today

The subject in the context of knowledge, power, ethics and aesthetics

2.1 Perspectives and reconceptions.
Foucault, Kant, Hegel, Bloch and Mbembe in dialogue

2.1.1 Limit and transgression. Michel Foucault's reception of Kant in view of philosophical metaphors[1]

2.1.1.1 Foucault and the critical tradition

The philosophies of Foucault and Kant attribute a special meaning to the metaphors 'limit' and 'transgression', which in turn contributes to a holistic understanding of these philosophical concepts and their views of philosophy in general; emphasises the distinctiveness of their respective thinking and clarifies the differences of their philosophical theories. Foucault's and Kant's specific insights will be examined in the context of the metaphorical environment, the systematic contexts and the argumentative direction of their philosophies – in particular when considering Foucault's reception of Kant with regard to the aspect of metaphors. Based on analysis of the differing application of the metaphors 'limit' and 'transgression', the relevance and function of these metaphors will be investigated in the context of Foucault and Kant's philosophies and the significance of their application for an understanding of the respective philosophical concepts will be analysed with

---

1   This section was published previously in German in a slightly modified version: Rainsborough, Marita: "Grenze und Überschreitung. Michel Foucaults Kantrezeption im Spiegel der philosophischen Metaphern". In: Cecchinato, Georgia; Figueiredo, Virginia de Araujo; Kauark-Leite, Patrícia; Ruffing, Margit (Eds.): *Kant and the Metaphors of Reason*. Hildesheim, Zurich, New York (Olms), 2015, pp. 531–545.

regard to their historical-philosophical implications. Using a pseudonym, Foucault writes about himself in an encyclopaedia *"To the extend that Foucault fits into the philosophical tradition of Kant, it is the* critical *tradition of Kant,* and this project could be called a *Critical History of Thought."*[2] Foucault repeatedly refers to Kant in his philosophical project, in particular with regard to the theorems of *Enlightenment* and *critique*, viewing Kant as the embodiment of a certain attitude of philosophical life, an ethos.[3] Foucault places Kant's critiques, his text on the Enlightenment and his philosophical work on history in an argumentative context within the framework of Kant's overall philosophical project and, when reflecting on the topicality of his project, discusses the essay *What is Enlightenment?* as the *crossroads* between critical philosophy and the philosophy of history. "The hypothesis I should like to propose is that this little text is located, in a sense, at the crossroads of critical reflection and reflection on history. It is a reflection by Kant on the contemporary status of his own enterprise."[4] Foucault thus assigns Kant's criticisms a role within the scope of his (Kant's) general project of Enlightenment.

> "Kant, in fact, describes Enlightenment as the moment when humanity is go-ing to put its own reason to use, without subjecting itself to any authority; now, it is precisely at this moment that the critique is necessary, since its role is that of defining the conditions under which the use of reason is legitimate

---

2   Foucault, Michel: "Foucault". In: Foucault, Michel: *Aesthetics, Method, and Epistemology (Essential Works of Foucault, 1954–1984, Vol. 2)*. Faubion, James (Ed.), London, New York et al. (The Penguin Books), 2000, p. 459.

3   "I do not know whether we will ever reach mature adulthood. Many things in our ex-perience convince us that the historical event of the *Enlightenment* did not make us mature adults, and we have not reached that stage yet. However, it seems to me that a meaning can be attributed to that critical interrogation on the present and on our-selves which Kant formulated by reflecting on the *Enlightenment*. It seems to me that Kant's reflection is even a way of philosophizing which has not been without its im-portance or effectiveness during the last two centuries. [...] it must be conceived as an attitude, an ethos, a philosophical life in which the critique of what we are is at one and the same time the historical analysis of the limits imposed on us and an experi-ment with the possibility of going beyond them [de leur franchissement possible]." In: Foucault, Michel: "What is Enlightenment?" In: Foucault, Michel: *Ethics: Subjectivity and Truth (Essential Works of Foucault, 1954–1984, Vol. 1)*. Rabinow, Paul (Ed.), New York (The New Press), 1997, pp. 318–319.

4   Foucault 1997: 309.

in order to determine what can be known [*connaitre*], what must be done, and what may be hoped."[5]

Kant's philosophy of history determines the direction of development and the objective of the process of Enlightenment. Andrea Hemminger writes in the epilogue to Foucault's *Introduction to Kant's Anthropology*[6] "[A]dopting Kant's gesture Foucault once again calls for a 'true critique' (ibid.), but he does not promote Kant, but Nietzsche as its model."[7] Foucault's genealogical research method stems from this reference to Nietzsche. Discussing the underlying agenda of Foucault's work, Hemminger speaks of 'a renewed critique'.[8] According to Hemminger, Deleuze also considers Kant's influence on Foucault is essential for understanding his philosophy. "Foucault takes a theoretical turn after reading Kant which is 'Foucault's major achievement' according to Deleuze: 'the conversion of phenomenology into epistemology'".[9] He changes "the critique from the transcendental to the historical" and "abandons the transcendental subject and replaces it with order, the mere fact 'that order exists'. [...] The sovereign's domain remains empty."[10] During his candidacy presentation for the *Collège de France* Foucault posed the following programmatic question

---

5   Foucault 1997: 308. Foucault continues "The critique is, in a sense, the handbook of reason that has grown up in *Enlightenment*; and, conversely, the *Enlightenment* is the age of the critique." (Ibid.)

6   Also with regard to Kant's anthropology, which he refers to as "the negative of the Critique" and which primarily deals with the mind (and whose deviations, weaknesses and diseases Foucault analyses), he looks for its place in the "organisation of knowledge" besides his work on its genealogy. In: Foucault, Michel: *Einführung in Kants Anthropologie*. Berlin (Suhrkamp), 2010c, pp. 59, 26. (Own translation) He assigns a transitional character to Kant's anthropology, referring in particular to Kant's *Opus Postumum*, as he moved towards his transcendental philosophy. According to Foucault, Kant's anthropology is therefore not to be understood in the sense of the subsequent contemporary scientific anthropology.

7   Hemminger, Andrea: "Nachwort". In: Foucault, Michel: *Einführung in Kants Anthropologie*. Berlin (Suhrkamp), 2010c, p. 126. (Own translation)

8   Hemminger 2010c: 127. (Own translation)

9   Ibid.; citing Deleuze, Gilles: *Foucault*. Frankfurt a.M. (Suhrkamp), 1987, p. 153. (Own translation)

10   Hemminger 2010c: 128; citing Foucault, Michel: *The Order of Things. An Archaeology of the Human Sciences*. London, New York (Routledge), 1989, p. XXII. (Own translation)

"What critique needs to look like 'when one aims to analyze it not in transcendental terms but in terms of history'. [...] This question is indeed the central question of archaeology, which can therefore be described as a transformation of Kant's critique. However, by shifting the level of analysis from the transcendental to the historical, the method of critique changes. It is no longer a matter of justifying the conditions of possible experiences, but of describing the conditions of actual experiences."[11]

Foucault summarizes this with the term *historical a priori*, in which conditions of reality are articulated for statements in a certain period of time, which are derived from the analysis of discourses in an archaeological process.

2.1.1.2   Metaphor of the limit in Kant's works

The metaphor[12] of the limit is central in Kantian thought and closely related to the understanding of philosophy and the project of critique. "Philosophy, ac-

---

11   Hemminger 2010c: 129–130. (Own translation) Hemminger cites Foucault, Michel: "Candidacy Presentation: Collège de France, 1969". In: Foucault, Michel: *Ethics: Subjectivity and Truth (Essential Works of Foucault, 1954–1984, Vol. 1)*. Rabinow, Paul (Ed.), New York (The New Press), 1997, p. 8.

12   In this context metaphor is understood in the sense of the concepts of Blumenberg's absolute metaphor and Ricœur's living metaphor. See Blumenberg, Hans: *Paradigms for a Metaphorology*. Ithaca (Cornell University Press; Cornell University Library), 2016 and Ricœur, Paul: *The Rule of Metaphor: Multi-Disciplinary Studies of the Creation of Meaning in Language*. London, New York (Routledge), 2003 [1975]. Both concepts of the metaphor are based on the relevance of metaphors for philosophical thought and their cognitive content, which cannot be replaced by linguistic terms. Blumenberg regards them as basic elements of the philosophical language which grasps reality in its entirety. According to Ricœur, living or impertinent metaphors offer new interpretations of the world. While Blumenberg focuses on the aspect of holistic understanding, Ricœur emphasizes the moment of novelty. Both conceptions are understood here as complementary. According to Haverkamp, both concepts of the metaphor are based on a hermeneutic paradigm. Cf. Haverkamp, Anselm (Ed.): *Theorie der Metapher*. Darmstadt (Wissenschaftliche Buchgesellschaft), 1996. Ribeiro dos Santos holds a similar view to Blumenberg "As metáforas determinam o ângulo de visão através do qual se vê a realidade, a natureza, a sociedade, o homem e o conjunto das suas representações e instituições. Eles constituem uma espécie de sistema de organisação perceptiva e cognitiva." In: Santos, Leonel Ribeiro dos: *Metáforas da razão ou economia poética do pensar kantiano*. Lisbon (Fundação Calouste Gulbenkian), 1994, p. 40.

cording to Kant, consists in *knowing its bounds*."[13] He is concerned with limiting the exercise of reason, a restriction which ensures in a positive sense that reason does not presume to determine something which goes beyond its possibilities of perception in a speculative manner. To define by setting limits plays an important role in this process "As the expression itself reveals, *to define* properly means to exhibit originally the exhaustive concept of a thing within its boundaries."[14] Foucault also describes Kant's enterprise on the basis of this aspect "[T]he first bold move that one must make when it is a matter of knowledge and knowing is to know what it is that one can know. This is the radicality and for Kant, moreover, the universality of his enterprise."[15] For him, this also involves a political dimension.[16] It is precisely this setting of boundaries which is the task of the critique of pure reason and at the same time creates the preconditions for philosophy to be practiced as science.

"Manfred Kuehn correctly emphasizes that Kant's speech on boundaries 'goes to the very heart of his philosophy'. [...] Already in his pre-critical phase Kant defines metaphysics as a 'science of the limits of human reason'; [...] Kant's plan for a text titled 'Die Grenzen der Sinnlichkeit und der Vernunft' (Limits of Sensuality and Reason) belongs to the history of the creation of the *Critique*. [...] In his critical writings, the debate on boundaries is omnipresent, as the project of critical reason is at its core the project of an

---

13   Konersmann, Ralf (Ed.): *Wörterbuch der philosophischen Metaphern*. Darmstadt (Wissenschaftliche Buchgesellschaft), 2011, p. 138. (Own translation) He cites Kant *Critique of Pure Reason* (KrV, B 755).

14   Kant, KrV A 727/B 755. In: Kant, Immanuel: *Critique of Pure Reason*. Guyer, Paul; Wood, Allen W. (Eds.), Cambridge (Cambridge University Press), 1998, p. 637.

15   Foucault, Michel: "What is Critique". In: Foucault, Michel. *The Politics of Truth*. Los Angeles (Semiotext(e)), 2007b, p. 80.

16   "[...] it now appears as a political problem." (Foucault 1997: 308) Further, Foucault writes "*Enlightenment* is thus not merely the process by which individuals would see their own personal freedom of thought guaranteed. There is *Enlightenment* when the universal, the free, and the public uses of reason are superimposed on one another. [...] The question, in any event, is that of knowing how the use of reason can take the public form that it requires, how the audacity to know can be exercised in broad daylight, while individuals are obeying as scrupulously as possible." (Foucault 1997: 307–308) According to Foucault, Kant proposes a type of contract to Friedrich II "[W]hat might be called the contract of rational despotism with free reason: the public and free use of autonomous reason will be the best guarantee of obedience, on condition, however, that the political principle which must be obeyed itself be in conformity with universal reason." (Foucault 1997: 308)

epistemological demarcation between the world of phenomena and the realm of things per se."[17]

In this process philosophy also reflects on itself: "This metaphor is an important means of self-reflection for the discipline that rates self-reflection among its essential provisions."[18] Thus for Kant setting limits is part of the philosophical process and closely connected to his fundamental philosophical standpoint. Particularly this aspect is often a point of criticism in the philosophical discussion on Kant.

> "If, according to Kant's self-perception, the metaphor of setting limits stands for disciplined philosophizing that abstains from all enthusiasm, its inversion by Kant's opponents serves as a proof of the narrow-mindedness and arrogance of the adherent of systematism, who believes he can force all possible forms of knowledge into his rigid order, and of the sceptic, who likes to humiliate human reason in its aspirations."[19]

For Foucault, the question of limits is closely linked to Kant's transcendental philosophy, his philosophical project in its entirety. "Transcendental philosophy, seeking to define the relationship between truth and freedom – that is, situating itself in the realm of the fundamental – cannot fail to come up against the problem of finitude, of *Grenzen*."[20] According to Kant, this setting of limits is, as Foucault states, a prerequisite for the appreciation of another domain "In Kant's opinion, however, this demarcation is not a pure negative as it necessarily points to the reality of a sphere beyond experience and thus reserves a place for faith."[21] It opens a domain for human hope "and establishing the 'limits of reason' gives meaning to that which 'one may hope for'."[22]

---

17   Pietsch, Lutz-Henning: *Topik der Kritik: Die Auseinandersetzung um die Kantische Philosophie (1781–1788) und ihre Metaphern*. Berlin, New York (De Gruyter), 2010, p. 238. (Own translation)

18   Konersmann 2011: 138. (Own translation)

19   Pietsch 2010: 248–249. (Own translation)

20   Foucault, Michel: *Introduction to Kant's Anthropology*. Nigro, Roberto (Ed.), Los Angeles (Semiotext(e)), 2008b, p. 106.

21   Pietsch 2010: 239. (Own translation)

22   Foucault 2008b: 82.

Also with regard to Kant's anthropology,[23] which deals primarily with the mind and examines its deviations, weaknesses and diseases – for Foucault "the negative of *Critique*" – Foucault looks for its place "in the organization of knowledge"[24] in addition to his preoccupation with its genealogy. According to Kant the task of anthropology is "[n]ot the description of what man is but what he can make of himself."[25] In this context, Foucault takes up Kant's concept of *free play*,[26] which has a metaphorical character. While Kant's concept primarily refers to the reconciliation of cognitive faculties in aesthetic pleasure, Foucault reinforces this idea in his philosophy in terms of discourse theory and practical life. "This notion of *Spielen* is singularly important: man is nature's play; it is the game that he plays, and is played by it."[27] According to Foucault, anthropology in Kant's works does not provide an answer to the question 'What is man?', which is among the three fundamental questions of logic in the *Transcendental Doctrine of Method*, as this question emerges "only once the organization of the *Philosophieren* in Kantian thought is complete – which is to say, in the *Logic* and in the *Opus Postumum*."[28] The question aims at the "*Vereinigung* of God and of the world in man and by man", "[t]his act of unification is therefore the synthesis of thought itself" and also a "universal synthesis, forming a real unity in which the personality of God and the objectivity of the world are rejoined, the sensible principle and the supra sensible."[29] Based on the *Opus Postumum*, Foucault assigns the metaphor of the *limit* to the mortality of humans in Kant's works.

"These three terms, God, the world, and man, in their fundamental relationship to one another, get these notions of *source, domain*, and *limit* going again – the organizational persistence and force of which we have already seen at

---

23 Foucault identifies a disparity in terms of quality between the critiques and anthropology, so that a structural comparison initially seems problematic, if not impossible.

24 Foucault 2008b: 66, 32.

25 Foucault 2008b: 52.

26 In the *Critique of Judgement* Kant speaks of a spontaneity in the play of cognitive faculties with regard to the mediation of the concept of nature and purpose by the concept of play. More generally, he uses the concept of play in anthropology, especially with regard to maintaining vitality in connection with human sociability. He attributes a pleasant character to play.

27 Foucault 2008b: 53.

28 Foucault 2008b: 76.

29 Foucault 2008b: 77, 78.

work in Kantian thought. It was these three notions which obscurely governed over the three essential questions of the *Philosophieren* and the *Critiques*; it was the same three notions which made explicit the content of the Anthropology".[30]

Foucault observes "Between the *Critique* and the *Anthropology*, the continuity is given by the fact that both insist on limitations, and on the inflexibility of the finitude that they gesture toward."[31] According to Foucault, limitations are primarily associated with finitude in the anthropological context of Kant's works.

2.1.1.3   Limit and transgression in view of metaphors in Foucault's and Kant's works

While Kant emphasises the aspect of boundaries, Foucault focuses on the interplay between limits and transgression and the aspect of crossing a limit; it is a means of expanding knowledge and experience.

> "There is no sovereign philosophy, it's true, but a philosophy or rather philosophy in activity. The movement by which, not without effort and uncertainty, dreams and illusions, one detaches oneself from what is accepted as true and seeks other rules – that is philosophy. The displacement and transformation of frameworks of thinking, the changing of received values and all the work that has been done to think otherwise, to do something else, to become other than what one is – that, too, is philosophy."[32]

He also speaks of a vivid and experimental philosophy, whose trademark is curiosity.[33]

> "Curiosity is a vice that has been stigmatized in turn by Christianity, by philosophy, and even by a certain conception of science. Curiosity is seen as fu-

---

30   Foucault 2008b: 105.

31   Foucault 2008b: 119.

32   Foucault, Michel: "The Masked Philosopher". In: Foucault, Michel: *Ethics: Subjectivity and Truth (Essential Works of Foucault, 1954–1984, Vol. 1)*. Rabinow, Paul (Ed.), New York (The New Press), 1997, p. 327.

33   "If this is the relationship that we have with truth, how must we behave? I believe that a considerable and varied amount of work has been done and is still being done that alters both our relation to truth and our way of behaving. And this has taken place in a complex situation, between a whole series of investigations and a whole set of social movements. It's the very life of philosophy." (Foucault 1997: 327)

tility. However, I like the word; it suggests something quite different to me [...] a certain determination to throw off familiar ways of thought and to look at the same things in a different way; a passion for seizing what is happening now and what is disappearing; a lack of respect for the traditional hierarchies of what is important and fundamental. I dream of a new age of curiosity."[34]

For Foucault, curiosity is a prerequisite for transgression in thought and action; it forms the motivational basis. Foucault explains the character of limits and transgression in general "The limit and transgression depend on each other for whatever density of being they possess: a limit could not exist if it were absolutely uncrossable and, reciprocally, transgression would be pointless if it merely crossed a limit composed of illusions and shadows."[35] Foucault illustrates the transgression of limits using the metaphors 'flash of lightning in the night'[36] and the 'wave'.[37] Each of these images focuses on a different kind of transgression – the sudden urgent and resounding and the persistent and continuous in crossing limits and a renewed retreat or falling back, whereby the experience gained has a transformative effect. In Foucault's philosophy, judgement is differently assessed than in Kant's. This is connected to a different approach to the metaphor of the 'court'.[38] Foucault's preference for imaginative

---

34   Foucault 1997: 325.

35   Foucault, Michel: "A Preface to Transgression." In: *Language, Counter-memory, Practice. Selected Essays and Interviews*. Bouchard, Donald F. (Ed.), Ithaca, New York (Cornell University Press), 1977, p. 34.

36   "Perhaps it is like a flash of lightning in the night which, from the beginning of time, gives a dense and black intensity to the night it denies, which lights up the night from the inside, from top to bottom, and yet owes to the dark the stark clarity of its manifestation, its harrowing and poised singularity; the flash loses itself in this space it marks with its sovereignty and becomes silent now that it has given a name to obscurity." (Foucault 1977: 35)

37   "Transgression incessantly crosses and recrosses a line which closes up behind it in a wave of extremely short duration, and thus it is made to return once more right to the horizon of the uncrossable. But this relationship is considerably more complex: these elements are situated in an uncertain context, in certainties which are immediately upset so that thought is ineffectual as soon as it attempts to seize them." (Foucault 1977: 34)

38   "I can't help but dream about a kind of criticism that would try not to judge but to bring an oeuvre, a book, a sentence, an idea to life; it would light fires, watch the grass grow, listen to the wind, and catch the sea foam in the breeze and scatter it. It would multiply not judgments but signs of existence; it would summon them, drag them from their sleep. Perhaps it would invent them sometimes – all the better. All the better. Criticism

criticism is not adequately reflected in the judges' red robes; he refers to images of nature such as growing grass, wind, flying foam, lightning and thunderstorms – images which symbolise movement. Kant's court metaphor describes the setting of limits in the context of a clear authority of judgement and sentencing – in this case in relation to an authority which mediates by making an arbitrary award – and is also connected to the phenomena of conflict and war. This allows a shift from epistemological to philosophical historical considerations.

At the same time, Kant's *unsociable sociability* and war as drivers of sociohistorical change can also be understood in terms of the teleological principle of his philosophy, which is perceived as an organic principle of development, and should thus be regarded in Kant's work as an expression of nature's cunning. The process of perfection is driven by *unsociable sociability*[39] in the interpersonal domain and by war at the level of states.[40] Both moments have an activating character.[41] The teleological principle, "history according to a specific plan of nature", can be regarded as the essence of Kant's conception of history *"All natural predispositions of a creature are determined sometime to develop themselves completely and purposively."*[42] Kant continues *"In the human being (as the only rational creature on earth), those predispositions whose goal is the use of his reason were to develop completely only in the species, but not in the individual."*[43] According

---

that hands down sentences sends me to sleep; I'd like a criticism of scintillating leaps of the imagination. It would not be sovereign or dressed in red." (Foucault 1997: 323)

39   "Here I understand by 'antagonism' the *unsociable sociability* of human beings, i.e. their propensity to enter into society, which, however, is combined with a thoroughgoing resistance that constantly threatens to break up this society. The predisposition for this obviously lies in human nature." (Kant, IaG, AA 08: 20. In: Kant, Immanuel: *Anthropology, History, and Education. The Cambridge Edition of the Works of Immanuel Kant.* Zöller, Günter; Louden, Robert B. [Eds.], Cambridge, New York [Cambridge University Press], 2007b, p. 109)

40   "Nature has therefore once again used the incompatibility of human beings, even of great societies and state bodies of this kind of creature as a means to seek out in their unavoidable *antagonism* a condition of tranquillity and safety; i.e. through wars [...] toward at first imperfect attempts [...] and enter into a federation of nations [...]." (Kant, IaG, AA 08: 24)

41   "Now it is this resistance that awakens all the powers of the human being, brings him to overcome his propensity to indolence [...]." (Kant, IaG, AA 08: 21)

42   Kant, IaG, AA 08: 18.

43   Kant, IaG, AA 08: 19.

to Kant, history is the place where all human predispositions are formed, not in the individual, but in the species, thus universal history.[44]

The ideas of a federation of nations[45] and perpetual peace[46] with their cosmopolitan orientation should serve as a guideline for human action. According to Kant, this also involves a republican constitutional concept; a concept of international relations; international law and socio-political change as a primarily reformatory process. The objective of this inconclusive teleological process is the civilisation, cultivation and moralisation of humanity.[47] Kant's historical-philosophical thinking is primarily illustrated by the metaphor of the organism or organic life. Like Kant, Foucault also uses the metaphor of the ocean, which he applies to characterise transgression by using the image of waves. This is particularly evident in the use of the metaphor of a disappearing face drawn in the sand, which is washed away by the sea waves.[48] With regard to the ocean metaphor, Foucault prefers the idea of transformation in the context of the constitution of knowledge in a process which cannot be completed, to which the human being as a construct also falls victim. Kant, on the other hand, emphasises the moment of demarcation between land and sea with the

---

44   His historical-philosophical considerations are particularly expressed in his writings: *Idea for a universal history with a cosmopolitan purpose* (1784), *Conjectural beginning of human history* (1786), *On the use of teleological principles in philosophy* (1788), *Review of J. G. Herder's Ideas for the philosophy of the history of humanity* (1785), *Perpetual peace: a philosophical sketch* (1795) and of course in his essay on the question: *What is Enlightenment?* (1784), which Foucault repeatedly refers to.

45   "But since they do not, according to their conception of international right, want the positive idea of a *world republic* at all [...] only the *negative* surrogate of a lasting and continually expanding *federation* that prevents war can curb the inclination to hostility and defiance of the law, though there is the constant threat of its breaking loose again [...]." (Kant, ZeF, AA 08: 357) In: Kant, Immanuel: *Toward Perpetual Peace and Other Writings on Politics, Peace, and History.* Doyle, Michael W.; Wood, Allen W. (Eds.), New Haven, London (Yale University Press), 2006, p. 81.

46   "[F]or this reason a special sort of federation must be created, which one might call a *pacific federation (foedus pacificum)*. This federation would be distinct from a *peace treaty (pactum pacis)* in that it seeks to end not merely *one* war, as does the latter, but rather to end *all* wars forever." (Kant, ZeF, AA 08: 356)

47   "This task is thus the most difficult of all. Indeed, its perfect solution is impossible: nothing entirely straight can be fashioned from the crooked wood of which humankind is made. Nature has charged us only with approximating to this idea." (Kant, IaG, 08: 23)

48   Cf. Foucault, Michel: *The Order of Things. An Archaeology of the Human Sciences.* London, New York (Routledge), 2005a, p. 422.

shore as a dividing line, using the linguistically evoked image of an island in the sea,[49] in which land symbolizes a safe haven for the seafarer in the boundless sea. The metaphors dream, sleep, slumber and veil[50] used by Kant and the associated awakening and uncovering illustrate his interest in the process of discovering the fundamentals of human knowledge, a process in which a secure foundation of knowledge emerges to enable the practicing of metaphysics as a science. Kant's architectural metaphors[51] of construction, foundation, building, etc. are related to his search for a safe starting point for philosophical reasoning, which involves adhering to limits, distinguishing between pure and impure – using the metaphor of purity[52] – and a clear differentiation between knowledge and hope. His architectural metaphors lead the reader from the architecture of reason to architectural reason. He believes that by philosophising he can construct a building which is safe and removed from time. According to this concept, taking the established solid foundation as their starting point, humans are constantly engaged in a process of optimisation or self-optimisation – until perfection in the ethical/practical sense is achieved. According to Kant's spatial model, safe knowledge is assigned to the inside in clear separation from the outside. Foucault, on the other hand, advocates a spatial concept of the *outside-inside* and the *heterotopic*, in which thresholds and fractures render limits as constantly shifting points of transition. Foucault's perspective moves away from the search for continuities towards the pursuit of fractures, discontinuities and transformations, thus making transgression more important to him than limits. Foucault continues "I shall thus characterize the philosophical ethos appropriate to the critical ontology of ourselves as a historical-practical test of the limits we may go beyond, and thus as work carried out by ourselves upon ourselves as free beings."[53] Foucault calls this *desubjugation*. The Kantian idea of Enlightenment is decisive for Foucault's project of *desubjugation*.

---

49   Cf. Kant, KrV A 235, 236/B 294, 295.

50   The metaphors dream, sleep and veil illustrate the forms of thinking which Kant wishes to replace with his critical philosophy (dreaming metaphysics, dreams of a spirit-seer, dogmatic slumber, etc.).

51   Taureck speaks with reference to Kant of "an anthropological metaphor of architecture". In: Taureck, Bernhard H. F.: *Metaphern und Gleichnisse in der Philosophie*. Frankfurt a.M. (Suhrkamp), 2004, p. 145. (Own translation)

52   Cf. Konersmann 2011: 300.

53   Foucault 1997: 316.

"Well, then!: critique will be the art of voluntary insubordination, that of re-flected intractability. Critique would essentially insure the desubjugation of the subject in the context of what we could call, in a word, the politics of truth. [...] And consequently, this definition of the *Aufklärung* is not simply going to be a kind of historical and speculative definition. In this definition of the *Aufklärung*, there will be something which no doubt it may be a little ridiculous to call a sermon, and yet it is very much a call for courage that he sounds in this description of the *Aufklärung*."[54]

According to Foucault, this attitude of courage must be developed and culti-vated. Transgressions and transformations can be accomplished using this ap-proach.

2.1.1.4   Foucault's reflections on limits

While Kant's philosophising is primarily characterised by logical, dialectical analysis and by its legislative, normative character, Foucault proceeds empir-ically, both as an archaeologist and as a genealogist and primarily focuses on real historical events.

---

54   Foucault 2007b: 47–48. He continues "I would have the arrogance to think that this definition, however empirical, approximate and deliciously distant its character in re-lation to the history it encompasses, is not very different from the one Kant provided: not to define critique, but precisely to define something else. It is not very far off in fact from the definition he was giving of the *Aufklärung*. It is indeed characteristic that, in his text from 1784, *What is the Aufklärung?*, he defined the *Aufklärung* in relation to a certain minority condition in which humanity was maintained and maintained in an authoritative way. Second, he defined this minority as characterized by a certain inca-pacity in which humanity was maintained, an incapacity to use its own understanding precisely without something which would be someone else's direction [...]." (Foucault 2007b: 47–48) On the *ethos* Foucault writes "This philosophical *ethos* may be charac-terized as a *limit-attitude*. We are not talking about a gesture of rejection. We have to move beyond the outside-inside alternative; we have to be at the frontiers. Criticism indeed consists of analyzing and reflecting upon limits. But if the Kantian question was that of knowing [*savoir*] what limits knowledge [*connaissance*] must renounce exceed-ing, it seems to me that the critical question today must be turned back into a positive one: In what is given to us as universal, necessary, obligatory, what place is occupied by whatever is singular, contingent, and the product of arbitrary constraints? The point, in brief, is to transform the critique conducted in the form of necessary limitation into a practical critique that takes the form of a possible crossing-over [*franchissement*]." (Fou-cault 1997: 315)

"This entails an obvious consequence: that criticism is no longer going to be practiced in the search for formal structures with universal value but, rather, as a historical investigation into the events that have led us to constitute ourselves and to recognize ourselves as subjects of what we are doing, thinking, saying. In that sense, this criticism is not transcendental, and its goal is not that of making a metaphysics possible: it is genealogical in its design and archaeological in its method."[55]

Hemminger notes "For both Kant and Foucault critique entails the reflection on limits. Kant developed critique in response to metaphysics being in a crisis. For him, its postulated realization of the unconditioned is problematic. Foucault, on the other hand, questions the disputed philosophy of the subject."[56] Foucault works on "a genealogy of the subject"[57] and investigates both the modes of subjectivation and objectivation.[58] Thus, according to Hemminger, he translates "Kant's three questions – 'What can I know? What should I do? What may I hope for?' into the historical".[59] She speaks of a "historicization of critique" in which, among other things, a "form of a critical history of the systems of thought" is elaborated.[60] The different forms of governmentality, of power and of the constitutional conditions of the subject in the discursive and dispositive, which become apparent in the historical orientation of the analysis, and the associated subject positions and historical forms of technologies of the self limit the subject's scope of freedom, but do not completely deprive them of their capacity to shape the self and society. Foucault is concerned with imaginative experimentation in the process of self-forming; the modes of cognition; desire and the configuration of social and societal realities in a non-universal way. Foucault's experimental attitude becomes increasingly modest:

"Yet if we are not to settle for the affirmation or the empty dream of freedom, it seems to me that this historico-critical attitude must also be an experimental one. I mean that this work done at the limits of ourselves must, on the one hand, open up a realm of historical inquiry and, on the other, put itself to the test of reality, of contemporary reality, both to grasp the points

---

55   Ibid.
56   Hemminger 2010c: 133–134. (Own translation)
57   Hemminger 2010c: 135. (Own translation)
58   Cf. Hemminger 2010c: 136.
59   Hemminger 2010c: 136. (Own translation)
60   Hemminger 2010c: 131–132. (Own translation)

where change is possible and desirable, and to determine the precise form this change should take. This means that the historical ontology of ourselves must turn away from all projects that claim to be global or radical."[61]

Foucault expresses a deep distrust of all comprehensive social change pro-grammes when he proclaims that they have "led only to the return of the most dangerous traditions".[62] Foucault's preoccupation with the dimension of the historical and his principle of *historical a priori* take him from transgression to limits, or to transgression conceived as 'limited', which is ultimately thought of as an ad hoc shift of limits.

2.1.1.5 Comparison of Kant and Foucault

Kant's preference for setting limits seems modest, disciplinary and strict, while Foucault appears playful, imaginative and excessive in an almost erotic way. In Foucault's works modesty, restraint and limitation are found in a dif-ferent way. "I do not know whether it must be said today that the critical task still entails faith in Enlightenment; I continue to think that this task requires work on our limits, that is, a patient labor giving form to our impatience for liberty."[63] It can be found in the modest, careful work on his historically focused projects; the selectively successful stylisations of lifestyles and the political ad-hoc orientation. An opposite trend can be observed in Kant's works. Kant dares to transgress by accepting the teleological principle of na-ture, which underlies the overall project of humans, humanity, the federation of states and world peace and is anchored in his metaphorical thinking of "as-if", analogy, symbol, schematism and the doctrine of ideas in the transcenden-tal orientation of his philosophy. In the *Critique of Pure Reason* Kant postulates the necessity of setting boundaries and does not permit the crossing of limits, but increasingly the metaphors transition, bridge, continuance and progress are granted a significant place in Kant's philosophy, which is connected to his concepts of morality and aesthetics and in particular to his concept of history in the context of his entire philosophical project. The quasi-utopian character of Kant's philosophy of history is completely immodest, almost presumptu-ous. While Kant's historical thinking entails a transition to the quasi-utopian

---

61   Foucault 1997: 316.
62   Ibid.
63   Foucault 1997: 319.

transgression, Foucault's historicization of philosophy has a limiting effect. Kant makes the real transgression.

2.1.2   Theme and variation. Foucault's historical apriority as criticism of Kant's concept of a priori[64]

2.1.2.1   Kant's apriority and the concept of *acquisitio originaria*

In his critique of Kant's apriority, Foucault's concept of history is based on a specific interpretation of Kant's a priori, which he uses as a starting point for the development of his understanding of the historical a priori. Kant's doctrine of the natural acquisition of a priori knowledge is simultaneously a criticism of the doctrine of innate ideas as expounded by, for example, Plato and Descartes, and of the empirical view of aposteriority represented by Aristotle or Hume. Kant's theory can be seen as a theory which mediates between empiricism and innatism, the latter both in the form of the concept of existing as well as also potentially inborn ideas.[65] Oberhausen writes in this context of Kantian conciliatory thought.[66]

---

64   This chapter has been previously published in: Rainsborough, Marita: "Theme and variation. Foucault's historical apriority as criticism of Kant's concept of a priori". In: Santos, Leonel Ribeiro dos; Louden, Robert B.; Marques, Ubirajara R. de Azevedo (Eds.): *Kant e o A Priori*. Marília, São Paulo (Oficina Universitária; Cultura Acadêmica), 2018, pp. 313–324.

65   "When Kant describes his doctrine of the origins of a priori thought as *acquisitio originaria* he is, on the one hand, thus making clear in what is almost a polemic manner that these ideas are *acquisiti* and thus cannot be inborn. On the other, while these ideas may be acquired, they are not, however, *derivative* from the senses as are empirical ideas, but rather *originarie* since they do not derive 'from things' but rather our cognitive capacity brings them 'out of themselves as a priori' (*Discovery* BA 68)." In: Oberhausen, Michael: *Das neue Apriori: Kants Lehre von einer 'ursprünglichen Erwerbung' apriorischer Vorstellungen*. Stuttgart, Bad Cannstatt (frommann-holzboog), 1997, p. 127. (Own translation)

66   Oberhausen 1997: 129. (Own translation). "The aspiration to solve contentious issues not by the mere refutation of one or more stances but rather to reconcile both conflicting viewpoints with one another following impartial examination, thus overcoming the dispute from the inside out, is an expression of the fundamentally conciliatory attitude which Kant shares with his peers." (Oberhausen 1997: 129; own translation) In this context Oldenburg refers to Herman Schmalenbach's work *Leibniz* (1921). Kant himself writes on this subject "When men of good understanding [...] state absolutely contrary opinions, then in accordance with the logic of all probabilities it is appropriate to direct the greatest attention to a certain middle way which allows both

"Kant's doctrine of the *acquisitio originaria* is not a completely new theory on the origins of cognition drawn from a radical rejection of all traditional explanations. Kant rather more combines elements of the empirical with elements of the innatist approach. In his own understanding he thus reconciles empiricism with innatism."[67]

This theory of the natural acquisition of apriority is demonstrated particularly clearly in the following quotation taken from Kant's work

"'Nevertheless, in the case of these concepts [sic. space, time and the categories], as in the case of all cognition, we can search in experience if not for the principle of their possibility, then for the occasional causes of their generation, where the impressions of the senses provide the first occasion for opening the entire power of cognition to them and for bringing about experience, which contains two very heterogeneous elements, namely a *matter* for cognition from the senses and a certain *form* for ordering it from the inner source of pure intuiting and thinking which, on the occasion of the former, are first brought into use and brings forth concepts' (B 118)".[68]

This theory addresses aspects concerning issues of the origin and validity of cognition and their extent. According to Kant, a priori ideas develop independently of objects deriving from the rules or laws of cognition; the nature of the

---

parties to remain in the right to a certain extent". (Kant, GSK, AA 01: 32) Hinske attributes Kant's antithesis to the Protestant controversy theory of the 17th and 18th centuries. Cf. Hinske, Norbert: *Kants Weg zur Transzendentalphilosophie: Der dreißigjährige Kant.* Stuttgart (Kohlhammer), 1982.

67   Oberhausen 1997: 132. (Own translation)

68   Oberhausen 1997: 118. (Own translation) Oberhausen argues that there is a certain similarity between Leibniz' concept of a virtual inborn cognition and Kant's idea of the *acquisitio originaria*. (Cf. Oberhausen 1997: 119) Leibniz is, however, not the only author in the history of philosophy to have adopted the premise of the potentially inborn idea. This theory of the dependency of Kantian argumentation on Leibniz' theory is, for this reason among others, not undisputed among researchers.

power of cognition and/or cognitive capacities;[69] through experience respectively on the 'occasion of experience'.[70]

> "Sensory impressions initiate action on the part of human reason; action which consists of the ordering of these impressions according to logical rules and laws. These rules, which are intrinsically integral to reflecting human understanding as a force, originate from a priori terms resulting from this activity. Put in other words – pure terms originate from the implementation of the *usus intellectus logicus*."[71]

He continues "The acquisition of space and time, pure forms of intuition, takes place analogue to this process."[72] They also presuppose sensory impressions.

Oberhausen notes "The laws of reason define cognition a priori."[73] Kant's a priori can thus, as Oberhausen correctly establishes, not be viewed simply

---

69   Kant's theory of laws which, independent of objects, have their origins in the nature of the power of cognition respectively the cognitive faculty, are based on Reimarus, who developed these ideas. (Cf. Oberhausen 1997: 105) "The question which, as a result, inevitably occurs concerning how definitions and statements correspond to the objects themselves is one which Reimarus admittedly did not pose but rather Kant." (Oberhausen 1997: 106; own translation) He continues "Kant was the first person to think the thought of the autonomy of reason through to the end and, by problemizing this congruence between laws of thought and nature, to identify the consequence of autonomizing reason." (Oberhausen 1997: 106–107; own translation)

70   Kant used the formulation 'on the occasion of experience' for the first time in 1766 in his essay *Träume eines Geistersehers* [Dreams of a Spirit-Seer]. (Cf. Oberhausen 1997: 115) "Experience is not the source of these terms but rather merely the cause for initiating the activity of the human mind. During this process pure terms are generated which are thus originally acquired." (Oberhausen 1997: 115; own translation) Kant does not, however, yet attribute any positive guidance of cognition to the pure terms in this essay. (Cf. Oberhausen 1997: 116) 'The occasion of experience' has, since Plato, also been constitutive for the doctrine of the inborn idea, which Kant does not, however, elaborate in his philosophic-historical argumentation. Oberhausen argues that this enables Kant to present his theory as a solution. "By integrating the momentum of the 'occasion of experience' into his approach he is able to present his theory of the *acquisitio originaria* as a model for conciliation and thus as the solution of the old dispute between innatism and empiricism." (Oberhausen 1997: 134; own translation) This hypothesis, however, is of a speculative nature and imputes a dishonest handling of the history of philosophy to Kant.

71   Oberhausen 1997: 117. (Own translation)

72   Ibid. (Own translation)

73   Oberhausen 1997: 105. (Own translation)

as synonymous with inborn in the sense of the doctrine of inborn ideas[74] as is the case when Kantian theory is interpreted as a variation of innatism. In his theory of acquisition Kant attributes a priori ideas to rules of thought, thus formal logic becomes the basis of transcendental logic. Logic for Kant is an a priori science; he no longer bases it in ontology. "Kant thus achieves the derivation of categories from the forms of judgement and ideas from the forms of conclusion contained in *The Critique of Pure Reason*, the so-called metaphysical deductions, on the basis of his theory of acquisition."[75] For Oberhausen, the *acquisitio originaria*[76] represents on the one hand a 'background theory' which was never fully developed and, on the other, the key to the epistemological turning point of 1772.[77] It allows Kant to avoid referencing God, who, as for example in Descartes' work, authenticates the validity of inborn ideas.[78] Kant rejects the "referencing of God as the explanation for the origin and validity of cognition"; merely assuming the validity of the laws of cognitive faculty which these are based on by reason of their nature, does, however, insofar refer to a connection to the doctrine of the inborn idea by rejecting "a purely empirical explanation for the origin of cognition."[79] This thus explains why Kant continues to employ certain terms derived from the doctrine of the inborn idea.[80] "The turning away from the basing of logic on ontology, which had, to all purposes, already been carried out by Reimarus, had, sooner or later, to result in a fundamental

---

74   Oberhausen writes on this subject in note 19 "Nevertheless the short-sighted equating of Kant's a priori with the inborn evidently persists." (Oberhausen 1997: 28; own translation)

75   Oberhausen 1997: 38. (Own translation)

76   Kant had already developed the basic idea for this theory in Paragraph 8 of his inaugural dissertation of 1770, first describing it as the *acquisitio originaria* in a polemical pamphlet aimed against Eberhard in 1790. "[T]he passage in the polemical pamphlet of 1790 is the only one in which Kant himself terms his theory of the origin of a priori thought as *acquisitio originaria*, whereby it can, in this context, also be assumed that the reason was the purely external one of being forced to engage with the opponents of his philosophy." (Oberhausen 1997: 122; own translation)

77   Cf. Oberhausen 1997: 37–38.

78   Oberhausen writes in this context "His principal objection is, however, that the assumption that certain ideas are God-given is incorrectly derived from an explanation which makes any further enquiry impossible, thus ruining philosophy." (Oberhausen 1997: 76; own translation) This type of explanation can be attributed to laziness and convenience.

79   Oberhausen 1997: 114. (Own translation)

80   Cf. Oberhausen 1997: 114.

reassessment of the relationship between the logical truth of terms and state-ments concerning the metaphysical truth."[81]

Together with the term *acquisitio derivativa* the term *acquisitio originaria* derives from natural law and thus juristic/juridical diction.[82] Kant trans-plants the term *acquisitio originaria* to the sphere of epistemology. "The manner in which Kant transplants the term *acquisitio originaria* from its established sphere to a completely new one of epistemology can, over and above this, serve as an example of Kant's idiosyncratic method of coining terms."[83] Kant himself refers to this conceptual origin in legal discourse

---

81   Oberhausen 1997: 111. (Own translation) Oberhausen asserts that Kant continued to assume the congruence between laws of thought and laws of things until 1772. "Not until 1772 does Kant draw the necessary conclusion from the autonomising of reason and invert the relationship between the logical and the metaphysical truth by, to use the well-known phrase from the preface to the second edition of the *Critique of pure reason*, only cognizing in things that which we place in them." (Oberhausen 1997: 112; own translation) Oberhausen continues "The doctrine of the *acquisitio originaria* is, however, based not only on this central change of direction in Kant's thinking but rathermore also supplies the solution for the problem of defining in their entirety the terms used to constitute the world of phenomena." (Oberhausen 1997: 112; own translation) And "Kant's so-called metaphysical deduction, the derivation of categories from types of judgement and of ideas from types of conclusion, is thus nothing more than the com-prehension of the *acquisitio originaria* of these terms." (Oberhausen 1997: 112; own trans-lation) The same applies to the *facultas cognoscendi inferior*, sensualism, with its pure forms space and time, which have their origins in the original establishment of this power of cognition. (Cf. Oberhausen 1997: 113) The laws of cognitive faculty may be in-born; "this may not, however, be understood in the sense that God created or implanted them." (Oberhausen 1997: 113; own translation)

82   In Paragraph 10 of the doctrine of right in *The Metaphysics of Morals* Kant writes "I acquire something when I bring it about (*efficio*) that it becomes *mine*. – Something external is originally mine which is mine without any act that establishes a right to it. But that *acquisition* is original which is not derived from what is another's. Nothing external is originally mine; but it can indeed be *acquired* originally, that is, without being derived from what is another's." (Kant, MS, AA 06: 258) On Kant's term 'original acquisition' in the doctrine see: Brocker, Manfred: *Kants Besitzlehre. Zur Problematik einer transzen-dentalphilosophischen Eigentumslehre*. Würzburg (Königshausen und Neumann), 1997, pp. 103–104. Oberhausen believes that the origins of the theory of original acquisition in the context of the development of legal doctrine is probable. (Cf. Oberhausen 1997: 129)

83   Oberhausen 1997: 121. (Own translation)

"'The Critique admits absolutely no implanted or inborn *ideas*. One and all, whether they belong to intuition or to concepts of the understanding, it considers them as *acquired*. But there is also an original acquisition (as the teachers of natural right call it), and thus of that which previously did not yet exist at all, and so did not belong to anything prior to this act. According to the Critique, these are, *in the first place*, the form of things in space and time, *second* the synthetic unity of the manifold in concepts; for neither of these does our cognitive faculty get from objects as given therein in themselves, rather it brings them about, a priori, out of itself' (*Discovery* BA 68)."[84]

The metaphysical deduction[85] of the categories based on forms of judgement relates to the aspect of the origins of ideas and, according to Oberhausen, has a place-holder function as regards the theory of *acquisitio originaria*, whereby the, in some cases, absence to a large extent of the term in Kant can be explained.

2.1.2.2   Foucault's historical a priori as a criticism of Kant's apriority

Foucault's recourse to Kant's a priori can be understood as a historicization of Kant's ideas of a priori and constitutes a clear modification of the idea of the *original acquisition*. Foucault's criticism of the Kantian assumption of a specific inventory of the a priori forms of sensualism; the categories of understanding and the ideas of reason based on the use of rules and/or laws of cognitive powers whose analysis allows a complete listing of a priori forms, terms and ideas through their referencing of formal logic allows an innovative understanding of apriority to become clear in Foucault's work. According to Foucault, apriority is subject to continuous societal and historical changes and can, also in its scope, only be more clearly conceived of within the scope of complex analytical procedures. This function is performed by discourse analysis, itself based on empirically given material, in an archaeological process which is, additionally, supplemented by a genealogical process of power analysis. In Foucault's work knowledge proves itself to be formed by discourses which are based on specific rules of formation, also offering subject positions for the individual, which in turn are subject to specific power strategies.

While Kant primarily bases his deduction of a priori ideas on logic, Foucault takes as his starting point the historic material of a given archive which

---

84   Oberhausen 1997: 123. (Own translation) "He then identifies this 'original acquisition' according to its Latin counterpart 'acquisitio […] originaria' (BA 71)." (Ibid.)

85   In common with 'antinomy' the term 'deduction' is also derived from a jurisprudential respectively a legal philosophy vocabulary. (Cf. ibid.)

contains all the rules characterising a discursive practice and which he views as the entirety of the factually formulated discourses of an epoch. In this context, Foucault not only takes into consideration linguistics; practices and rituals – the medial basis is also incorporated by means of the 'dispositive'. The examination of monuments results in the development of fundamental categories, rules, relationships, subject positions, etc. for an era. Foucault seeks in particular to identify the rules of in- and exclusion; of the distribution of standpoints and their scarcity through which the discourses of an era are structured. In this context fundamental statements are not only of a linguistic nature but rather can, for example, take the form of graphic curves or mathematical formulae.

In contrast to Kant Foucault's concern is not to undertake a precise examination of the specificity of individual cognitive powers but rather to identify their structuring according to fundamental, historically differing rules of formation in cognitive processes within the scope of which they are likewise addressed. Space and time in Foucault's work, for example, are thus not solely sensory concepts but rather phenomena which are linked to all cognitive abilities and, in historical terms, are differently conceived of and shaped. For Foucault the history of knowledge is also the history of space; he combines space and the ordering of knowledge. He develops a topological foundation for all thought; Foucault's theory of space must thus be viewed as the basis for understanding his philosophy overall. The absolutely unthinkable respectively the unspeakable of an era cannot be contained in its knowledge system; it can only appear on the fringes. Discourses must thus be organised according to rules which are specific to a given epoch in order for them not to be excluded from the sphere of the speakable, thus, for example, to be considered as madness. The outcome is an order of things based on time-specific oppositions such as, for example, true and false, normal and pathological, reasonable and mad. The outcome is a historical a priori which defines the cognitive possibilities of an epoch. The endowment with reason itself is subject to historical conditions. In *The Order of Things* Foucault defines the term 'historical a priori'[86] as follows

"This a priori is what, in a given period, delimits in the totality of experience a field of knowledge; defines the mode of being of the objects which appear

---

86   Foucault already uses the term 'historical a priori' in 1957 in his essay "Scientific research and psychology". In it he writes on a "historical a priori of psychology". Cf. Foucault, Michel: "La recherche scientifique et la psychologie". In: Foucault, Michel: *Dits et Écrits I. 1954–1975*, Paris (Gallimard), 2001a, pp. 137–158.

in that field; provides man's everyday perception with theoretical powers and defines the conditions in which he can sustain a discourse about things which is recognized to be true."[87]

In addition to this, he clarifies the term within the context of his methodological work *The Archaeology of Knowledge* in the chapter 'The historical *a priori* and the archive', in which he presents his method of archaeology and clarifies the central terms such as discourse, discursive formation, statement, archive, etc.

"Moreover, this *a priori* does not elude historicity: it does not constitute, above events, and in an unmoving heaven, an atemporal structure; it is defined as the group of rules which characterize a discursive practice [...]. The *a priori* of positivities is not only the system of a temporal dispersion; it is itself a transformable group."[88]

Each archaeological analysis poses the question of its fundamental historical a priori "What historical a priori provided the starting-point from which it was possible to define the great checkerboard of distinct identities established against the confused, undefined, faceless, and, as it were, indifferent background of differences?"[89] He also poses the question

"What the conditions of this emergence were, the price that was paid for it, so to speak, its effects on reality and the way in which, linking a certain type of object to certain modalities of the subject, it constituted the historical a priori of a possible experience for a period of time, an area and for given individuals."[90]

The search for conditions leaves room for the question of power. Foucault's concept stands in the tradition of criticism of the Kantian understanding of

---

87   Foucault 2005a: 172. To do so he examines the three fields of affluence, natural history and general grammar.

88   Foucault, Michel: *Archaeology of Knowledge*. London, New York (Routledge Classics), 2002a, p. 144.

89   Foucault 2005a: XXVI.

90   Foucault, Michel: "Foucault". In: *Aesthetics, Method, and Epistemology (Essential Works of Foucault, 1954–1984, Vol. 2)*. Faubion, James D. (Ed.), New York (The New Press), 1998, p. 460. In 1984 Foucault contributed an article to an encyclopaedia of philosophy concerning his own philosophy, which is the source of this quotation.

the a priori which, although it attacks this understanding's transtemporal validity, however wishes to retain the constitutive character for cognition as the requirement for the possibility of knowledge and thus Kant's transcendental question.[91] "What we end up with, in this tradition, is thus a relativized and dynamical conception of the a priori [...], but which nevertheless retain the characteristically Kantian constitutive function of making the empirical natural knowledge thereby structured and framed by such principles first possible."[92] In this regard, Foucault's theory of the historical a priori demonstrates similarities to Thomas Kuhn's theory of the paradigm shift.[93] Kuhn also references Kant

> "Though it is a more articulated source of constitutive categories, my structured lexicon [= Kuhn's late version of 'paradigm'] resembles Kant's a priori when the latter is taken in its second, relativized sense. Both are constitutive of *possible experience* of the world, but neither dictates what that experience must be. [...] The fact that experience within another form of life – another time, place, or culture – might have constituted knowledge differently is irrelevant to its status as knowledge."[94]

While Kuhn primarily focuses on the history of science and paradigms which evoked its changes over time, Foucault is, over and above this, concerned with the constitution of knowledge in general; he presents a new, modified form of epistemology which does not take its cue from the cognitive subject and incorporates practices of the constitution of knowledge and the handling of knowledge. Foucault's apriority is thus simultaneously linked with a new conception of the subject.

---

91   Kant writes "I call all cognition transcendental which is occupied not so much with objects but rather with *our mode of cognition* of objects *insofar as this is to be possible* a priori." (KrV, B 25)

92   Friedman, Michael: "Transcendental Philosophy and A Priori Knowledge: A Neo-Kantian Perspective". In: Boghossian, Paul; Peacocke, Christopher (Eds.): *New Essays on the A Priori*. Oxford, New York (Oxford University Press), reprinted 2008, p. 370.

93   See Kuhn, Thomas: *The Structure of Scientific Revolutions*. Chicago (University of Chicago Press), 2012.

94   Kuhn, Thomas: "Afterwards". In: Horwich, Paul (Ed.): *World changes: Thomas Kuhn and the Nature of Science*. Cambridge, Mass. (MIT Press), 1993, pp. 331–332.

2.1.2.3 Foucault's and Kant's apriority

While in Kant's work, as in Foucault's, the acquisition of a priori cognition increases with experience, Kant envisages the activation of a specific inventory of pure forms, terms and ideas, while in the case of Foucault a historical openness of the a priori must be assumed which even human beings, as epistemes, are subject to. It is not the endowment of the human cognitive ability which is examined but rather the defined structuring of discursive formations. These include the historically variable constitutive conditions of the subject itself to an equal extent. The archaeological search for historical a priori is thus a continuous task, representing, in particular with regard to the relevant present, a socio-political function and, in terms of our own formation, also an ethical-political one. While Foucault initially identifies epistemes as epoch-structuring historical a priori, he differentiates between types of historical a priori for individual discourses which become increasingly more precise in their diversity and particularity.

In contrast to Kant's apriority, which concerns in equal measure the concept of the subject, ethics, aesthetics and socio-historical processes in general, Foucault transfers his concept of historical apriority to his theory of knowledge; does not, however, apply it to the field of power, a fundamental theory in his philosophy. In Foucault's work apriority remains primarily linked to the field of cognition and to processes relating to the formation of the subject. While Kant, for example with regard to ethics, questions the generalisability of personal maxims and views moral laws, the categorical imperative, as a given in a priori terms, for Foucault ethics are sited in particular in the application of technologies of the self for the forming of the self, also as a moral subject in the socio-historical context and linked to the concept of life as art. Foucault differentiates between historical forms of power and historical combinations of forms of power, his discursive analytical instruments are not, however, made accessible for his genealogical work and referenced to the power practices which constitute them. While in Kant's work the concept of apriority must be viewed as constitutive for his entire philosophy, in Foucault's case it remains primarily limited to discursive analysis and thus to the field of knowledge. In other areas Foucault only discusses the idea of historicity and processuality in general without further modifying, developing, and specifying the concept of apriority. His theorems of the empty form of salvation and parrhesia reveal a tendency to transfer this concept of the philosophy of knowledge to the philosophy of the subject and indicate a thinking of historical apriority in its ethics. The link between knowledge, power and subject could, taking the concept of historical apriority as its starting point, be defined more precisely and further developed. It can thus be concluded that Foucault does not consider Kant's apriority sufficiently, failing to exploit any possible lessons to be derived from Kant – also in terms of critical content. Seen from a different perspective, Foucault's drawing of boundaries regarding the usability of the concept of apriority can be understood in the sense of the Kantian critical stance. The concept is subjected to a pragmatic reduction of its radius of application and thus also its usability and significance. The apriority resulting from Foucault's work is, in the final instance, a paradigmatic consolidation of experience; is an apriority in aposterity.

2.1.3   Freedom, nature and history. On the relationship of nature and history in Kant's and Foucault's works[95]

2.1.3.1   Freedom, nature and history in Kant's and Foucault's works

While freedom and nature are equally relevant to Kant's philosophy of history, the concept of nature appears to entirely lose its significance in Foucault's work. History undergoes a process of detachment from nature and seems to have dissolved into the cultural, social and political responsibilities of humans and into the randomness of events. While for Kant nature is anchored in the historical process and natural teleology enables historical progress in the first place, for Foucault nature ceases to play a fundamental role and the concept of nature consequently loses its central position in his overall concept. Nature disappears from his works and is absorbed by the cultural and socio-historical. Further, Foucault wishes to detach himself from anthropological assumptions and from the episteme of humans, which structures knowledge, when he speaks of the 'death of man' and the 'death of the subject'. Does Foucault also abandon Kant's concept of freedom with his conception of power as well as the discursive and dispositive constitution of humans, to whom certain subject positions are assigned? Thus, for example, on the one hand Foucault turns against Kant's concept of freedom as the starting point of ethical action according to

---

95   This chapter has been previously published in German in a slightly modified form. See Rainsborough, Marita: "Freiheit, Natur und Geschichte. Zum Verhältnis von Natur und Geschichte bei Kant und Foucault". In: Marques, Ubirajara Rancan de Azevedo (Ed.): *Estudos Kantianos. Edição Especial em homenagem a Leonel Ribeiro dos Santos*, Marília, 2017, pp. 339–350. Retrieved from: http://www2.marilia.unesp.br/revistas/index.php/ek/article/view/7095.

the law of practical reason on the basis of its associated universality and status as a philosophical fundamental assumption and, on the other, he relies on Kant for his theories of *desubjugation* and critical ethos. How can this be explained? Are Kant's key terms revisited in a modified form or is there a paradigm shift? What role do nature and history play in this context?

2.1.3.2   Kant's concepts of freedom and nature

In Kant's philosophy there is a "parallelism between theoretical and practical reason"[96] which exists in various respects in the organising, structuring, and contextualising action of reason. At the centre of Kant's concept of freedom is rational action, independence from sensory determination. In Kant's *Critique of Pure Reason*, he remarks "The human power of choice is indeed an *arbitrium sensitivum*, yet not *brutum* but *liberum*, because sensibility does not render its action necessary, but in the human being there is a faculty of determining oneself from oneself, independently from necessitation by sensible impulses."[97] It is necessary to detach oneself from the sensible affectedness, from the sensible inclinations which make up our nature as human beings.[98] Since sensibility, affects and emotions[99] cannot guarantee reliability and universality in ethical action, practical reason is required a priori. In the domain of morality, this prevails in the form of the categorical imperative. Kant's varying formulations of the categorical imperative demonstrate the close link between

---

96   Timmermann, Jens: *Sittengesetz und Freiheit: Untersuchungen zu Immanuel Kants Theorie des freien Willens*. Berlin, New York (De Gruyter), 2003, p. 4. (Own translation)

97   Kant, KrV, A 534/B 562.

98   Kant notes "Now, however, we find our nature as sensible beings so constituted that the matter of the faculty of desire (objects of inclination, whether of hope or fear) first forces itself upon us, and we find our pathologically determinable self, even though it is quite unfit to give universal law through its maxims, nevertheless striving antecedently to make its claims primary and originally valid, just as if it constituted our entire self." (Kant, KpV, AA 05: 74)

99   "There is a specific distinction between affects and passions. Affects are related merely to feeling; passions belong to the faculty of desire, and are inclinations that hinder or render impossible all determinability of the power of choice through principles." (Kant, KU, AA 05: 272, Note 7) In: Kant, Immanuel: *Critique of Judgement*. Walker, Nicholas (Ed.), Oxford (Oxford University Press), 2007a, p. 102. According to Kant, human freedom is more affected by passions than by affects, reason is exploited by them. He argues that only respect for the law, which abides by a verdict, qualifies as a feeling conducive to morality. By acknowledging this sentiment, Kant simultaneously solves the problem of motivation for ethical action, the problem of the *incentive (Triebfeder)*.

morality, the notion of the human being an *end-in-itself* and the purposiveness of nature in his philosophy. Kant's concept of freedom has different aspects – freedom from coercion;[100] freedom as the possibility of choosing maxims; as spontaneity of self-directed action; as the ability of acting according to the requirements of reason; as practical, transcendental or absolute freedom and as autonomy consisting of moral self-legislation.[101] A distinction can be made between a negative and a positive concept of freedom. Timmermann notes "A negative concept of freedom is in itself 'unproductive' and does not give insight into the 'essence' of freedom. [...] It only states what man is free from in his actions, not what he is also free to do."[102] In this context, the question of the various links between nature and freedom in Kant's works is relevant. Kant emphasises the difference between freedom based on regularity and blind or wild freedom

> "One represents freedom, i.e., a power of choice that is independent of instincts or in general of direction by nature. So freedom is in itself a rulelessness and the source of all ill and all disorder where it is not itself a rule. Freedom must accordingly stand under the condition of universal conformity to rules and must be an intelligent freedom, otherwise it is blind or wild."[103]

According to Kant freedom does not imply independence from laws of nature, but instead must be conceived based on their validity. "It is difficult to reconcile a 'subjectively unconditioned', i.e. a negative free choice which does not see itself determined by natural causes, with the universal determination of nature according to causal laws."[104] For Kant, positive freedom, which determines the meaning and purpose of freedom, is linked to the exercise of reason, especially in moral contexts. Freedom is the *ratio essendi* of moral law, according to which freedom is both a necessary and a sufficient condition for the validity of moral law, and moral law is the *ratio cognoscendi* of freedom, which he understands as an awareness of moral commitment, both being directly connected.[105]

---

100   This should be understood as independence from sensible influences or sensible inclinations.
101   The latter is developed in Kant's *Groundwork of the Metaphysics of Morals*.
102   Timmermann 2003: 22. (Own translation)
103   Kant cited in Timmermann 2007: 176 (Kant, Refl, AA 19: 289). In: Kant, Immanuel: *Notes and Fragments*. Guyer, Paul (Ed.), Cambridge (Cambridge University Press). 2005, p. 473.
104   Timmermann 2003: 24. (Own translation)
105   Cf. Kant, CPR, AA 05: 5.

"Since freedom initially means freedom from natural causality, but freedom without laws is impossible, and since we also have good reasons to consider free will by means of causality to be lawful, we must look for the specific causal law of causality through freedom."[106]

At this point, the autonomy of the will as *lawgiving of its own* through the categorical imperative is fundamental. The will is the ability to act according to the principles of reason; Kant also speaks of a *capacity for ends*. "Because free will is not heteronomously determined, it must be a rule for itself."[107] This consists of the legislative form and its universalisation. Morality and freedom mutually refer to each other. Timmermann notes that morality is the *ground of cognition* for freedom and freedom is the *ground of being* for morality.[108] Kant develops a concept of rational and moral freedom as the capacity to act independently of natural causes. Free and responsible action is possible even if the actor has limited options. Responsibility is not bound to the possibility of acting differently, but instead to reflected and independent will. For Kant, "a lack of reason is at the same time a reduction of freedom."[109] Recki speaks of an ethics of autonomy in Kant's work.[110] Timmermann notes on the relationship between freedom and morality "Only morally motivated actions are fully autonomous, since only then can the will give itself the law of reason."[111] He continues "Thus, strictly speaking, human autonomy is realised only by acting out of duty and out of respect for moral law."[112] Sensibility is restrained by adherence to the law. Therefore it is not independence from constraint which is significant, but the type of constraint imposed. "Whoever is subject to the constraint of reason thereby obtains freedom."[113]

---

106   Timmermann 2003: 30. (Own translation)

107   Timmermann 2003: 31. (Own translation)

108   Cf. Timmermann 2003: 37.

109   Timmermann 2003: 39. (Own translation)

110   Cf. Recki, Birgit: *Die Vernunft, ihre Natur, ihr Gefühl und der Fortschritt.* Paderborn (mentis), 2005, p. 55.

111   Timmermann 2003: 43. (Own translation) Further he remarks "Independent, rational decisions demonstrate that reason, like nature, proceeds according to laws." (Timmermann 2003: 53; own translation)

112   Timmermann 2003: 43. (Own translation)

113   Timmermann 2003: 56. (Own translation) Further he notes "Kant does not find determinism as such frightening, but rather a certain manifestation of nature. If all human action were nothing other than a consequence of natural causes and their effects, then,

For Kant, the concept of nature also has various meanings. Nature as a mechanism based on causal laws; nature as cosmology; nature as an organism which develops according to the nucleus it contains and nature as a teleological process oriented towards a specific purpose. Recki points out that in the *Critique of Judgement* in which Kant presents his aesthetic theory he develops a different understanding of nature, which includes the idea of a purposively constructed nature, nature as a *system of ends*. The appreciation of sensibility through the assumption of the free play of cognitive faculties in disinterested delight, of the genuinely aesthetic experience of purposiveness without purpose, is primarily demonstrated using the example of experiences in nature. In this context Recki conceives the model of a non-hierarchical relationship to nature and a rehabilitation of sensibility, identifying the possibility of natural ethics. The idea of a functional nature, which is connected to the fundamental assumption of teleology, refers to the structure of the organism as a meaningful entity, to the idea of nature as a system and to the beauty in nature.[114]

> "On the basis of purposiveness, nature at large is assumed to be rational in its actions, and thus is also the form of reason, based on which we need to respect ourselves as acting beings. The notion of the purposiveness of nature basically means that we think of nature as rationally arranged according to the model of our own practical self-concept".[115]

Recki further notes "During aesthetic reflection we thus experience and think of ourselves as sensible rational beings in a sensible rational context."[116] This allows humans to experience "fitting into the world as rational beings."[117] From this Recki infers an ethical implication for aesthetics, also in the sense of an ethical respect for nature, an appreciation of nature. According to Recki, however, teleological thinking remains an *as-if*, since it refers to ourselves, meaning that the starting point of teleology remains anthropocentric. "Anthropocentrism particularly cannot be overcome by reflective teleological thinking, but is almost affirmed, since it is a condition of its existence and purpose. Therefore, we cannot dispose of anthropocentrism through teleological thought or

---

according to Kant, there would be no capacity within itself to put the commandments of reason into practice." (Ibid.; own translation)

114   Cf. Recki 2005: 60.
115   Recki 2005: 61. (Own translation)
116   Ibid. (Own translation)
117   Ibid. (Own translation)

by reversing it into the normative."[118] Foucault historicises this anthropocentrism by placing it in a particular period of thought and also sharply criticises it, which has considerable consequences for his concept of history.

2.1.3.3 Foucault's concepts of freedom, nature and history

Similarly to Kant, Foucault's concept of freedom can be understood both negatively in the sense of liberation from restrictions and positively as a practice of freedom for the purpose of creation. Under certain circumstances, the act of liberation can be regarded as a prerequisite for the exercise of freedom. "Freedom can be practiced in resistance, in subordination, counter-conduct, as well as ethical subjectivation."[119] He conceives "freedom as 'ongoing work'".[120] Freedom must always be seized in specific situations. In this context, resistance is a practice of freedom. In Foucault's work, freedom proves to be embedded in the logic of power and not, as in Kant's case, based on human reason, in particular on a practical level. Han states with reference to the relationship between power and freedom in Foucault's work "Thus, an ethos of freedom stops power from solidifying into domination and makes sure that it remains an open game."[121] He accuses Foucault of using "the concept of 'freedom' in an emphatic sense"[122] without adequately deriving it.

> "There is an argumentative vagueness in Foucault's *silent transition from freedom as a structural presupposition of power relations to an ethics of freedom*. Foucault tacitly transforms freedom as a structural element of power relations into something *ethical*. But such an ethical quality does not inhere power as such. With the help of this very fragile transition of power to the ethics of power, Foucault introduces a difference between power and domination."[123]

---

118   Recki 2005: 62. (Own translation)

119   Simons, Jon: "Power, Resistance, and Freedom". In: Falzon, Christopher; O'Leary, Timothy; Sawicki, Jana (Eds.): *A Companion to Foucault*. Chichester (Wiley-Blackwell), 2013, p. 314.

120   Taylor, Dianna: "Introduction: Power, freedom and subjectivity". In: Taylor, Dianna (Ed.): *Michel Foucault: Key Concepts*. Durham (Routledge), 2011, p. 6. Further "Freedom for Foucault is not a state we occupy, but rather a practice that we undertake. Specifically, it is the practice of navigating power relations in ways that keep them open and dynamic and which, in doing so, allow for the development of new, alternative modes of thought and existence." (Taylor 2011: 4–5)

121   Han, Byung-Chul: *What is power?* Cambridge (Polity), 2019, p. 86.

122   Ibid.

123   Han 2019: 89.

Foucault's pathos formula of freedom turns out to be a legacy of Kant's philosophy and his concepts of *critique* and *Enlightenment*. Foucault is particularly concerned with the quality of power relations and domination. This is based on the idea that it is possible to affect conditions of constitution and thus provides an opportunity for liberation from external influences and for self-formation. In contrast to Kant, there is no anthropological essence which represents a natural faculty, since one can assume a fundamental, inevitable constructedness. A natural essence cannot be identified, as is, for example, also apparent in Foucault's criticism of the theory of sexual repression. The distinction between natural and cultural dispositions becomes obsolete. In contrast to Kant, Foucault does not presuppose an organic and teleological conception of nature and does not require this idea to argue for propositions such as the perfection of humans and historical progress towards perpetual peace.

This is replaced by Foucault's concept that history is constructed through discourses, dispositives and the associated power practices. Kant's question of how freedom and nature can be conceived as compatible, in which nature can and should be regarded as an 'accomplice' to the human project of ethical, cultural, and political/historical perfection thus shifts to the question of how detachment from a specific constitution is attainable and consequently how the individual can influence their way of being formed and how partial liberation is possible. Foucault's concept is characterised by profound modesty and pragmatism.[124] Thus, Foucault focuses primarily on socio-political and historical processes. Initially nature is conceived only as a knowledge of nature from the point of view of its social constitution through discourses and dispositives. Foucault focuses on the analysis of historically evolving epistemological categories and processes in the natural sciences, such as biology or medicine, which are also set in the context of power practices related to, among others, life and the human body, as becomes evident in the example of biopolitics. Nature is not an independent theorem and constitutes a blind spot in Foucault's philosophy. It presents itself neither as an antipode to freedom

---

124   "Yet if we are not to settle for the affirmation or the empty dream of freedom, it seems to me that this historico-critical attitude must also be an experimental one. I mean that this work done at the limits of ourselves must, on the one hand, open up a realm of historical inquiry and, on the other, put itself to the test of reality, of contemporary reality, both to grasp the points where change is possible and desirable, and to determine the precise form this change should take. This means that the historical ontology of ourselves must turn away from all projects that claim to be global or radical." (Foucault 1997: 316)

nor as a secret ally; for Foucault nature is absorbed by culture. He thus focuses primarily on history, investigating individual events and considering them as an archive of monuments and events. Even though in contrast to Kant, Foucault's philosophy does not envisage a presupposed direction of development in the sense of progress towards a republican constitution, a federation of states and perpetual peace, the constitution of human life as an individual and in coexistence in different contexts is nevertheless subject to human responsibility and thus a project of human formation and emancipation.

On the other hand, it can be observed that Foucault's terminology is largely determined by natural sciences, in particular biology, and their associated technologies. The proximity to Darwin's concept of the struggle for existence, the struggle for opportunities in life, as manifested in adaptation and evolution[125] is striking. Philipp Sarasin succeeded in uncovering Foucault's recourse to Darwin,[126] which Foucault himself did not highlight, and in analysing Foucault's terminology and metaphors in relation to natural sciences. Sarasin notes that "Foucault felt a tendency to refer methodologically to natural sciences which was never explicitly expressed, but nevertheless cannot be overlooked"[127] and mentions in this context the key terms of Foucault's philosophy – 'event', 'series', 'regularity', 'conditions of existence', 'function' and 'transformation'.[128] These manifest the epistemological stance of natural sciences.[129] This "bridge", which Foucault builds "between biology and culture"[130] in particular is also reflected in the metaphors of nature employed in Foucault's philosophical language, as discussed in chapter 2.1 in comparison to Kant's use of metaphors with regard to the aspects of limit and transgression.

---

125   According to Sarasin, Foucault rejects the term evolution and opposes at the same time also the erroneous interpretation of Darwin's concept of evolution as a developmental logic. For Darwin, evolution entails randomness and discontinuity, it is about the reconstruction of a factual line of development. Cf. Sarasin, Philipp: *Wie weiter mit Michel Foucault? (»Wie weiter mit … ?«)*. Hamburg (Hamburger Edition HIS), 2016b, p. 31, 38.

126   Cf. Sarasin, Philipp: *Darwin und Foucault. Genealogie und Geschichte im Zeitalter der Biologie*. Frankfurt a.M. (Suhrkamp), 2009.

127   Sarasin 2016b: 11. (Own translation)

128   Cf. Sarasin 2016b: 21. Sarasin cites the anatomist Xavier Bichat and the biologist Georges Cuvier as Foucault's references. According to Sarasin, Foucault refers to Darwin for the concepts of power and resistance. (Cf. Sarasin 2016b: 34–35)

129   Cf. Sarasin 2016b: 21.

130   Sarasin 2016b: 43. (Own translation)

Foucault also incorporates the materiality of the world and its various phenomena, such as discursivity. His neglect of the concept of nature thus does not result in an idealistic and speculative constructivism. On the contrary, in Foucault's works the production of knowledge and procedures of power are always anchored in materiality. This is clearly reflected in his concept of dispositives. For Foucault, culture is therefore always also materially determined. Consequently, the concepts of nature and materiality reappear in a modified form, anchored in the concept of culture itself, in the concept of the dispositive, and in the theoretical-scientific study of natural phenomena in the context of analysing discourses in natural sciences. In addition, it is also reflected in the theorems of Foucault's philosophy, in its theoretical terminology and metaphors of nature. In Foucault's work, the absorption of matter and nature into culture originates from the idea of the materiality of cultural processes in the sense of an ontologisation of culture as a form of cultural realism. Foucault, however, does not adequately emphasise the agency, power and potency of nature itself, as demanded by new realism "According to post-humanism, culture is not the source of all change and thus does not deny nature any kind of agency and historicity".[131] This form of capacity in the evolution of nature is, as Barad notes, not sufficiently substantiated in Foucault's theory. "Matter is produced and is productive, it is created and is procreative. Matter is an agent and not a fixed being or quality of things."[132] According to Barad, the limit as defined by Foucault must always be reassessed at the intersection of culture and nature.[133]

2.1.3.4   Nature, freedom and history in Foucault's and Kant's works. A conclusive comparison

Although Foucault uses a significantly modified form of Kant's concept of freedom in the formula of the ethos of freedom, in addition to his power-logical interpretation of freedom, he does not revert to Kant's concept of nature. Nature is somewhat disregarded by Foucault; even though it is relevant in terms of epistemology and power theory, it is not relevant in ethical, aesthetic and political-historical regards. Kant's philosophy ascribes a central role to nature in a

---

131   Barad, Karen: *Agentieller Realismus*. Berlin (Suhrkamp), 2012, p. 13. (Own translation)

132   Barad 2012: 14–15. (Own translation)

133   "In fact, [post-humanism] rejects the notion of a natural (or even a strictly cultural) division of nature and culture, and calls for an explanation of how this limit is actively defined and constantly redrawn." (Barad 2012: 14; own translation)

number of ways – as the world which integrates humans and functions according to the laws of nature; as cosmology;[134] as sublimity in aesthetic experience and beauty, evoking human action according to the laws of reason; and as an element supporting human projects in global and forward-looking regards. As a result, Kant's organic and teleological concept of nature offers hope for the development of the human species towards ethical perfection and peaceful coexistence in a federation of states in accordance with his cosmopolitan concept. Human action is attributed the fundamental capacity to achieve this, and rational action can proceed from a world structured according to it. Even though Kant regards nature as an element to be controlled, the human conception of nature goes beyond this in aesthetic and ethical experience. Kant's philosophy of history is therefore based on both his concept of freedom and his concept of nature, each in its different facets.

In Foucault's work, history is also regarded as a human task which involves shaping the world, the social community and the self, and presupposes human freedom, whilst nature is neglected. Analysis of nature is primarily reduced to the aspect of the epistemic approach to natural phenomena; the investigation of the constitution of body and desire through power practices; and discursive moments. It appears as if the philosophical concept of the Anthropocene[135] was already indirectly conceived in Foucault's thinking, manifesting itself as the disappearance of nature or its profound transformation through human influence, but this is not addressed at the level of natural philosophy, geology or ecology, but instead at the level of epistemology. Here we see Foucault's paradox of the overemphasis of the human in an attempt to supposedly overcome this exaggeration; his anthropomorphism in the struggle to avoid anthropocentric thinking. Foucault also fails to sufficiently perceive technological and ecological implications,[136] as Karen Barad in particular points out

---

134 "The cosmology which [Kant] proposes does not wish to explain the genesis of the living, but instead only the mechanical and cosmic conditions under which such an existence of living and conscious beings comes into existence." In: Meillassoux, Quentin: "Metaphysik, Spekulation, Korrelation". In: Avanessian, Armen (Ed.): *Realismus Jetzt: Spekulative Philosophie und Metaphysik für das 21. Jahrhundert*. Berlin (Merve), 2013, p. 31. (Own translation)

135 The term refers to a genealogical epoch in which human interventions directly or indirectly determine nature. Cf. Kersten, Jens: *Das Anthropozän-Konzept: Kontrakt – Komposition – Konflikt*. Baden-Baden (Nomos), 2014.

136 Foucault's approach to the material and technological dimension is conceived particularly in the concept of the *dispositive* and could certainly be expanded.

within the framework of her concept of agential realism.[137] She criticises the neglect of the materiality and reality of the world and therefore considers Foucault's philosophy outdated. His failure to theoretically incorporate nature into his work is a sign of a gap in his reasoning and a shift towards a materialisation of the spiritual and the social, while at the same time neglecting the agentiality of nature and matter.

Despite similarities in the concept of freedom and in the amended project of the Enlightenment, when compared to Kant there is a paradigm shift with respect to the understanding of nature and history in Foucault's work, and thus a detachment from Kant's teleologically oriented philosophy of history towards a pragmatic philosophy based on the theorem of a history structured by events. Despite the prominent position that Kant assigns to humans, human modesty towards nature is apparent in Kant's work, on whose harmony and cooperation humans can hope. In contrast to Kant, Foucault's theory also does not offer the possibility of natural ethics and a domination-free relationship to nature. Thus, in Foucault's work, besides the 'death of man' and the 'death of the subject' – again in a methodological sense – one can also speak of the 'death of nature'. His tendency to materialise the cultural, however, creates a bridge to nature. The path away from nature could certainly lead back to it in a further shift, comparable to the theoretical movement in his subject-philosophy. Foucault, however, ceases to follow this path. Using Foucault's work it is necessary at this point to extend our thinking beyond him.

---

137   Cf. Barad 2012.

2.1.4 From utopia to heterotopia. Foucault's philosophical concept of history as a response to Kant and Hegel[138]

2.1.4.1 A comparison of Foucault's, Kant's and Hegel's concepts of history

Foucault's analysis of history is oriented towards individual events, in which history is not regarded as a sensible, teleologically motivated process of meaning, but rather as an archive of monuments and events which is examined with regard to its regularity and is directed against the utopian core of Kant's and Hegel's views of history. This can be observed in particular in the teleological or logical principle underlying the historical process. Kant's view of history is based on his vision of the perfection of humankind, of the federation of states and of perpetual peace on the basis of his conception of organicity. When combined with an inherent development of humans as a species,[139] his two-worlds theory, which grants humans freedom for ethical perfection and an orientation towards ideas and ideals in the unfolding of their natural dispositions, this view of history clearly has a teleological character which is based on a teleological concept of nature. The "idea of progress [serves] as a 'guide' to explain the intricate game of human affairs".[140] Hegel shifts the utopian character of history into a system of a dialectical process of the return of the absolute mind to itself and thus to the end of history as self-ablation, a process in which beginning and end merge, and when studying his work a logical principle can be

---

138   This section has been published as an essay in a shortened and slightly modified version. See Rainsborough, Marita: "From Utopia to Heterotopy. Foucault's philosophical conception of history as an answer to Kant and Hegel". In: Arndt, Andreas; Bowman Brady; Gerhard, Myriam; Zovko, Jure (Eds.): *Hegel Yearbook*. Vol. 2017. Berlin (De Gruyter), 2017, pp. 430–434. It has also been published in Portuguese: "Da Utopia à Heterotopia. Conceção Filosófica da História de Foucault como Resposta a Kant e Hegel". In: Afonso, Filipa; Marques, Ubirajara Rancan de Azevedo; Santos, Leonel Ribeiro dos (Eds.): *Filosofia & Atualidade: Problemas, Métodos, Linguagens: Jornadas Filosóficas Internacionais de Lisboa 2015*. Lisbon, CFUL, 2015, pp. 203–214; retrieved from: http://repositorio.ul.pt/bitstream/10451/22762/1/Jornadas2015.pdf.

139   Kant remarks "All natural predispositions of a creature are determined sometime to develop themselves completely and purposively." In: Oksenberg Rorty, Amélie; Schmidt, James (Eds.): *Kant's Idea for a Universal History with a Cosmopolitan Aim: A Critical Guide*. Cambridge, New York (Cambridge University Press), 2009, p. 11.

140   Hübner, Dietmar: *Die Geschichtsphilosophie des deutschen Idealismus: Kant – Fichte – Schelling – Hegel*. Stuttgart (Kohlhammer), 2011, p. 21. (Own translation)

discerned at the centre of his thought.[141] The utopian in history can therefore be characterised more specifically as meaningfulness, purposefulness, and a process regarded as being connected to the development of humans and humanity as a whole in the sense of making progress towards the idea of a desirable final state. In Hegel's case this means the end of history within the scope of the process of developing absolute reason towards itself and within itself. Foucault resolutely opposes this very notion of history. According to Habermas, abandoning the utopian is typical of the general *Zeitgeist*.

> "Today it seems as if the utopian energies have been used up, as if they had withdrawn from historical reflection. The horizon of the future has now narrowed itself and in doing so has fundamentally changed both the *Zeitgeist* and politics, at least in Western Europe. The future is occupied with the merely negative [...]. At issue, then, is Western culture's confidence in itself."[142]

Has Foucault ultimately transcended the utopian element of the teleological or logical in philosophical historical thought?

2.1.4.2   History in Foucault's and Hegel's works

Hegel is generally understood as Foucault's antipode "The actual philosophical antipode of Foucault[143] is Hegel, [...] particularly also Hegel in his role as a philosopher of history."[144] For Hegel, the absolute is shaped in the self-production of reason in an objective totality in historical stages[145] of *Entäußerung* and the return of the absolute to itself, which is shaped by the dialectical principle of the 'identity of identity and non-identity',[146] which follows the pattern of

---

141   Cf. Labarrière, Pierre-Jean: *L'Utopie Logique*. Paris (L'Harmattan), 1992.

142   Habermas, Jürgen: "The New Obscurity: The Crisis of the Welfare State and the Exhaustion of Utopian Energies." In: *Philosophy & Social Criticism*, Vol. 11, Issue 2, 1986, p. 2.

143   His analysis is primarily based on Hegel's phenomenology of the mind.

144   Seitter, Walter: "Michel Foucault – von der Subversion des Wissens". In: Foucault, Michel: *Von der Subversion des Wissens*. Frankfurt a.M. (Fischer), 1983, p. 123. (Own translation)

145   The spirit evolves historically from the stage of the "subjective spirit' to that of the 'objective spirit' to the third stage of the 'absolute spirit'.

146   Hegel writes "Hence, the Absolute itself is the identity of identity and non-identity". In: Hegel, Georg Wilhelm Friedrich: *Difference Between Fichte's & Schelling's Philosophy*. New York (State University of New York Press), 1977, p. 156.

opposition and sublation,[147] the *An-sich-Sein*, *Für-sich-sein* and *An-und-für-sich-Sein*, and the theorem of the 'cunning of reason'.[148] Dialectic "is both the fundamental formula of the system of philosophy and the structural principle of the absolute in reality".[149] In Hegel's work, the philosophy of history is only possible if "reason is in history". The separation of thinking and being is eliminated in the historical process, in which an immanent telos operates "The dialectical three-step process thus becomes, in particular in Hegel's work, the pattern of historical progress."[150] Aposteriori and apriori unite in the historical process.[151] The *Absolute* is eventually realised at an advanced stage of development in philosophy itself, which is thus part of this process.

"The cultural forms of art, religion and philosophy, however, operate on the level of the absolute spirit, where the spirit realises its self-discovery in the first place, although philosophy in particular has the advantage of carrying out this essential self-discovery of the spirit in the truest form, which is the concept. Thus, Hegel's world history as a spiritual history contains two parallel levels, the political level of the objective spirit and the cultural level of the absolute spirit, while the subjective spirit of the individual consciousness, for understandable reasons, does not have a direct historical dimension."[152]

---

147 "To sublate and being sublated (the idealized) constitute one of the most important concepts of philosophy. It is a fundamental determination that repeatedly occurs everywhere in it, the meaning of which must be grasped with precision and especially distinguished from nothing. [...] The German *'aufheben'* (*'to sublate'* in English) has a twofold meaning in the language: it equally means *'to keep'*, *'to preserve'*, and *'to cause to cease'*, *'to put an end to'*." In: Hegel, Georg Wilhelm Friedrich: *Science of Logic*. Di Giovanni, George (Ed.), Cambridge, New York (Cambridge University Press), 2010, pp. 81–82.

148 Hübner 2011: 185. This theorem can be found in Hegel's lectures on the philosophy of world history. The 'cunning of reason' is comparable to Kant's 'intention of nature' in terms of its argumentative function.

149 Hübner 2011: 148. (Own translation)

150 Hübner 2011: 183. (Own translation)

151 Cf. Hübner 2011: 199. Hübner remarks "On this basis in particular, it is possible to grasp empirical history a priori, i.e. to understand historical reality as the unfolding of the spirit in 'world history' according to its own laws". (Hübner 2011: 199; own translation)

152 Hübner 2011: 182–183. (Own translation) Hegel himself says about this process "Here it is sufficient to state that the first step in the process presents that immersion of Spirit in Nature which has been already referred to; the second shows it as advancing to the consciousness of its freedom. But this initial separation from Nature is imperfect and partial, since it is derived immediately from the merely natural state, is consequently related to it, and is still encumbered with it as an essentially connected element. The

This development is based on a specific concept of history, which must be understood in the context of his philosophy. "It thus transcends 'original history', i.e. the mere chronology of successive events, and also 'reflective history', i.e. the arrangement of these events under certain external and ultimately arbitrary points of view, such as moral ones."[153]

Foucault criticises Hegel's dialectical thinking, which must be escaped from due to its prevailing influence.

"But truly to escape Hegel involves an exact appreciation of the price we have to pay to detach ourselves from him. It assumes that we are aware of the extent to which Hegel, insidiously perhaps, is close to us; it implies a knowledge, in that which permits us to think against Hegel, of that which remains Hegelian. We have to determine the extent to which our anti-Hegelianism is possibly one of his tricks directed against us, at the end of which he stands, motionless, waiting for us."[154]

Foucault criticises Hegel's dialectical thinking because of the latter's assertion of the absoluteness of knowledge; of totality and continuity: because of its systemic character and its localisation in the subject of knowledge, in self-consciousness and in the absolute spirit, even if these are understood in a process-oriented manner – a reasoning which Foucault locates historically in the order of knowledge at the beginning of the 19th century, thereby historicising it and depriving it of the claim to a universal understanding of the world.

"The exceptional significance of the concept of totality in Hegel's system is directly illustrated by the fact that knowledge with a claim to absoluteness (which also includes the historical process) can only be realised if it can formally combine necessity, completeness and logical stringency of its moments. An attempt which is not only doomed to failure from a historical point of view, because it must presuppose an 'end point' of knowledge

---

third step is the elevation of the soul from this still limited and special form of freedom to its pure universal form; that state in which the spiritual essence attains the consciousness and feeling of itself." In: Hegel, G.W.F.: *The Philosophy of History*. Kitchener (Batoche Books), 2001a, pp. 72–73.

153   Hübner 2011: 199. (Own translation)

154   Foucault, Michel: "The Discourse on Language". In: Foucault, Michel: *Archaeology of Knowledge*. New York (Pantheon), 1972, p. 235.

creation, but also remains problematic within the system, since, as will become apparent, it condemns the development of thinking to the standstill of circular reproduction."[155]

Foucault contrasts Hegel's dialectical, system-related and circular or spiral thinking with his own conception of history

"My aim was to analyse this history, in the discontinuity that no teleology would reduce in advance; to map it in a dispersion that no pre-established horizon would embrace; to allow it to be deployed in an anonymity on which no transcendental constitution would impose the form of the subject; to open it up to a temporality that would not promise the return of any dawn. My aim was to cleanse it of all transcendental narcissism; it had to be freed from that circle of the lost origin, and rediscovered where it was imprisoned."[156]

Shaun Gallagher, however, notes a similarity between Foucault and Hegel in the specific consideration of the particular "Hegel rejects the philosophical starting point of first seeking out the universal (or the future utopia) and then applying it to the particular situation. The starting point must be with the particular situation, because there is no way for a philosopher to go beyond it."[157] And even more pointedly "The universal can be found only within the particular."[158] Further he remarks "Foucault, not unlike Hegel, offers a model of critique that takes its point of departure from historical contents rather than from utopian schemas or the metanarratives of totalitarian theories. Critique, according to Foucault, needs to reveal the historical knowledge that is displaced or hidden by functionalist or systematizing thought."[159] Beatrice Han also draws attention to a similarity of thinking between Foucault and Hegel. "[She] argues that some of Foucault's formulations reactivate the type of Hegelian schema so dis-

---

155 Künzel, Werner: *Foucault liest Hegel: Versuch einer polemischen Dekonstruktion dialektischen Denkens*. Frankfurt a.M. (Haag + Herchen), 1985, p. XII. (Own translation)

156 Foucault 2002a: 223–224.

157 Gallagher, Shaun: "Hegel, Foucault, and Critical Hermeneutics". In: Gallagher, Shaun (Ed.): *Hegel, History and Interpretation*. Albany (State University of New York Press), 1997, p. 149.

158 Ibid.

159 Gallagher 1997: 155.

liked by him, in which power knowledge takes different historical forms."[160] Hegel's thesis of the end of history as the end of the history of the spirit contrasts with Foucault's thesis of the 'end of man' as the end of the episteme 'man'. For both, history does not end here, but assumes a new character.

The similarities in the appreciation of the particular and the acceptance of specific historical forms do not, however, render Foucault's critique of Hegel's philosophy a universalist theory, whose implications must be overcome, or superfluous and/or inconsistent.[161] In Hegel's recourse to logic, the mediation of the general and the particular is not elaborated clearly enough. In Foucault's works, the general, based on an investigation of individual phenomena using archaeological and genealogical methods, appears to be appropriately analysed in methodological terms – as epistemes underlying a certain period.[162] Furthermore, Foucault's productive theory of strategic power relations distances itself from Hegel's theory of power, which is based on a model of repression. "Hegel and Foucault differ fundamentally on the question of the nature of power and domination."[163] Similarly, the "collectivist character of Hegel's philosophy"[164] stands in contrast to Foucault's preference for the individual as the starting point for political critique in his ethics or aesthetics of being. "For Foucault, reason cannot be found in history, but rather reason is historical."[165]

---

160   Oksala, Johanna: *Foucault on Freedom*. Cambridge, New York (Cambridge University Press), 2005, p. 104.

161   "It is true that Foucault, like Lyotard, would list Hegel's discourse as one of the 'globalizing discourses' that he attempts to struggle against." (Gallagher 1997: 156)

162   After the development of discourse analysis, Foucault speaks of discourse rules.

163   Gallagher 1997: 159. "On this point only a general remark is required here. The welfare of a state has a justification that is totally different from that of the welfare of the individual. The determinate being [Dasein] of the ethical substance or the state—i.e. its right—is immediately embodied in an existence [Existenz] that is not abstract but concrete, and the principle of its conduct and behaviour can only be this concrete existence and not one of the many universal thoughts supposed to be moral commands. When politics is alleged to clash with morals and so to be always wrong, the doctrine propounded rests on superficial ideas about morality, the nature of the state, and the state's relation to the moral point of view." In: Hegel, G. W. F.: *Outlines of the Philosophy of Right*. Oxford, New York (Oxford University Press), 2008, p. 314.

164   Hübner 2011: 178. (Own translation)

165   Baberowski, Jörg: *Der Sinn der Geschichte: Geschichtstheorien von Hegel bis Foucault*. München (C. H. Beck), 2013, p. 196. (Own translation) He further states "Foucault's significance for the historical sciences primarily stems from the historicization of rational-

2.1.4.3 Kant's critique and its historicization in Foucault's work

Unlike Hegel, Kant is not understood as Foucault's antipode, but as his ancestor. Hemminger says "Kant develops his critique as a reaction to a crisis of metaphysics. For him, the postulated knowledge of the unconditional is problematic. Foucault, on the other hand, examines the philosophy of the subject."[166] He develops "a genealogy of the subject" and analyses both the modes of subjectivation and of objectivation.[167] "In addition to the level of knowledge at which we constitute ourselves as subjects of knowledge, Foucault's genealogy of the subject includes the level of power at which we constitute ourselves as subjects who influence others, as well as the level of ethics at which we constitute ourselves as moral agents."[168] Foucault thus assigns a distinctive meaning to history within the framework of his reasoning. History is at the core of his philosophical thought. Foucault still considers the attitude of courage demanded by Kant to be desirable today. Foucault's project of desubjugation is based on Kant's concept of Enlightenment. He is concerned with imaginative experimentation in the process of self-forming; the modes of cognition; desire; and the shaping of social and societal realities in a non-universal way. According to Schmidt "Foucault wishes to revive the spirit of the Enlightenment, the spirit of freedom, the spirit of rebellion against the contemporary way of being governed".[169] Foucault's concern for Kant's cosmopolitan concept of perpetual peace, however, is marked by considerable modesty. "Foucault looks for another way of philosophising, a modest philosophy which does not aim to develop an alternative order based on philosophical thought [...]. Foucault's modest philosophy strives only to preserve the En-

---

ity and the realisation that subjects are constituted in cultural practices constituting a system of power." (Baberowski 2013: 203; own translation)

166   Hemminger in Foucault 2010c: 133–134. (Own translation)

167   Hemminger in Foucault 2010c: 135. (Own translation) Cf. also p. 136.

168   Hemminger in Foucault 2010c: 136. (Own translation) Hemminger refers to: Foucault, Michael: "Zur Genealogie der Ethik: ein Überblick über laufende Arbeiten, Foucaults Gespräch mit Hubert L. Dreyfus und Paul Rabinow." In: Dreyfus, Hubert L.; Rabinow, Paul (Eds.): *Michel Foucault. Jenseits von Strukturalismus und Hermeneutik.* Frankfurt a.M. (Suhrkamp), 1987, p. 275.

169   Schmidt, Christian: "Kritik als Lebensform: Foucaults Studien zu Kant und revolutionärer Subjektivität." In: Schmidt Christian (Ed.): *Können wir der Geschichte entkommen? Geschichtsphilosophie am Beginn des 21. Jahrhunderts.* Frankfurt, New York (Campus), 2013, p. 112. (Own translation)

lightenment critique of the existing".[170] He does not adopt Kant's teleology, which is rooted in his concept of nature,[171] or his concept of a federation of states and world citizenship.

> "Foucault [rejects] most of Kant's solutions but asks the same questions. What does it mean to be enlightened? How enlightened am I? And above all, What are the prerequisites for Enlightenment? What are the subjective forces which advance Enlightenment, and how is it possible to unleash them?"[172]

Foucault refers to Kant's 'radicalisation of self-reflection', as Schmidt calls it, and develops an interpretation concerning him as a person "Foucault reads more or less between the actual lines How enlightened am I? And How enlightened can I be under the given circumstances?"[173] Like Kant, Foucault relies on the importance of the public in this process. Unlike Kant, however, Foucault believes that Enlightenment and Critique always depend on the emancipatory effect of practices of the self which affectively embed critical and resistive behaviour in the subject and physically inscribe it. They cannot be regarded solely as rational practices which depend on insight and a social possibility for realisation through political freedom. They require the subject's self-design in various dimensions such as affect, intellectual and psychological endowment, and physicality. In his final creative period, Foucault explores ancient technologies of the self, such as asceticism, fortune telling, meditation and dietetics, which can serve as role models but should not be copied, in order to explore the subject's possibilities for forming the self, which enable critique as a form of

---

170   Schmidt 2013: 113. (Own translation)
171   Kant states "One can regard the history of the human species in the large as the completion of a hidden plan of nature to bring about an inwardly and, to this end, also an externally perfect state constitution [...]." (Kant, IaG, AA 08: 27) According to Kant, the practical and moral legitimisation of the idea of progress, the practical 'guideline', is indispensable for the implementation of nature's intentions. This is where ethics, politics and history meet. The historical process is also based on a theoretical-regulatory principle, a theoretical 'guideline', as a development principle. Natural mechanisms such as war and misery, the civil constitution of states with its legal structure and psychosocial factors such as *unsociable sociability* favour progress. (Cf. Hübner 2011: 23–24)
172   Schmidt 2013: 127–128. (Own translation)
173   Schmidt 2013: 115. (Own translation)

life. Foucault is concerned with the development of practices of freedom using means which we enable us to constitute ourselves as autonomous subjects.[174]

> "It is important to note that for Foucault this question cannot be resolved once and for all. It is a new question for every historically occurring form of subjectivity. Therefore, freedom requires an attitude of 'permanent critique of ourselves'. That is why the practices of freedom also have an ascetic trait and must be perpetuated in the *ethos*."[175]

According to Foucault, ethos is an experimental attitude. In this context, he clearly opposes comprehensive programmes of societal change, which, as can be observed in historical processes, only have negative consequences. Foucault presents a project of social change which begins with the individual and the concrete, taking small steps towards individual and social development and is not based on Kant's historical-philosophical concept of perpetual peace. "Critical hermeneutics involves struggle which is immediate in two ways: it is struggle at a local level, and it is not oriented toward a future."[176] In concrete terms, this means the abandonment of a specific, idealised image of society, but not the departure from responsibility for shaping a future worth living in, in which individuals are given the opportunity to define their own way of life, and in which friendly coexistence is possible; a society in which the critical ethos can be lived. "To give up the power of an ought that derives from an already known universal, from the future already dreamed, is not to give up the responsibility to act in response to existing conditions."[177]

2.1.4.4 Foucault's concept of history as heterotopia

The Kantian attitude of courage towards change detaches Foucault from the overall teleological framework of Kant's philosophy. The sole direction of the intended transformation of the self in the aesthetics or ethics of the self is the emancipatory objective of liberation from given power procedures and self-determination. "As a starting point, the present does not lead to consensus or to a perfect future, but to the possibility of critical refusal. [...] Thus, Foucault suggests, critique takes the form of a 'possible transgression'."[178] The di-

---

174   Cf. Schmidt 2013: 125.
175   Schmidt 2013: 126. (Own translation)
176   Gallagher 1997: 165–166.
177   Gallagher 1997: 166.
178   Gallagher 1997: 165.

rection which the individuals repeatedly set for themselves in a stylisation of their way of life, in which they cannot escape the socio-historical processes of constitution, reveals a conception of appreciation for the autonomy of the self and for an ethical relationship to the other on the basis of the model of friendship – moments which society as a whole cannot and should not leave untouched. Like Kant, Foucault calls for 'moral politics'[179] which provide the individual with scope for aesthetic-ethical self-design. Even though he renounces a teleological or logical principle in his theory of history, Foucault does not completely turn away from the utopian aspects of Kant's and Hegel's concepts of history, reverting to the topical, atopic or dystopian. In Foucault's work, Hegel's dialectical progress of history, which emphasises reconciliation, becomes a fractured succession of periods based on specific epistemes or formation rules of discourse, specific power practices, constitutional processes of the subject and technologies of the self. These superseding periods are not embedded in a given comprehensive system, thus have no intended direction of development, but nevertheless serve to organise monuments and events. They create an orderly system of the historical process which is accessible for analysis. At the edges of the topical, the *new* and *other* emerges, and heterotopic places of knowledge, power and subject formation are possible in the topical. Foucault strengthens this area of the heterotopic in his historical-philosophical considerations and for him utopia becomes a heterotopia in historical development.

2.1.5   Projecting the future. Hope in Kant's, Bloch's and Foucault's philosophy

2.1.5.1   On the phenomenon of hope

Hope, as an emotive attitude respectively an emotive form of motivation for action, is linked to a positive orientation towards the future. To shape the future we must be confident in our feelings, thoughts and actions as the basis for rearranging the existing order; this applies equally to the individual and the

179   Hübner points decisively to the moral foundation of politics: "In *Zum Ewigen Frieden*, Kant emphasises the extent to which his political philosophy is committed to a moral perspective in two different ways. Firstly, he confrontationally rejects the claims of a strictly pragmatic policy towards the binding nature of moral law; secondly, he affirmatively formulates substantive principles for a moral policy with recourse to his ethics." (Hübner 2011: 46; own translation) In his critique and in his political actions, Foucault also links politics in a moral sense to a particular standard.

general societal sphere. Without positive expectations; without human hope for desirable changes which are not merely the outcome of coincidental twists of fate but rather are subject to human planning and a belief in their achievability, a 'project of the future' is inconceivable.[180] Just as, on the other hand, fear of an uncertain, perhaps tragic, future can also define emotive actions while motivations for action in a positive manner, can, however, also generate apathy, despair and hopelessness. Human emotions concerning projections of the future can thus oscillate between the utopian and the dystopian or apocalyptic; between hope and fear. In hope, humans behave optimistically with regard to the temporality of their personal existence and human existence in general, expecting the fulfilment of their desires, aspirations and ideas. Kant, Bloch and Foucault offer very different approaches to understanding hope. What functions are assigned to hope in the different philosophical concepts of Kant, Bloch and Foucault; how do the authors understand hope and what meaning does hope have for each philosophical system and its argumentative context? What connection can be established between Foucault and Kant's and Bloch's philosophy based on this aspect? In this context Foucault's reception of Bloch, which has hitherto been overlooked, will be examined. Is the engagement of these three philosophers with the phenomenon of hope still relevant today for individual questions regarding how to cope with life and in the contemporary broader societal or global context?

2.1.5.2   Hope in Kant's work and the future of the human race

In Kant's work hope is closely linked to the question of knowledge; it begins where knowledge reaches its limits. Hope commences where certain knowledge is no longer possible, arising from a need of human reason. It is thus anchored in anthropology. Kant's central concerns with regard to hope are, on the one hand, ethics and, on the other, the philosophy of history. His concept of "worthiness to be happy" is based on the hope that morally appropriate actions will be compensated for at some later point; which should follow

---

180   Hope is not always associated with positive connotations in the historical philosophical context. In Greek antiquity for example there was a general scepticism concerning unjustified, illusionary hopes (e.g. in Plato's *Philebos*). Aristotle argues that it can also be linked to a subdued mood of the soul. In Seneca's work it has an undefined character. Christianity assigns a specific role to hope in the context of believing in God, also as an antithesis to apocalyptic thought. The Christian definition of hope can still be found in the existentialist philosophy of Gabriel Marcel. In his work hope represents the answer to the despair triggered by borderline experiences in human life.

dutiful action. Acting according to the categorical imperative creates the need for compensation for renunciations associated with moral action. Hope becomes a central component of Kant's morality. Also within the framework of Kant's philosophy of history, hope is related to the model of perpetual peace, as the moment which makes future-oriented action possible in the first place by creating optimism. Here it focuses on the expediency of nature, which corresponds to human action and is not at odds with human objectives. Hope, like respect for moral law as a moral sentiment, is thus a constitutive emotive element of Kant's philosophy, which is conceived as being linked to rationality and originates from reason itself.

In Kant's concept of reason emotions are, in contrast to affects and passions[181] of "integral significance".[182] Kant's criterion to evaluate different emotions refers to the corresponding degree of losing the freedom to act or the fostering of liberty. Affects and passions should be regarded as irrational or unreasonable forms of motivating action, which differ from each other in their spontaneous, temporary or habitual nature. Kant writes "To be subject to affects and passions must always be considered an *illness of the mind* since both preclude mastery of reason."[183] Emotions, however, as an emotive form of motivation, are of vital importance to the extent that they are indispensable for his critique of reason both in the realm of morality and in the aesthetic orientation of humans within the framework of a general world orientation and by demonstrating the connection between moralisation and culture.[184] "Because emotions, regardless of the influence of reason, cannot be conceived of in any

---

181   "The affect, as he defines it, is the 'feeling of desire or reluctance in the present state which prevents the subject from reflecting (the rational consideration of whether to yield or resist this feeling)'." In: Recki, Birgit: "Wie fühlt man sich als vernünftiges Wesen? Immanuel Kant über ästhetische und moralische Gefühle". In: Herding, Klaus; Stumpfhaus, Bernhard (Eds.): *Pathos, Affekt, Gefühl: Die Emotionen in den Künsten*. Berlin, New York (Walter de Gruyter), 2004, p. 276. (Own translation) Here Recki quotes Kant, Anth, AA 07: 251. On the difference between affect and passion in Kant's work Recki remarks "While passion is comparable to a river 'which carves itself ever deeper into its bed' affect is 'like water bursting through a dam'; passion has similar effects to consumption or wasting whilst affect, in contrast, is like a stroke." (Recki 2004: 276; own translation) Recki refers here to Kant, Anth, AA 07: 252. Kant writes of 'an apoplectic fit' and 'emaciation'.

182   Recki 2004: 275. (Own translation)

183   Kant, Anth, AA 07: 251.

184   Recki correctly speaks of Kant's aesthetics as an "aesthetics of pure emotion". (Recki 2004: 278; own translation)

other way than as a sensory state. Only a sensual, and that means physical, being can feel at all."[185] The emotional and action-guiding feelings which do not oppose humans' rational orientation but even promote it by, on the one hand, doing justice to the duality of the human character as a being of both reason and senses and, on the other hand, supporting humans' further development as individuals and as a species, in addition to respect for the moral law within us, an appreciation of beauty, which is more specifically defined as impartial pleasure, an experience of the sublime, and in particular the feeling of hope. Kant's analysis of rational feelings can be found in his epistemology, moral philosophy, aesthetics and his philosophy of history while his anthropology is concerned in particular with irrational feelings such as pathos, affects and passions without, however, developing a theory about them. Kant employs differing approaches and arguments within the individual areas of his philosophy with regard to the phenomena of hoping and hope. While, in order to make metaphysics possible as a science, his epistemology differentiates between the spheres of knowledge and hope to prevent theoretical reason from exceeding its boundaries and becoming speculative, in Kant's moral and historical philosophy hope, with its political and educational implications, is an integrative, fundamental element of philosophical considerations, promoting moral behaviour and historical progress. In the area of morality, Kant asserts the hope for happiness based on the moral subject's worthiness of being happy *"Do that through which you will become worthy to be happy.* Now the second question asks: Now, if I behave so as not to be unworthy of happiness, how may I hope thereby to partake of it?"[186] In Kant's work the phenomenon of hope becomes relevant in a philosophical sense and the term assumes a systemic significance within the overall framework of his philosophy. As one of the three initial questions on which Kant's philosophical work is based, the question 'What can I hope?' already highlights the significance of hope for Kant.[187] It refers in a specific way to the congruence of sensuality and reason; to the laws of nature and morals and to the postulates of the immortality of the soul, the existence of God and the freedom of the will. In the *Logic* hope is assigned to religion and the three fundamental questions are extended by the comprehensive anthropological question "What is a human?" On the basis of these considerations we

---

185   Recki 2004: 287. (Own translation)
186   Kant, KrV A808-809/B836-837.
187   The other two questions are 'What can I know?' and 'What should I do?'

are faced with the question, 'How and regarding which aspects do Bloch and Foucault revert to Kant's ideas?'

2.1.5.3   Bloch's philosophy of hope and the utopian

In Bloch's work, Kant's conception of hope is expanded and becomes the fundamental principle of his philosophy, which is linked to the blueprint and shaping of the future in general, particularly reflected in the terms 'abstract' and 'concrete' utopia as well as 'not-yet'. Kant's philosophy and its ideas of the categorical imperative, the kingdom of ends and perpetual peace becomes a utopia in Bloch's work. Bloch regards hope on the one hand as a fundamental anthropological principle and, on the other, as a concept which permeates all areas of human life equally. His philosophy explores daydreams, wishes and yearnings in everyday life; art as an illusion and social utopias. The terms 'being according to possibility' and 'being within the scope of possibility' reflect the discrepancy between the desirable and the feasible. Hope as defined by Bloch manifests itself as a feeling of confidence, which is linked with anticipation of the future to create an attitude of positive expectation. He argues that the anticipatory consciousness of humans means that they are beings who are primarily focused on the future. The starting point for hope in Bloch's work is the experience of affliction, lack and need. Hope should, in this context, be viewed both as affect and a cognitive act whose antithesis in the affective is fear and in the cognitive memory. Memory refers to recognition of what lies in the past, whereby what has not yet come to pass could possibly occur. "Hope makes remembrance fruitful; knocks the beautiful, the perpetually significant out of it."[188] It becomes clear that Bloch focuses in particular on a transformation of society's historical development by means of utopian thought. To this end hope is anthropologically founded and permeates human endeavours, particularly in the process of cultural creation, in which, among other things, works of art and literature reveal a better world. Bloch's utopia of hope in *The Principle of Hope* begins with a reformulation of the Kantian questions "Who are we? Where do we come from? Where are we going? What do we expect? What awaits us?"[189] In Bloch's work, the temporal nature of his fundamental questions, which relate to the human

---

188   Bloch, Ernst, *Philosophische Aufsätze zur objektiven Phantasie*. Frankfurt am Main (Suhrkamp), 1985, p. 145. (Own translation)

189   Bloch, Ernst: *Das Prinzip Hoffnung: Erster Band*. Frankfurt am Main (Suhrkamp), 1978, p. 1. (Own translation)

past, present and future, becomes clear, emphasising in particular the temporal dimension of humans, nature and the world.

The correlation to human hope presupposes a subject-object dialogue, whereby the world and historical process both have a dimension of possibility. Hope can, however, also be disappointed over and over again, causing its attitude of 'nevertheless' to become opportune. This makes it possible to endure breaks; unexpected avenues of development and the corresponding disappointments. Hope is always linked to indeterminacy and focused on the world's process character with the anticipatory goal which manifests itself in the realm of possibilities. Hope, an expectation affect, is, according to Bloch, linked to a call to action, intervention and change and thus has an activating character. The overcoming of anxiety and fear is also linked to hope. Hope is always on the boundary to the 'not-yet'. The utopian moment linked to hope requires a utopian existence as its principle of being; this can be understood as a 'not yet', a 'has not yet become', a latency of being. In this context Bloch refers to Aristotle's category of possibility, in particular with regard to the essence of substance[190] as "movement according to the 'concept of possibility'" (*kata to dynaton*) and "the being possible" (*dynamei on*).[191] Bloch speaks of subjective potency and objective potentiality[192] to clarify the harmonization of humans, nature and the world. He argues that the anthropological principle of hope in its different forms – from the day dream to considered hope as a form of act of recognition, the *docta spes* – simultaneously corresponds to a social and natural principle, an interaction which Bloch uses the term 'homeland' to define. Reason alters hope from a best possible condition of the world into a focused activity connected to norms, which can be subordinated to communicative negotiation processes.

2.1.5.4 Hope and heterotopia in Foucault's work

Foucault's revised subject theory, in contrast, argues that the future as an intentional project is obsolete. The constitution of the subject through knowledge discourses and power strategies limit personal room for manoeuvre. Autonomy has to be painstakingly wrested from heteronomy. It is not possible to

---

190   Bloch prefers to speak of *world-substance*. Cf. Bloch in Traub, Rainer; Wieser, Harald (Eds.): *Gespräche mit Ernst Bloch*. Frankfurt am Main (Suhrkamp), 1975, p. 288.

191   Bloch in Traub/Wiesner 1975: 285–286. (Own translation) Bloch cites 'the disruptive' as the third Aristotelian category of substance.

192   Cf. Bloch in Traub/Wiesner 1975: 288.

develop a vision of the future, either in the sense of Kantian perpetual peace or Bloch's concrete utopia. Within the scope of the historical process the future is unforeseeable. Does Foucault's theory, which proclaims the death of the subject, nevertheless allow room for hope? It becomes clear that Foucault's definition of heterotopia is located between the topical and the utopian and that his ad-hoc theory allows for a critical dimension within the political in the sense of Kant's *Enlightenment* as the basis for human hope. A hope which also encompasses the formation of the self in ethics respectively the aesthetics of the self. Foucault's quasi-utopian focus, which is based on the perfecting of the self and of society in equal measure, cannot function without referencing Kant. Unlike Bloch's work, Foucault's work does not view Kant's philosophy as merely a documentation of the utopian in order to illustrate his own fundamental standpoint but rather, by integrating the Kantian theory of criticism, becomes a cornerstone for his hopes. Besides Kant, Bloch is also of vital importance in this context

> "Tout simplement la lecture d'un livre déjà ancien que je n'avais pas encore lu, et que, à la faveur d'un accident et d'une convalescence, j'ai eu le temps de lire avec soin l'été dernier et c'est le livre de Ernst Bloch *Le Principe Espérance* [...]. Ça m'a beaucoup frappé, parce que c'est un livre qui est finalement assez peu connu en France, a eu relativement peu d'influence, et qui me paraît poser un problème tout à fait capital."[193]

Foucault refers to Bloch's work *The Principle of Hope* in the context of exploring possibilities for resistance with regard to the Iranian Revolution. Here he alludes to Bloch's concept of *Vorschein einer besseren Welt* "[...] une ouverture, un point de lumière et d'attraction qui nous donne accès, dès ce monde-ci, à un monde meilleur."[194] *Vorschein* in history inspires hope for social change "[...] quel-que chose comme une Révolution était possible."[195] Similarly to Kant, Foucault understands revolutionary events as signs rather than as desirable actions.

In Foucault's work the dimension of hope is manifested in the sphere of illusion, imagination, fantasy and dream, in particular in heterotopia. In his lec-

---

193   Foucault in: Foucault, Michel; Sassine, Farès: "Foucault en l'entretien". [1979] 2014. Retrieved August 30, 2024, from: http://fares-sassine.blogspot.de/2014/08/entretien-inedit-avec-michel-foucault.html.
194   Foucault in Foucault/Sassine 2014: 2.
195   Ibid.

ture *Les hétérotopies*, the heterotopias, which in *The order of things* initially represent distinct systems of language and thought, become counter-spaces, often
in conjunction with heterochronies. They are spaces of transition, transformation, states of crisis and deviation. Due to their revealing nature they also have
an impact on the perception of reality as a whole. In his lecture *Le corps utopique*
Foucault defines the human body as the principal protagonist of all utopias.

> "It [the body] is the small utopian core at the centre of the world from which I
> embark; from which I dream, speak, fantasise, perceive things in their place
> and, thanks to the limitless power of the utopias I conceive, also negate."[196]

It is the basis not only of the topical but also of the heterotopian and the
utopian. In Foucault's work thinking other thoughts in the heterotopian is
the starting point for a change to, transition of and correction of the existing
order. His idea of heterotopia can be compared with Bloch's concept of *concrete
utopia*. In contrast to Bloch, Foucault emphasises in particular the spatial
character of heterotopia. He does not stop at a purely spatial definition, however. Foucault's analysis of existing discourse formations, dispositives, subject
constitutions and forms of power in specific domains of historical situations
provides an instrument for potential changes in forms of government, subject
forms and social conditions, opening up possibilities for freedom of thought
and action.[197] In his concept of critique, which references Kant, Foucault
intends to make the autonomy of the self conceivable. This heterotopian
space is, among other things, a place of hope, where resistance is possible. In
this context, Foucault rejects utopian ideas which strive for comprehensive
socio-political change and usually fail. He prefers a policy of small steps, of
restraint.[198]

---

196 Foucault, Michel: *Die Heterotopien: Les hétérotopies: Der utopische Körper: Le corps utopique:
Zwei Radiovorträge*. Frankfurt am Main (Suhrkamp), 2005c, p. 34. (Own translation)

197 In Foucault's work the experience of otherness is possible particularly in the fields of
literature and art.

198 "But if we are not to settle for the affirmation or the empty dream of freedom, it seems
to me that this historico-critical attitude must also be an experimental one. I mean
that this work done at the limits of ourselves must, on the one hand, open up a realm
of historical inquiry and, on the other, put itself to the test of reality, of contemporary
reality, both to grasp the points where change is possible and desirable, and to determine the precise form this change should take. This means that the historical ontology of ourselves must turn away from all projects that claim to be global or radical." In:

2.1.5.5   Projecting the future. A comparison of Kant, Bloch and Foucault

Similarly to Kant, Bloch presupposes that nature makes concessions so that human actions, motivated and guided by hope, represent an objective-real option; a form of alliance between the world, nature and human beings. While in Kant's work the postulatory nature of the desired harmony is emphasised and hope refers specifically to this aspect, the anthropological and ontological congruence in Bloch's work is argued to be an element of his materialistic ontology. Bloch does not subscribe to Kantian caution. Bloch, as does Kant, employs biological-organic metaphors to express this congruence when, in the context of process immanence, he writes of "germinating content" and a "seed" which has not yet flowered.[199] He also references Kant's aesthetics with its differentiation between the naturally beautiful and the naturally dignified in order to interpret them as a promise. Hope's openness to reason respectively its character of reason is a further similarity in Bloch and Kant's work. While Bloch highlights a specific form of hope, the *docta spes*, in Kant's work hope in the context of moral philosophy is explicitly singled out as an emotion which is accessible to reason respectively beneficial to reason; an emotion which aids human morality. Similarly to Bloch, Kant's historical philosophy, which has a league of nations and perpetual peace as its objectives, includes a historical-philosophical concept as well as a utopian or quasi-utopian character. In contrast to Bloch Kant, however, does not discuss economic-social disparities as the trigger for international conflicts and, unlike Bloch, does not differentiate between the struggle for real-utopian goals, which should be viewed positively, and war as a phenomenon which must be combatted but rather, taking his theory of *unsocial sociability* as the starting point, views war as a historical motor which could be overcome through the process of increasing the legal regulation of inter-state relationships by means of forming a league of nations. The positive assessment of trade relations to promote peace is also absent in Bloch's work. The economic sphere in particular is, in Bloch's view, the starting point for conflict and military disputes. Bloch himself regards his work as a form of *critique of practical reason*.[200] This should, however, not be understood

---

Foucault, Michel: "What is Enlightenment?" In: Rabinow, Paul (Ed.): *The Foucault Reader*. New York (Pantheon Books), 1984, p. 46. Foucault argues that these have in reality "led only to the return of the most dangerous traditions." (Foucault 1984: 46)

199   Cf. Bloch in Traub/Wiesner 1975: 260, 286.

200   Cf. Braun, Eberhard: "Ernst Bloch – der philosophische Schriftsteller des Exils". In: Zeilinger, Doris (Ed.): *Grenzen der Utopie? Krieg der Hoffnung? Ernst Bloch zum 25. Todestag.*

as moral philosophy, as in Kant's case, but rather as a form of action theory. In contrast to Kant's organisational-legal concept of a league of nations, Bloch's objective has a Marxist-anarchic focus. Bloch counters the Kantian doctrine of the schemata expounded within the scope of the theory of perception with a "processing doctrine of schemata"[201] – with the basic category 'possibility'. Bloch emphasises the grounding of openness and changeableness in the categorical; Foucault subsequently achieves the absolute historiography of categories with his concept of historical a priori. For him, possibility should no longer to be understood categorically, but rather in the openness of the historical process.

Bloch and Foucault's philosophies are linked by the term 'transition', which Foucault defined as the key concept of his philosophy of the subject, of power and knowledge to characterise a transition, which can also take place unexpectedly, whereas Bloch embedded it in the concept of hope. Both work with the concept of horizon, which includes an orientation towards the future and the emergence of the different, the possible and the marginalised. Bloch and Foucault reject abstract utopias, the grand visions of changing the world. While Bloch strives for the concrete utopia as a realizable utopia in the sense of socialist humanism, Foucault formulates a modest programme involving a form of ad-hoc change to society which is concerned with an increased autonomy for the individual who can and should change themself like a work of art and influence the shaping of society as a whole. Foucault's interest is in experimental trial and error[202] of ways of life, forms of living together and bringing about of socio-political changes which facilitate a partial liberation from systems of power, thus preventing power structures from solidifying into forms of government. Based on the concept of the constructiveness of knowledge and the constitution of the subject through knowledge and power in discursive as well as dispositive contexts, Foucault considers an anthropological definition of humans, which Bloch employs with his principle of hope as the definition of the essence of humans, to be inconceivable. Foucault regards humans as nothing more than a 'face in the sand'; a metaphor which alludes to human openness. In contrast to Kant and Bloch, humans can no

Berlin, Vienna (Philo & Philo Fine Arts), 2004, VorSchein: Almanac of the Ernst-Bloch-Assoziation. No. 24/2003, p. 192.

201   Bloch in Traub/Wiesner 1975: 261. (Own translation)
202   Bloch also assigns a key role to experimentation within the scope of the real-utopian process. Cf. Bloch in Traub/Wiesner 1975: 265.

longer hope for, or expect, a harmonisation of humankind, nature and the world, and their acts are no longer the key to historical progress even if not entirely devoid of influence.

While Bloch understands power as repression, Foucault regards power as a strategic-relational concept. Bloch's definition of power is the basis for a concept of resistance aimed at realising a concrete utopia, which primarily means liberation from a repressive government. In Foucault's work, in contrast, resistance requires engagement with oneself and, equally, entails changing oneself as well as the social context. For Foucault, hope is a human emotion shaped and malleable through knowledge and power practices and technologies of the self. Hope must thus be defined not only by changing contextual references and functions in both the individual and the social context but rather by the changeability of the character of emotion and cognition itself. Foucault criticises Bloch

> "Alors, euh, ce thème m'a beaucoup intéressé car je le crois historiquement vrai, même si Ernst Bloch ne donne pas de tout cela une démonstration très satisfaisante en termes de science historique. Je crois que c'est une idée, qui est tout de même ..."[203]

However, Foucault does not completely suspend the moment of the concrete utopian and hopeful but transforms and historicises it. In Foucault's work, hope cannot be assigned to emotions associated with cognition, as in Bloch and Kant's work, but rather, in accordance with his idea of the constructed nature of emotion, it must always be inscribed both in the sensual and the cognitive, as well as physically, and at the same time be presented in a form which can be shaped by technologies of the self. For Foucault, there is a fundamental relationship between feeling and cognition based on his concept of the unity of body and soul. Hope itself must be viewed as historically open and characterised in different ways. The hope for a self, which is able to free itself from heteronomous constraints and a socio-political framework which enables this thus proves to be a project of shaping the future without a pre-determined direction,[204] a common task of mankind.

Rorty states that a 'loss of faith' has occurred recently with regard to the belief in the achievability of global justice and that it is linked to the lack of

---

203   Foucault in Foucault/Sassine 2014: 2.
204   Bloch uses the term 'homeland' to define the objective.

persuasiveness of historic narratives which, on the one hand, express the insufficient persuasive power of the Marxist model and, on the other, reflect the failure of Western democracies' economic-technical model to achieve equality in the global context. Utopian thought has lost its most important roots in our contemporary situation.

> "It seems to me that loss of faith in both of the alternative scenarios that were supposed to culminate in an egalitarian utopia plays a much greater role in our concern about globalization than do either the movements grouped together under 'identity politics', or any specific philosophical theory."[205]

Rorty argues that current philosophical topics reflect this loss of hope "This seems to me the result of a loss of hope – or, more specifically, of an inability to construct a plausible narrative of progress. A turn away from narration and utopian dreams toward philosophy seems to me a gesture of despair."[206] The validity of the hope that utopian thought could find other forms of expression as the motor for the development of new forms of political thought and action which could mobilise and modify an existing theory of hope-oriented utopian

---

205   Rorty, Richard: *Philosophy and Social Hope*. London (Penguin Book), 1999, p. 231

206   Rorty 1999: 232. He points out the significance of the term 'impossibility' in the political philosophy of Chantal Mouffe and Ernesto Laclau. Rorty uses the significance of global capital, which lies in the hands of the *global overclass*, to outline the current social situation. "The absence of a global polity means that the super-rich can operate without any thought of any interests save their own." (Rorty 1999: 233) Rorty emphasizes the necessity of a global polity and the creation of global institutions – "We should probably be doing more than we are in dramatizing the changes in the world economy which globalization is bringing about, and to remind our fellow citizens that only global political institutions can offset the power of all that marvellously liquid and mobile capital." (Rorty 1999: 233–234) He believes that this is the only option if we are to achieve the goal of global justice in the future – "But I suspect that is the only chance for anything like a just global society." (Rorty 1999: 234) Rorty continues "Although I think that historical narrative and utopian speculation are the best background for political deliberation, I have no special expertise at constructing such narratives and speculations." (Ibid.) The focus on the topics of 'identity' and 'difference' is, for Rorty, an expression of the old egalitarian utopian thought – "As I see it, the emergence of feminism, gay liberation, various sorts of ethnic separations, aboriginal rights, and the like, simply add further concreteness to sketches of the good old egalitarian utopia." (Rorty 1999: 235) Rorty shows here that utopian thought in the contemporary situation can, and does, undoubtedly take other forms.

thought and that new philosophical-political concepts could be developed, becomes clear in the pragmatic philosophy of Foucault. While this philosophy lacks the utopian pull of a Kant or Bloch[207] it does, nevertheless, offer a concept of hope following the end of the utopian and real-utopian narratives. In Foucault's work the primacy of the future becomes the primacy of the present without losing sight of the significance of the future. The end of utopia[208] is not the end of hope.

2.1.6   Projecting the future. Kant, Foucault and Mbembe on critique, violence and progress in history and politics

2.1.6.1   Projecting the future. Kant, Foucault and Mbembe

For the philosophical reflections of Michel Foucault and the postcolonial African philosopher Achille Mbembe, who refers to him, recourse to Kant is of equal importance and demonstrates not only the actuality of Foucault's thought but also Kant's relevance for the examination of contemporary questions and problems in a global context.

Similarly to Kant, Foucault and Mbembe see the concept of critique as connected on the one hand to analysis of human knowledge and, on the other, to a critical attitude as an Enlightenment impetus. While Kant's investigation of the cognitive faculty – the cognitive powers of sensuality, understanding and reason – focuses particularly on the elaboration of their a priori, Foucault and Mbembe are concerned with a discourse analysis in which, according to Foucault, the epistemes which structure the thought of an epoch, the historical a priori, and, according to Mbembe, the underlying principles respectively

---

207   Arabatzis, for example, thus asserts that Bloch has lost significance in the present day – "I begin with the thesis that Bloch is no longer current today. He has, in fact, lost his following." In: Arabatzis, Stavros: "Zur Aktualität Ernst Blochs". In: Zeilinger, Doris (Ed.): *Grenzen der Utopie? Krieg der Hoffnung?: Ernst Bloch zum 25. Todestag.* Berlin, Vienna (Philo & Philo Fine Arts GmbH), 2004, VorSchein: Almanac of the Ernst-Bloch-Assoziation. No. 24/2003, p. 102. (Own translation) According to Anne Frommann engagement with Bloch's philosophy is today characterised by disdain and a cynical attitude. The 'Principle of Hope' has been degraded into a platitude. Cf. Frommann, Anne: "Augenblick – dreifach". In: Zeilinger, Doris (Ed.): *Grenzen der Utopie? Krieg der Hoffnung?: Ernst Bloch zum 25. Todestag.* Berlin, Vienna (Philo & Philo Fine Arts GmbH), 2004, VorSchein: Almanac of the Ernst-Bloch-Assoziation. No. 24/2003, p. 156.

208   This formulation references Marcuse, Herbert: "Das Ende der Utopie". In: *Psychoanalyse und Politik.* Frankfurt am Main (Suhrkamp), 1968, pp. 69–78.

paradigms are to be found. In his work *Critique de la raison nègre* (2013) Mbembe thus, contrary to the intertextual dialogue with Kant suggested by the title, references a Kant who has been modified in the tradition of Foucault by critically examining the discourse on black people, both in terms of the external perspective and their internal perspective, while also taking the dispositive level into consideration. Self-criticism of African thinkers' retention of the racial theory in relation to Africans themselves is expanded to include a critique of the perpetuation of the notion of victimhood; of the lack of willingness to accept complicity in the traumatic events of the past or to admit Africans' own guilt; and the lack of willingness to take responsibility for shaping their own lives, Africa and the world. Despite the concept of the constitution of the subject, Mbembe and Foucault take human autonomy and majority in the moral/political context as their starting point – in line with Kant's philosophy. Kant's, Foucault's, and Mbembe's concepts of violence, critique, and progress will be examined in this context, as will the interrelationships between the terms respectively the phenomena. To what degree do the contemporary philosophers reference Kant? What are the functions of this recourse? In what way do they criticise Kant and what is the significance of this critique for their philosophical positions?

2.1.6.2   Kant on revolution, violent resistance, critique and progress

When deliberating on violence, Kant begins by examining the subject of revolution and the differentiation between war and peace. In contrast to Foucault, who emphasises the perpetuation of suffering, Kant rejects violent revolution on the grounds, in particular, that violence destroys the legal structure of the state. In his view, *perpetual peace* still, despite the tendency to an *unsociable sociability* between the states, remains conceivable and desirable as a universal human project of a federation of free states with a cosmopolitan focus. Kant is known as a firm opponent of the right of resistance, propounding the fundamental duty of obedience to sovereignty.[209] The legitimation of state power

---

209 Kant only tolerates resistance in the shape of the legally envisaged form which was, itself, embedded in the dualistic state form of the medieval feudal state, in which the people participate in the exercise of power via their representatives. This resistance is, postulates Kant, enshrined in law and serves to maintain and improve the state; it is the embodiment of a legally regulated violence. It is, de facto, the actively legitimised right of resistance of the estates, not of the people. In this context Kant references the teachings of the Monarchomachs and the general theory of the state of his era. Cf. Kersting, Wolfgang: *Wohlgeordnete Freiheit: Immanuel Kants Rechts- und Staatsphilosophie.* Paderborn (mentis), 2007, p. 357–387.

through constitutional-philosophical contractualism would, due to its subjective interpretation of justice, open the floodgates to anarchy if the subjects could themselves define the limits of obedience. For Kant, resistance is, particularly for logical reasons, incompatible with the principles of state power – he himself refers to *self-contradiction*.[210] He thus only legitimates the binding nature of the claim to obedience vis-à-vis the sovereign

> "From this it follows that any resistance to the supreme legislative power, any incitement to have the subjects' dissatisfaction become active, any insurrection that breaks out in rebellion, is the highest and most punishable crime within a commonwealth, because it destroys its foundation. And this prohibition is unconditional, so that even if that power or its agent, the head of state, has gone so far as to violate the original contract and has thereby, according to the subjects' concept, forfeited the right to be legislator inasmuch as he has empowered the government to proceed quite violently (tyrannically), a subject is still not permitted any resistance by way of counteracting force."[211]

This aspect of Kant's work demonstrates conflicting theoretical requirements between the Leviathan-based concept of rulership; the concept of justice; contractualism and a constitutional foundation.[212] Seen from a legal point of view,

---

210 Cf. Kant, MS, AA 06: 320–322. Kersting states "Kant's proof of impossibility of the right of resistance under constitutional law is based on a coherent, easily comprehensible, logical argument. The legal possibility of a right of resistance to the power of the state implies the authorization of the holder of the right to define the conditions of his obedience himself. It establishes the holder of the right as master of the instance of resistance, thus equipping him with sovereignty." (Kersting 2007b: 362–363; own translation) Kant comments as follows on this: "[T]here would have to be a public law that would permit this resistance of the people; i.e. the supreme legislation included a provision that it was not supreme and in the same judgement made the people as subjects sovereigns over that which is subservient; this is a contradiction in itself and the contradiction soon becomes apparent in the form of the question of who should be the judge in this dispute between the people and the sovereign." (Kant, MS, 06: 320) It is, furthermore, also not possible to derive the right of resistance from the right of self-defence, which Kant differentiates from emergency law. (Cf. Kersting 2007b: 378)

211 Kant, TP, AA 08: 299–300.

212 "The outcome of this twin-track procedure is a differentiated legal-philosophical position that attempts to unite the 'Hobbes Ideal' with the 'Rousseau Ideal', thus incorporating both a constitutional basis of the true republic and theory of righteous dominion as well as also a theory of validity of positive law that makes itself independent

in the methodological-systematic parallel foundation of constitutional law to private law, the issue of the root cause of state rulership becomes secondary;[213] its origin remains irrelevant with regard to legitimation theory. Despite the fundamental "illegality of a revolutionary improvement of the state",[214] violent revolutionary[215] seizure of power does not permit any other evaluation in terms of the right of resistance. Kant argues that subjects have an obligation of obedience to these rulers respectively a ban on resistance. The natural legal position[216] itself does not, according to Kant, justify a right of resistance but rather only a legal obligation on the part of the ruler to respect the citizen's

---

of standards of justice." (Kersting 2007b: 355; own translation) Kant even concedes the right of violent restoration of power to a deposed monarch. Kersting rightly views this as a failure in Kant's argumentation: "This would make him the only citizen who had a right to revolution and resistance. With a single stroke of the pen Kant thus declares his entire concept of constitutional law to be invalid. The right of power is suddenly no longer defined as a public law imperium but as a civil law dominium." (Kersting 2007b: 368; own translation)

213   "Moreover, once a revolution has succeeded and a new constitution has been established, the lack of legitimacy with which it began and has been implemented cannot release the subjects from the obligation to comply with the new order of things as good citizens, and they cannot refuse honest obedience to the authority that now has the power." (Kant, MS, 06: 323)

214   Kersting 2007b: 374. (Own translation)

215   Kant does not differentiate between tumult, insurrection and revolution; in his work the term 'revolution' encompasses all forms of violent protest and overthrow.

216   Natural law can be viewed as a right to freedom based on the universal principle of justice and providing the foundation for the right to property. In contrast to Locke, in the natural condition these rights are of a merely provisional character. Taking Rousseau's concepts as its starting point, in Kant's work rights are guaranteed by the social contract, understood by Kant as hypothetical respectively transcendental and in the sense of a posit. Korsgaard argues that, as reciprocal guarantees, they are thus based on social relationships. Cf. Korsgaard, Christine M.: "Taking the Law in Our Own Hands: Kant on the Right to Revolution." In: Reath, Andrews; Herman, Barbara; Korsgaard, Christine (Eds.): *Reclaiming the History of Ethics: Essays for John Rawls.* Cambridge, New York, Melbourne etc. (Cambridge University Press), 1997, pp. 301, 305. It must, furthermore, be possible to assert these individual rights by means of a general will based on an established legal foundation and/or coercion. This general will is understood in procedural terms. (Cf. Korsgaard 1997: 313) Taking this as the starting point, there is an obligation for coexistence in a civil society. (Cf. Korsgaard 1997: 302–303) "To put it another way, justice, which is the condition in which we have guaranteed one another our rights, exists only where there is government. Government, then is founded on our presumptive general will to justice." (Korsgaard 1997: 303)

natural rights. Kant postulates that the quality of rulership is demonstrated by the ruler's willingness to participate in self-enlightenment; the guaranteeing of a mutually limiting liberty of the citizen and the establishment of a culture of publicity. In this regard Kant also believes in an evolutionary process of gradual improvement. Revolution would represent a relapse into the natural condition, which would in turn imply the abolition of law and the advent of violence – "before a public lawful condition is established, individual human beings, peoples and states can never be secure against violence from one another". (Kant, MS, AA 06: 312) Kersting emphasizes that "The tyrant thus progresses from being the summum malum to the lesser evil – insofar as differentiating political ethics that allow a normative differentiation of the various forms in which state power can be exercised are still in existence and do not content themselves with a general theory of legitimation as regards state power."[217] In Kant's work, the natural condition functions as the summum malum.[218] He argues that the grounding of violent resistance in positive law signifies the self-dissolution of the state; a condition of lawlessness, injustice, and instability since, according to Kant, the state guarantees the freedom of all its citizens – "act externally that the free use of choice can coexist with the freedom of everyone in accordance with the universal law."[219] The only justification for the use of coercive means is to ensure the reciprocal exercise of freedom. Kant states

---

217   Kersting 2007b: 375. (Own translation) "If we define the attack on the moral integrity of the subjects as a characteristic of tyrannical rulership, then it can be posited that Kant, and all modern constitutional philosophy, has been unable to develop a solution to the problem of tyrants. Their rulership is imposed undiminishedly and directly on the individual. Whereas in classical politics the tyrant was the ruler who perverted the purpose of the state and could thus legitimately be driven out of power and, where necessary, killed; in Kant's work he represents a practical test for the moral subject." (Kersting 2007b: 374; own translation)

218   "In modern constitutional philosophy, in contrast, the natural condition assumes the summum malum function. Its contrasting concept is not bad because it betrays the political purpose of rulership but rather anarchy. Modern thought must thus, as a matter of principle, be an enemy of resistance since any form of resistance destroys order and serves to promote anarchy." (Kersting 2007b: 374–375; own translation)

219   Kant, MS, AA 06: 231. "Justice (Right) thus involves 'the sum of the conditions under which the choice of one can be united with the choice of another in accordance with a universal law of freedom.' (MS 230) The universal law of justice, the categorial imperative of justice, is thus: 'so act externally that the free use of your choice can coexist with the freedom of everyone in accordance with a universal law.' (MS 230–31)." (Cummiskey 2009: 220)

"if a certain use of freedom is itself a hindrance to freedom in accordance with universal laws (i.e. wrong), coercion that is opposed to this (as a hindering of a hindering to freedom) is consistent with freedom in accordance with universal laws, that is, it is right. Hence there is connected with Right by the principle of contradiction an authorization to coerce someone who infringes it ... one can locate the concept of Right directly in the possibility of connecting universal reciprocal coercion with the freedom of everyone (MS 231–32)".[220]

Kant postulates that the exercising of violence to establish a just civil society is undoubtedly permissible; however, once the natural condition has been overcome he favours normative-legalistic, institutional means, espousing an evolutionary process of gradual reforms. Kant's primary fear in conjunction with the occurrence of a lawless condition is the advent of violence and destruction as well as the termination of peace within the context of the political system. Kant sees violence and war from a natural-teleological point of view and thus included in his concept of progress. They are initially the motor for the path to a cosmopolitan world order, however subsequently become an obstructive, dispensable means. Growing global trade relationships; the right of citizens from different states to hospitality; increasing political cooperation between states with the aim of establishing a federation of free states; and the fact that the republican participation of citizens will, in the final instance, prevent thoughtlessly initiated, avoidable wars demanding huge sacrifices from the population allow the hope for peace and the avoidance of the use of violence to appear justified. Institutional and legal measures; changes in ways of thinking and the growth of human morality are linked to this development towards perpetual peace. This process in turn advances the development of human capabilities and is supported by nature itself, since, as argued by Kant, human beings may

---

220 Cummiskey 2009: 221. In common with, for example, Sarah William Holt, Cummiskey posits the theory that the Kantian concept of justice legitimates resistance under certain circumstances. This view assumes the independence of the derivation of justice on the one hand and, on the other, law, whereby justice already exists in the natural condition. "[T]hese actions are direct violations of justice and do not depend on civil society for their legitimate external enforcement." (Cummiskey 2009: 221) According to Kant, however, justice and law can only be considered in conjunction with one another; in my view it is thus not possible to identify any logical contradiction in his argumentation on this point. Coercion does not originate from the idea of justice itself but rather must be institutionally and legally substantiated.

hope that nature facilitates and favours the acting out of higher human ambitions.

Despite his rejection of revolution and violence Kant viewed the French Revolution as a sign of historical progress and increasing morality in terms of the rise in moral enthusiasm which it engendered on the part of spectators.[221] Kant's assessment took place on the historical-philosophical meta-level and was not concerned with the theoretical action level of politically active adversaries in terms of the sacrifices demanded by the Revolution[222] and the ramifications for the rule of law as guaranteed by the state. Kant hoped for improvements to the state on the one hand thanks to reforms of the political-legal system within the scope of a continuous process of progress and, on the other, as a result of the increase in autonomy, self-determination and morality of all citizens and the sovereign himself. In this context, Kant refers to a revolution in the manner in which humans think, resulting in a massive reorientation in thought; an abrupt break with what had gone before. The ban on resistance does not, however, mean unconditional obedience

"Kant thus naturally demands that obedience be refused if the ruler's commands collide with moral obligations. The general ban on active resistance does not, in itself, mean that the subject's obedience must be limitless. [...]

---

221   "The revolution of a gifted people which we have seen unfolding in our day may succeed or miscarry; it may be filled with misery and atrocities to the point that a sensible man, were he boldly to hope to execute it successfully the second time, would never resolve to make the experiment at such cost – this revolution, I say, nonetheless finds in the hearts of all spectators (who are not engaged in the game themselves) a wishful participation which borders on enthusiasm, the very expression of which is fraught with danger; this sympathy, therefore, can have no other cause than a moral disposition in the human race." (Kant, SF, AA 07: 85) In: Kant, Immanuel: "The Conflict of the Faculties (Der Streit der Fakultäten)". Translation and Introduction Mary J. Gregor, New York (Abaris Books), 1979, p. 153. In this context Kant focuses on human morality as a sign of hope. "But if revolution is wrong, how can 'wishful participation' be right? And we know that Kant himself was one of the most enthusiastic of these wishful participants. His personal obsession was both the French and the American Revolutions". (Korsgaard 1997: 299–300) Korsgaard argues that revolutionaries must be viewed as responsible for their actions – "A revolutionary must see himself as the author of the loss of life and limb, the social disorder, and the suspension of the juridical condition that results from revolution." (Korsgaard 1997: 315)

222   They make clear that human beings are often viewed as a means to an end within the scope of revolutionary processes.

Kant also believes that the sovereign's demand for obedience expires at the point at which normative laws reach their limits. Only that which is an object of the law is subject to the ruler's legislative disposition. The legal irresistibility of the monarch's authority thus ends where the domain of moral reason begins."[223]

It is at this point that critique is assigned its logical-argumentative position in the system of Kantian philosophy. Critique can, initially, be understood in the sense of examining the condition of the possibility for human comprehension and morality. Over and above this, critique – understood as a form of socio-

---

223   Kersting 2007b: 371. (Own translation) He continues "In the event of a collision between the obligation to be obedient and fundamental moral obligations, human beings subject to moral law are, without doubt, not only entitled but explicitly obliged
to give precedence to moral obligations. In other words and moreover, a collision, between the obligation to be obedient and moral obligations is only ever apparent since
the higher degree of obligation is inherent in the latter. If, therefore, the state demands
a breach of moral obligations then resistance may and must take place. This resistance
is, however, of a solely passive nature; it is not an active termination of obedience but
rather a suffering refusal to obey." (Kersting 2007: 372; own translation) In my opinion,
resistance in Kant's work should be understood as a critical attitude which can be interpreted as passive. In concrete terms this means, for example, resigning from office
and expressing one's own critical position via public media but not, however, violent
actions in the form of insurrection or revolution – resistance in the form of a public
critique. "It is erroneous to view Kant's theory of resistance as the documentation of
a morally monstrous authoritarian ethos." (Kersting 2007b: 373; own translation) He
continues "In addition to this, Kant did not postulate the legal impossibility of limiting a subject's obedience but rather the illegality of a revolutionary improvement
of the state." (Kersting 2007b: 374; own translation) The political instrument of a vote
of no confidence in today's parliamentary democracies can be viewed as a legally organised process in the sense of the Kantian understanding of resistance. In my opinion the resistance originating from Kantian philosophy cannot be interpreted in the
sense of a moral refusal to be obedient and an ethos of public critique but rather in
the more restricted sense of the political-legal. There is a logical limit to obedience if
the legal constitution of a state is abolished by the sovereign himself, with the result
that, in basic terms, a natural condition exists. According to Kant violence must pre-
dominate at this point and the issue of the creation of constitutional structures would
reemerge. As is known, Kant envisages a coercive law to facilitate the establishment of
legally grounded states which implies and legitimises the use of violence – "the right
to use violent means to bring about a civil society." (Cummiskey 2009: 220) He continues "Justice involves the authorization to use coercion to promote lawful freedom."
(Cummiskey 2009: 221)

political autonomy of thought – is given a specific form as a mode of accessing one's own comprehension within the framework of society, in particular
within the scope of the publicity-seeking position of the scholar in the general
sense of a specialist in a specific area, in line with the principle of publicity –
defined as a critical attitude on the part of a citizen. Critique thus becomes
an ethos. This form of critique can, and should, affect all areas of human coexistence. In Kant's era, which he defined as striving for *Aufklärung* [Enlight-
enment], enfranchisement and critique were closely related. Although Kant attributes a mobilising character to the exercising of violence[224] within the scope
of military conflicts, positing that it motivates humans to even greater efforts,
violence must, due to its destructive character, be rejected on both legal and hu-
man-moral grounds, only becoming acceptable through a teleology supported
by nature[225] and pointing to 'perpetual peace'. In the field of nation-state politics Kant gives preference to the legal option as a means to achieve progress
which simultaneously promotes human morality.

---

224   "For Kant progressive violence exercised in the cause of a moral-legal progress [...] is
      inconceivable." (Kersting 2007b: 369; own translation) He continues "Kant juxtaposes
      the revolutionary pathos of the clean slate; of the necessary final battle; the enthusias-
      tic presumptuousness of creating the new state from the ruins of the old order; as the
      unsullied embodiment of justice detached from all ties to the corrupt old regime with
      the sober forcefulness of the inalienable universal right to peace, order, and freedom
      from violence." (Kersting 2007b: 370; own translation)

225   Kant writes "when nature herself produces revolutions". (*Perpetual Peace*, Ak VIII, 350)
      He continues "The history of mankind can be seen, in the large, as the realization of Na-
      ture's secret plan to bring forth a perfectly constituted state." (Kant, IaG, 08: 27) Beck
      asserts "The unsocial sociability of mankind, the competition among tribes and states
      which leads to war, and revolutions – all of which are judged, juridically and moralisti-
      cally, to be evil – are the means nature uses in realizing her 'secret plan' for mankind."
      In: Beck, Lewis W.: "Kant and the Right of Revolution". In: Beck, Lewis W. (Ed.): *Essays on
      Kant and Hume*. New Haven, London (Yale University Press), 1978, p. 182. Discussing rev-
      olution Beck refers to Kant's *Kritik der Urteilskraft* – "The organization of nature, Kant
      tells us, has nothing analogous to any causality known to us, but it throws light on 'a
      complete transformation, recently undertaken, of a great people into a state'. (Ibid.)
      Beck argues that in this context Kant emphasises the aspect of transformation into a
      single whole. However, he rejects the use of human beings as a means to an end, em-
      phasising human nature as an 'end in itself'. (Cf. ibid.)

2.1.6.3   Resistance, violence and critique in the work of Michel Foucault

For Foucault violence is one of the possible forms of resistance and is theoretically anchored in his concept of power. His concept of violence is wide-ranging, also including, for example, symbolic forms of violence. When discussing revolution Foucault unambiguously rejects physical violence which perpetuates suffering. It is "[a] marvelous and formidable promise" and he poses the question "[b]ut is this revolution really such a desirable thing?"[226] He continues

> "It constituted a gigantic effort to domesticate revolts within a rational and controllable history: it gave them a legitimacy, separated their good forms from their bad, and defined the laws of their unfolding: it set their prior conditions, objectives, and ways of being carried to completion. Even the status of the professional revolutionary was defined: By thus repatriating revolt, people have aspired to make its truth manifest and to bring it to a real end."[227]

Foucault displays a preference for non-violent forms of resistance, emphasising the necessity of integrating the technologies of the self into socio-political change processes and change on the part of the subject himself. Foucault, however, argues that neither revolutions nor the exercising of violence in its various forms can, as a matter of principle, be avoided; various historical-social implementations and areas of their exercising can be observed. Foucault writes "Revolts belong to history. But, in a certain way, they escape from it. The impulse by which a single individual, a group, a minority, or an entire people says, 'I will no longer obey,' and throws the risk of their life in the face of an authority they consider unjust seems to me to be something irreducible."[228]

---

226   Foucault, Michel: "Useless to revolt?". In: Foucault, Michel: *Power. (Essential Works of Foucault 1954–1984. Vol. 3)*. Faubion, James D. (Ed.), London (Penguin Books), 2002b, p. 450. In this context Foucault references Max Horkheimer; he develops his considerations as a reaction to the fall of the Shah's regime and the revolution of the ayatollahs in Iran. "Because they are thus 'outside history' and in history, because everyone stakes his life, and his death, on their possibility, one understands why uprisings have so easily found their expression and their drama in religious forms. Promises of the afterlife, time's renewal, anticipation of the savior or the empire of the last days, a reign of pure goodness – for centuries all this constituted, where the religious form allowed, not an ideological costume but the very way of experiencing revolts." (Ibid.)

227   Ibid. Here Foucault refers to the so-called "era of the 'Revolution' since the 18th century".

228   Foucault 2002b: 449. He continues "And because the man who rebels is finally inexplicable; it takes a wrenching-away that interrupts the flow of history, and its long chains

In contrast to Kant, Foucault views revolutions within the scope of the overall historical process of their event-like nature. When discussing the experiential aspect for participants he highlights the overlaying of political and religious promises of salvation, in which "the secular power is always accused."[229] Unlike Kant, in Foucault's work revolutions are not viewed under the aspect of a relapse into the natural condition, as a break in the legal system and, simultaneously, as a sign of morality on global society's path to a federation of free states and perpetual peace but rather, as a historical fact, they remain part of the history in the making.

> "No one has the right to say, 'Revolt for me; the final liberation of all men depends on it.' But I am not in agreement with anyone who would say. 'It is useless for you to revolt; it is always going to be the same thing.' One does not dictate to those who risk their lives facing a power. Is one right to revolt, or not? Let us leave the question open. People do revolt; that is a fact."[230]

Foucault asserts that history is not an evolutionary process, stating "A question of ethics? Perhaps. A question of reality, without a doubt. All the disenchantments of history won't after the fact of the matter: it is because there are such voices that the time of human beings does not have the form of evolution but that of 'history', precisely."[231] For Foucault history has the character of an event and cannot be interpreted in the progress mode. It is thus also not possible to identify specific strategies for a concept to improve the world. This does not, however, mean passive acceptance but rather is linked to ad-hoc forms of socio-political action in both the personal and the general societal context. "So my position leads not to apathy but to a hyper- and pessimistic activism."[232] Foucault argues that power in all its forms, in particular the cemented form of rulership, must be subjected to limitations.[233]

---

of reasons, for a man to be able, 'really', to prefer the risk of death to the certainty of having to obey." (Foucault 2002b: 447)

229   Foucault 2002b: 450.

230   Foucault 2002b: 452.

231   Ibid.

232   Foucault, Michel: "On the Genealogy of Ethics: an Overview of Work in Progress". In: Rabinow, Paul (Ed.): *Foucault Reader*. London (Penguin Books), 1991, p. 343.

233   "The rules that exist to limit it can never be stringent enough; the universal principles for dispossessing it of all the occasions it seizes are never sufficiently rigorous. Against power one must always set inviolable laws and unrestricted rights." (Foucault 2002b: 453) Foucault outlines his task as an intellectual in this context as follows "I am an in-

Foucault's concern is "to elaborate new modes of critique, new modes of questioning, to attempt something else."[234] He poses the question "since I am in one sense a historian of ideas and science, of what effect are these relations of power in the order of knowledge?"[235] Archaeological critique serves to identify the epistemes and discourse rules which form knowledge; genealogical critique examines the having-become of principles of thought, forms of power, methods of subjectification and their interplay and thus has a historical focus in order to facilitate a critique which takes present society as its starting point; "philosophical critique of the present in a genealogical form" in the "mode of historical philosophizing".[236] To quote Foucault, "I would like to do the genealogy of problems, of *problématiques*."[237] He continues "And in a certain way, what I wanted to speak to you about is this critical attitude as virtue in general"; of a "critical attitude".[238] Foucault defines this more clearly as follows

tellectual. If I were asked for my conception of what I do, the strategist being the man who says, 'What difference does a particular death, a particular cry, a particular revolt make compared to the general necessity, and, on the other hand, what difference does a general principle make in the particular situation where we are?', well, I would have to say that it is immaterial to me whether the strategist is a politician, a historian, a revolutionary, a follower of the shah or of the ayatollah; my theoretical ethic is opposite to theirs. It is 'antistrategic': to be respectful when a singularity revolts, intransigent as soon as power violates the universal. A simple choice, a difficult job: for one must at the same time look closely, a bit beneath history, at what cleaves it and stirs it, and keep watch, a bit behind politics, over what must unconditionally limit it. After all, that is my work; I am not the first or the only one to do it. But that is what I chose." (Foucault 2002b: 453)

234   Foucault, Michel: "Interview with Christian Panier and Pierre Watté". In: Foucault, Michel: *Wrong-Doing, Truth-Telling: the Function of Avowal in Justice*. Brion, Fabienne; Harcourt, Bernard E. (Eds.), Chicago (The University of Chicago Press), 2014, p. 249.

235   Foucault 2014: 251.

236   Saar, Martin: *Genealogie als Kritik: Geschichte und Theorie des Subjekts nach Nietzsche und Foucault*. Frankfurt, New York, (Campus), 2007, pp. 159, 161. (Own translation)

237   Foucault, Michel: "The Subject and Power". In: Foucault, Michel: Power (Essential Works of Foucault 1954–1984. Vol. 3). Faubion, James D. (Ed.), London (Penguin Books), 2002c, p. 343.

238   Foucault 2007b: 43, 42. "After all, critique only exists in relation to something other than itself: it is an instrument, a means for a future or a truth that it will not know nor happen to be, it oversees a domain it would want to police and is unable to regulate." (Foucault 2007b: 42) Foucault continues "However, above all, one sees that the core of critique is basically made of the bundle of relationships that are tied to one another, or one to the two others, power, truth and the subject." (Foucault 2007b: 47) He elaborates "I will say that critique is the movement by which the subject gives himself the right

"[A]s compensation, or rather, as both partner and adversary to the arts of governing, as an act of defiance, as a challenge, as a way of limiting these arts of governing and sizing them up, transforming them, of finding a way to escape from them or, in any case, a way to displace them, with a basic distrust, but also and by the same token, as a line of development of the arts of governing, there would have been something born in Europe at that time, a kind of general cultural form, both a political and moral attitude, a way of thinking, etc. and which I would very simply call the art of not being governed or better, the art of not being governed like that and at that cost. I would therefore propose, as a very first definition of critique, this general characterization: the art of not being governed quite so much."[239]

Foucault concludes "Well, then!: critique will be the art of voluntary insubordination, that of reflected intractability. Critique would essentially insure the desubjugation of the subject in the context of what we could call, in a word, the politics of truth."[240] According to Foucault this definition corresponds to Kant's definition of *Aufklärung*, whose central momentum is, in turn, critique. Kant focuses on the aspect of minority as the incapability of being able to use one's own reason without the guidance of others, without being ruled by authorities. On the one hand he emphasizes the interest of the ruler in maintaining the condition of minority and, on the other, the lack of courage on the part of those concerned to change this state of affairs. Foucault posits that *Aufklärung* in Kant's work is a "call for courage."[241] Within the scope of this Kantian project critique in the sense of recognition of the limits of one's own possibilities of knowledge is linked to the *Aufklärung*. Kant understands critique as the examination of the conditions for the possibility of theoretical knowledge; of the principle of human morality and the justification of basic teleological assumptions, also with regard to the entitlement to assume human progress within the scope of the historical development process. Foucault argues that Kant's three critiques lie at the heart of the enterprise and are incorporated into the project

---

to question truth on its effects of power and question power on its discourses of truth." (Ibid.)

239   Foucault 2007b: 44–45. Foucault elaborates on this attitude with regard to its historical origins – "Let us say that critique is biblical, historically." (Foucault 2007b: 46) In the context of natural law it is, furthermore, a legal matter as well as confronting authority. (Cf. Foucault 2007b: 46)

240   Foucault 2007b: 47.

241   Foucault 2007b: 48.

of *Aufklärung*. He says "Nevertheless, in his attempt to desubjugate the subject in the context of power and truth, as a prolegomena to the whole present and future *Aufklärung*, Kant set forth critique's primordial responsibility, to know knowledge."[242] By posing the question of the conditions and limits of knowledge the orientation of Foucault's archaeological search for the historical a priori demonstrates a significant analogy to the Kantian procedure. Stating that the Kantian appeal for *Aufklärung* has been neglected, Foucault formulates his programme for the examination of power. "It may take the question of the *Aufklärung* as its way of gaining access, not to the problem of knowledge, but to that of power. It would proceed not as an investigation into legitimacy, but as something I would call an examination of *eventualization (evenementialisation)*."[243] It is at precisely this point that the methods of archaeological and genealogical critique can be applied to investigate the "connections between mechanisms of coercion and contents of knowledge";[244] "the nexus of knowledge-power".[245] This also includes an exploration of the conditions of acceptability.[246] Foucault thus attempts to resume the Kantian project of Aufklärung.[247]

---

242   Foucault 2007b: 50.

243   Foucault 2007b: 59.

244   Ibid.

245   Foucault 2007b: 61. "Let us say, roughly, that as opposed to a genesis oriented towards the unity of some principal cause burdened with multiple descendants, what is proposed instead is a genealogy, that is, something that attempts to restore the conditions for the appearance of a singularity born out of multiple determining elements of which it is not the product, but rather the effect." (Foucault 2007b: 64)

246   Foucault 2007b: 62.

247   "In conclusion, given the movement which swung critical attitude over into the question of critique or better yet, the movement responsible for reassessing the *Aufklärung* enterprise within the critical project whose intent was to allow knowledge to acquire an adequate idea of itself – given this swinging movement, this slippage, this way of deporting the question of the *Aufklärung* into critique – might it not now be necessary to follow the opposite route?" (Foucault 2007b: 66–67) The following quotation clarifies the connection with the question of domination: "And if it is necessary to ask the question about knowledge in its relationship to domination, it would be, first and foremost, from a certain decision-making will not to be governed, the decision-making will, both an individual and collective attitude which meant, as Kant said, to get out of one's minority. A question of attitude." (Foucault 2007b: 67)

2.1.6.4   Projecting the future. Violence, critique and progress in the context of Mbembe's *afropolitanism*

Mbembe also discusses violence, among other things in the form of epistemic violence, arguing that a decolonisation of thought is required, particularly "in a historical context in which violence has touched not only material infrastructures but psychological infrastructures too, through the denigration of the Other, through the assertion of the latter's worthlessness."[248] For him, postcolonial thought represents a critique in the form of deconstruction of processes of thought and judgements; the analysis of the processes which form identity and subject; and an examination of European humanism and universalism. On the other hand, in Mbembe's work critique has an equal bearing on the African discourse – "And so, if you like, it's a way of reflecting on the fractures, on what remains of the promise of life when the enemy is no longer the colonist in a strict sense, but the 'brother'? So the book is a critique of the African discourse on community and brotherhood."[249] The paratextual echoing of Kant's critiques in his work *Critique de la raison nègre* suggests the purpose behind the examination of 'black reason' in supposed Kantian tradition; can, however, be defined as discourse analysis in the Foucauldian sense – as a grounding of critique in discourse analysis. Mbembe differentiates between "material and mental war" and makes clear "that the colonial project was not reducible to a simple military-economic system, but was underpinned by a discursive infrastructure, a symbolic economy system, a whole apparatus of knowledge the violence of which was as much episteme as it was physical."[250] The objective of critique is to develop alternative forms of knowledge and thus, among other things, to transform the world as a whole.[251] In this context the institutionalisation of law is not, as is the case in Kant's work, the central basis for the improvement of society. For Mbembe there is a close link between law and injustice – "It was also the place where law had nothing to do with justice but,

---

248   Mbembe, Achille: "What is postcolonial thinking? An interview with Achille Mbembe". In: *Eurozine*. 2008, p. 8, retrieved August 14, 2024, from: http://www.eurozine.com/pdf/2008-01-09-mbembe-en.pdf.

249   Mbembe 2008: 11; Mbembe refers here to his book *On the Postcolony* (2005). He also pursues the project of examining the 'African' discourse in his book *Critique de la raison nègre* (2013).

250   Mbembe 2008: 6. "The cultural analysis of the discursive infrastructure and of the colonial imagination would gradually become the very subject of postcolonial theory and give rise to severe criticism from intellectuals". (Mbembe 2008: 6)

251   Cf. Mbembe 2008: 3, 5.

on the contrary, was a way of starting wars, continuing them and perpetuating them."[252] Mbembe also argues that it is impossible to differentiate between 'good violence' and 'bad violence' – "There is no 'good violence' that can follow on automatically from 'bad violence' and be legitimized by it. All violence 'good' or 'bad', always sanctions a disjunction. The reinvention of politics in postcolonial conditions first requires people to depart from the logic of vengeance, above all when vengeance wears the shabby garb of the law."[253] Violence and war, argues Mbembe, often take on indirect forms which conceal them; in this context critique has an exposing function. It also serves to analyse the particular effects of power, whereby Mbembe differentiates between 'power' and 'force' – "As a result it could be said of postcolonial thinking that it is not a critique of power as usually understood, but of force – a force that is incapable of transformation."[254] The focus of Mbembe's investigation of power theory is on coercive, oppressive forms of power which are linked to the exercising of violence. His analysis of present forms of power and counter-power leads him to develop the concept of necropolitics,[255] incorporating forms of terror, genocide and suicide bombers. Necropower is viewed as a critique, expansion and updating of the Foucauldian definition of power. The use of the human body as a weapon – e.g. in the case of the suicide bomber – procures a sovereignty which consciously employs death as a means of power. Mbembe thus updates and expands Foucauldian forms of power such as disciplinary power, pastoral power and biopower in order to facilitate an appropriate power theory-related discussion of present societal situations. Mbembe argues that it is impossible today to differentiate between war and peace since war-like states of violence are omnipresent. He furthermore states

> "It might be that we will have to live with violence. [...] So, if you look from the historical point of view, there will never be a moment when we are at peace with ourselves and our neighbors, and that the kind of social, economic and

---

252 Mbembe 2008: 2. "In order to enable those who were on their knees not long before, bowed down under the weight of oppression, to arise and walk, justice must be done. So there is no escape from the need of justice." (Mbembe 2008: 9)

253 Mbembe 2008: 8.

254 Mbembe 2008: 3.

255 Cf. Mbembe, Achille: "Necropolitics". In: *Public Culture*, 15(1), 2003, pp. 11–40.

political formations that are emerging in the continent and elsewhere too, will always be a mixture of civil peace and violence."[256]

In this context and with regard to Africa he demands "the demilitarization of politics" and "the democratization of its politics",[257] criticising "the combination of militarism and mercantilism".[258] Mbembe also discusses a crisis of emancipation theories in conjunction with this – "All of this creates a terrible crisis in the foundational theories of emancipation we used to rely on in order to further a kind of politics of openness and equality."[259] He therefore demands an imagining of the possible with regard to the future as a critical potential for change – "So we wanted to recapture the category of the future and see to what extent it could be remobilized in the attempt at critiquing the present, and reopening up a space not only for imagination, but also for the politics of possibility."[260]

While echoing Kant's cosmopolitan concept of world citizenship; the federation of free states and the right to hospitality, in contrast to Kant Mbembe primarily relates his concept of *afropolitanism* to one continent, Africa, which is, however, open to the world. "In any event the future, viewed from this angle, is not some sort of afro-centrism, but what I'd call afropolitanism – a way of being 'African' open to difference and conceived as transcending race."[261] Africans' cosmopolitanism, the outcome of abduction, exile and diaspora, and current forms of cosmopolitan nomadism are the starting points for his cosmopolitan concept which is concerned with overcoming racial categorisation. In his *afropolitanism* Mbembe develops the idea of Africa as the centre of its own self,[262] one which, thanks to the simplification of intercontinental and

---

256 Mbembe, Achille: "Africa and the Future: An Interview with Achille Mbembe". In: *Swiss-future* 03/2013a, p. 3, retrieved August 14, 2024, from: http://africasacountry.com/2013/11/africa-and-the-future-an-interview-with-achille-mbembe/.

257 Mbembe 2013a: 4.

258 Mbembe 2013a: 3.

259 Mbembe 2013a: 2.

260 Ibid. He writes on this as follows: "In such an age the old division between subject and object is no longer as clear as it used to be and that in fact, if we look carefully at the operations of consumption world-wide today, we might observe that, many people want to become objects, or be treated as such, if only because becoming an object one might end up being treated better than as a human." (Ibid.)

261 Mbembe 2008: 10.

262 "The ultimate challenge, however, is for Africa to become its own center." (Mbembe 2013a: 4)

global mobility, should be, and become, a magnet for people from all over the world. "As Europe closes its borders, Africa will have to open its borders."[263] The focus on Africa is thus linked to an openness towards the world which should lead to a return to Africa. His particular concern is the simplification of crossing borders; of residence rights and the acquisition of state citizenships in order to promote global coexistence. He rejects exclusion and isolation, speaking in favour of diversity and plurality. In his re-conceived humanism, the world's population is viewed as a brotherhood, in the Christian sense of the word. African cosmopolitan incorporates a progressive concept which differs from that understood by Europeans and Americans, in particular as regards its rejection of a technical-materialistic focus and the associated paternalism. In his *politics of possibility* Mbembe references in particular the term 'future' – a future which has hitherto been denied to Africa.[264] Foucault in contrast does not develop any concept of a world future; his focus is on context-related, ad hoc improvements to create a society which facilitates a self-determined form of life viewed as a work of art. A Kantian inspired vision of an increasingly individual autonomy which must be conceived in the context of technologies of the self. While Kant takes the idea of 'perpetual peace' as the basis for his deliberations, substantiating it legally and politically in the sense of a contract, whereby he provides human moral and political activity with a range of instruments to assist this process – state, inter-state and supra-state regimentation and institutionalism; legal provisions and teleological concepts concerning nature – Mbembe argues that humans are primarily dependent on their insight, their morality and their willingness to exchange information and to cooperate when attempting to achieve peace. When discussing coming to terms with colonial and postcolonial history he places his faith in a dialogue with the traumas; own guilt; overcoming of victimhood and the power of forgiveness, aspiring to socio-political transformation processes for a greater sense of responsibility; participation; justice and sharing. Mbembe argues that we still require Kant today in two respects – on the one hand as a proponent of *Perpetual Peace* who opens up the horizon of a global community, a global society which should be viewed as a kind of community of owners; on the other as

---

263   Ibid.
264   Mbembe 2013a: 2.

a proponent of human beings as sovereign creatures of reason who are able to master their passions and affects and arrive at a moral judgement.[265]

2.1.6.5   Conclusive observations. Criticism, violence and progress in Kant, Foucault and Mbembe

Critique is a key element of the three philosophical concepts of Kant, Foucault and Mbembe. While Kant examines the faculty of understanding – the cognitive powers of sensibility, understanding and reason – with a particular focus on the elaboration of apriority, Foucault and Mbembe investigate issues relating to a critique of knowledge and power theory, examining time-specific, socio-historical forms. In contrast to Foucault, who is concerned with Western thought as a whole in terms of its fundamental epistemes or discourse rules, Mbembe's postcolonial theory respectively philosophy focuses on an examination of the African and afro-diasporic discourse and hegemonic Western discourse, primarily in the context of the first and second waves of colonisation and of globalisation. Even if both share Kant's epistemological concern, in contrast to Kant, however, they posit a socio-historic constructedness of knowledge; their objective is still to use critique to achieve social change. For each philosopher, critique is in equal measure incorporated in the cultivation and moralisation of human beings; they are viewed as instruments of social change. In contrast to Kant and Mbembe, with their cosmopolitan respectively afrocosmopolitan vision, Foucault does not formulate a concept of progress in the wider social sense but instead remains within the individual framework of a desired aestheticization or moralisation of the subject and their desubjugation.[266] In Kant's work violence in the political context is viewed primarily as a restriction of the freedom of others which must be prevented by means of institutional and legal restrictions and their legitimate coercive instruments in order to facilitate private ownership and free trade which, in turn, form the basis of a state regimentation which displays a republican character and, in addition to this, a tendency towards a federation of free states and the realisation of

---

265   Cf. Mbembe, Achille: "Was bleibt von Immanuel Kant?" In: *ZEIT ONLINE*, 2015, p. 1; retrieved August 17, 2024, from: http://www.zeit.de/2015/49/philosophie-immanuel-kant-vermaechtnis-philosophen.

266   Foucault, however, clearly links this process to the hope for a freer society which offers the individual space to develop their own potential.

perpetual peace. Kant argues that the universalistic regulatory nature of law[267] also binds power; which he understands in the sense of rulership. Kant wishes to use structural violence and its coercive means to limit physical violence, in particular for the benefit of the law and political institutionalism. Foucault and Mbembe, however, demonstrate that hegemonic power has penetrated the legal/juridical field, thus deconstructing the latter in its function as a positive counterweight. Both philosophers argue that structural coercive means have, in general, become obsolete.

Foucault, and with him Mbembe, are particularly interested in hidden forms of violence such as, for example, epistemic violence which determines thought and, within the scope of subjectification processes and in addition to forming by means of body practices, also has an influence on the body, emotionality and desire and is incorporated into evaluation processes. Critique should reveal these forms of being ruled and provide support in actively bringing about change – in the sense of increased autonomy. This is also linked to processes of changed norms and revaluation. In this context, the self-design of the individual in Foucault's work references technologies of the self, such as reading, writing, etc., in conjunction with a concept of life as art in the sense of an aesthetic-ethical work. Critique in both Foucault's and Kant's work thus proves to be a key element of their philosophy. Mbembe is primarily concerned with critique as a dialogue with history and experienced trauma and with the processes of forgiveness and exoneration. In contrast to Foucault his argumentation is less aesthetic and/or ethical but instead based more on psychology and, in some cases, religion, demanding the establishment of institutions for historical reappraisal. Parallel to this, in the tradition of Kantian cosmopolitanism he places his faith in political measures to bring people from different cultures together and unite them behind the common project of 'the future' – in Mbembe's work primarily with regard to Africa. It becomes apparent in this context that Mbembe's *afropolitanism* is not free from a certain Afrocentrism. Kant in contrast overcomes the Eurocentrism of his philosophy by means of the fundamental theories of world citizenship; the federation of free states and the right to hospitality, which, in the final analysis, transcend this Eurocentrism.

---

267 "Progress in history is not measured by the happiness of the people but by the formal criterion of the rule of law and the scope of juridical freedom." (Beck 1978: 181)

2.2   Between autonomy and heteronomy. Subject, ethics and aesthetics in the work of Michel Foucault

2.2.1   Recognise yourself. Anthropological perspectives in Hegel's aesthetics and in Foucault's aesthetics and ethics

2.2.1.1   Anthropological perspectives and self-recognition in Hegel's and Foucault's works

For Hegel, the theorem of 'know yourself' is the basic principle of his philosophy of the mind and knowledge of the human being. His concern is to understand truth per se and the human as a primarily spiritual being. In his aesthetics, Hegel describes the development of art as a materially dependent stage in the progress of the mind. It proceeds in a spiral movement of alienation and return of the mind to itself leading to spiritual growth until art itself ends. 'Know yourself' as a spiritual principle is based on an increasing spiritualisation of those who are alienated, also as a fundamental anthropological moment, which increases the ability to recognise the spiritual as spiritual by means of the spiritual – as a way to truth. The central foundation of anthropology is located in Hegel's principle of the mind. Foucault's aesthetics and ethics attempt to demonstrate a method of self-formation of the subject using the analogy of works of art and life in order to make greater individual autonomy conceivable. In his critique of 'know yourself' he refers to the Greek/Roman concept of care of the self and the associated technologies of the self. For Foucault, the human being is "a face drawn in sand"[268] and is a structuring episteme of modernity in the historical process of thinking and speaking. He sees the human being as "a face in the sand" which is a structuring episteme of modernity in the historical process of thinking and speaking. In this context, Foucault speaks of "la fin de l'homme".[269] In his radical concept of the historicization of humans, humans represent a task for themselves, referencing Kant's concept of Enlightenment. According to Foucault, the aim is to develop a lifestyle which comes close to Kant's concept of ethos and implies a liberation from heteronomy and an increase in autonomy. Foucault's aesthetic thus evolves into a form of ethics. How can the principle of 'know yourself' be understood in Hegel and Foucault's work, in particular with regard to their

---

268   Foucault 2005a: 422.
269   Foucault, Michel: "La naissance d'un monde". In: Foucault, Michel: Dits et Écrits I. 1954–1975. Paris (Gallimard). 2001a, p. 816.

aesthetic considerations? What anthropological perspectives are associated with this and how are they reflected in Hegel's aesthetics and in Foucault's ethics or aesthetics? What concept of anthropology can be discerned among philosophers in this context? What conception of art forms the basis of their considerations?

2.2.1.2 'Know yourself'. Anthropological perspectives in the aesthetics of Hegel

The absolute spirit, which is the principle of Hegel's philosophy, simultaneously constitutes the essence of humans "Hegel's principle is the spirit. [...] As the absolute, it is also the true and universal essence of man. And it is only under the condition of the 'inner universality', which is the spirit, that the external peculiarities of human beings can be recognized."[270] Hegel criticises the focus of the philosophy of the Enlightenment on humans and mankind.[271] As a result of Hegel's philosophical fundamental idea and his philosophical concept and system, anthropological considerations are not at the heart of his thinking, but are assigned a clearly defined space in the entirety, which, when considered overall, is of limited significance. Thus, the most important anthropological considerations of Hegel[272] are embedded in the subsection of the philosophy of the mind, thematically related to the analysis of the human soul in the chapter 'The subjective mind'. The soul, which "is potentially all things",[273] is metaphorically described as the sleep of the spirit, since it "is not yet mind."[274] The natural

---

270   Löwith, Karl: *From Hegel to Nietzsche: The revolution in nineteenth-century thought.* New York (Columbia University Press), 1991, p. 307. Löwith refers here to Hegel's *Encyclopaedia* § 384 and § 377. Cf. Hegel, Georg Wilhelm Friedrich: *Encyclopaedia of the Philosophical Sciences in Basic Outline.* Brinkmann, Klaus; Dahlstrom, Daniel O. (Eds.), Cambridge, New York (Cambridge University Press), 2010.

271   Cf. Löwith, Karl: "Its absolute standpoint is, rather, 'man and mankind'. Philosophy, nevertheless, cannot halt at this empirical mankind and its superficial ideality, relinquishing the absolute 'for the sake of its beloved mankind'. What is usually called 'man' is merely a 'determinate finite object', not the 'spiritual focus of the universe'." (Löwith 1991: 307)

272   In the philosophy of law, Hegel specifically deals with the common understanding of man as a person, family member and citizen in civil society.

273   Hegel, Georg Wilhelm Friedrich: *Hegel's Philosophy of Mind.* Translated by W. Wallace and A. V. Miller; introduction by M. J. Inwood, Oxford (Oxford University Press), 2007, p. 34.

274   "But here in Anthropology we have not yet to consider the fulfilment that accrues to waking consciousness but waking only in so far as it is a natural state." (Ibid.)

determination of the soul, which includes physical and spiritual disparities – predisposition, temperament, character[275] and race,[276] people and nation[277] – is understood as a "copy of the concept".[278] Anthropology in the narrower sense therefore primarily comprises body-related experiences[279] and should be understood as a "representation of the natural spirit".[280] In Hegel's work the field of anthropology is thus narrowly defined. It does not encompass all areas of the human in the sense of a comprehensive consideration of humans and humankind, whereby its determination of essence by the spirit – as its foundation and a form of extended concept for the determination of the human – underlying the anthropological characterisations in a broader sense. "The human being is therefore not the bearer of the spirit but is himself spirit."[281] According to

---

275   "All the same, it cannot be denied that it has a *natural* foundation, that some people are more naturally prone to a strong character than others. For this reason, we had the right to speak of character here in Anthropology, although it is only in the sphere of free mind that it obtains its full unfolding." (Hegel 2007: 52–53)

276   For Hegel, the difference between the races is based in particular on geography and climate. Hegel distinguishes between the Caucasian, Ethiopian, Mongolian, Malay and American races and describes their different characteristics in a judgemental and hierarchical manner. In the Caucasian race, to which Europeans belong, the spirit, according to Hegel, comes to absolute unity with itself; it enables self-determination and development and brings forth world history. (Cf. Hegel 2007: 42) "*Negroes* are to be regarded as a nation of children who remain immersed in their uninterested and indifferent naïveté." (Hegel 2007: 41) On the other hand, Hegel emphasises the rationality of all human beings as a common characteristic of the species: "But descent affords no ground for the entitlement or non-entitlement of human beings to freedom and to dominion. Man is implicitly rational; herein lies the possibility of equality of right for all men,—the futility of a rigid distinction between races that have rights and those that have none." (Hegel 2007: 40)

277   Cf. Hegel 2007: 45–49.

278   Hegel 2007: 34. The problem arises of "how anthropology can be represented as a philosophy of corporeality (of the soul) in general within the philosophy of spirit. For Hegel understands this anthropology as the doctrine of the spirit insofar as it is natural – as the doctrine of the 'natural spirit' (10.38/§387). Within this anthropology, for example, there is talk of natural qualities, natural changes, natural states, and then also of sensation, self-feeling, illness, etc., all determinations that were already thematic within natural philosophy in the third part of 'Organic Physics'." In: Lomar, Achim: *Anthropologie und Vernunftkritik: Hegels Philosophie der menschlichen Welt.* Paderborn, Munich, Vienna, Zürich (Schöningh), 1997, p. 222. (Own translation)

279   Cf. Lomar 1997: 245.

280   Lomar 1997: 222. (Own translation)

281   Lomar 1997: 205. (Own translation)

Hegel the anthropological point of view is merely conditional; the metaphysical determinations of humans go beyond it. "The genus, on the other hand, truly realises itself in the spirit, in thinking, this homogeneous element of it. In the anthropological, however, this realisation, since it takes place in the natural individual spirit, still has the manner of naturalness."[282] In this respect Hegel speaks of the unity of genre and reason.[283] The definition of humans as spirits in the Hegelian sense should not be understood anthropologically, but theologically or metaphysically in the sense of a philosophical theology which focuses on the unconditional. Löwith states in this regard "This sentence occurs on the first page of the philosophy of religion, giving an external indication of the fact that Hegel's notion of the spirit is not intended anthropologically, but theologically, as the Christian Logos. It thus is 'superhuman'."[284]

Hegel refers to the incarnation of God in this context. In this respect, humans are, amongst other things, simultaneously part of the process of disembodiment of the absolute idea in the form of nature and the return to themselves in the stages of the subjective, objective and absolute spirit, a process of self-knowledge of the spirit. Humans, with their different moments, are involved in this process at various stages, especially as creators of culture; also as producers and recipients of art.

Hegel refers to the humanisation of God here. Also in this respect, humans are simultaneously part of the process of the disembodiment of the absolute idea in the form of nature and the return to themselves in the stages of the subjective, objective and absolute spirit, a process of the self-discovery of the spirit. Humans with their different moments are involved in this process on different levels, in particular as creators of culture; also as producers and recipients of art. Along with religion and philosophy, art should be regarded as one of the forms of the absolute spirit through which humans transcend the realm of the 'narrow' anthropological, moving towards an approach to the spiritual which determines their being.

Art as a spiritual requirement is in its three art forms (symbolic, classical and romantic) a form of expression of the absolute spirit upon its return to

---

282   Hegel 2007: 54.

283   Cf. ibid.

284   Löwith 1991: 308. Löwith refers here to Hegel XI, p. 3. Löwith further states "In Hegel's philosophical theology, the universal definition of man's essence is, and remains, that man is spirit (Logos), understood in the Christian sense, not merely a human being with earthly needs." (Löwith 1991: 309)

itself. In art, the immediate synthesis of nature and spirit manifests itself in contemplation, particularly of classical art, where beauty is viewed as a reconciliation between idea and creation in the representation of the human form in ancient Greek sculptural art. The sublimity of the Egyptians' symbolic art, on the other hand, with its predominance of the physical-material reveals the inappropriateness of idea and design, which in other ways, especially in poetry, is equally prevalent in Romantic art due to the increasing dematerialisation of art. The anthropological perspectives in Hegel's aesthetics, which in a narrower sense refer to humans' naturalness and in a broader sense to their spiritual nature, are closely connected to the process of 'know yourself'. Self-awareness in the human context refers primarily to the recognition of the human being's spirituality. The process of the absolute spirit's disembodiment and return to itself must be seen as a process of self-knowledge overall. "But, looked at in a higher speculative way, it is *the absolute spirit itself* which, in order explicitly to be knowledge of itself, makes distinctions *within* itself, and thereby establishes the finitude of spirit, within which it becomes the absolute object of the knowledge of itself. Thus it is absolute spirit in its community, [...] the actual Absolute as spirit and self-knowledge."[285] At the same time, however, self-awareness is, in relation to the human being, also reflected in the actuality of this process as an activity involving knowledge and manifests itself, among other things, in artistic creation and in perception of works of art. The genuine originality of a genius creates works of art which embody the sensual appearance of the idea in the ideal of artistic beauty reconciling the inner and the outer or materiality and spirituality in such a way that it can be experienced in the perception of art. The production and reception of art are therefore integrated into the process of self-experience of the spiritual as a form of self-knowledge. This is, however, surpassed in its further development by the more intellectual forms of religion and philosophy. The significance of artistic creativity and the process of reception for mankind consists of reconciliation of nature and spirit, the increasing transcendence of the merely natural. The further development of art itself therefore brings with it an expansion of spiritualisation and dematerialisation, especially in poetry. Art, in particular when it depicts human action, the human body and human sensation, satisfies both sides of humanity and is thus part of the process of growing spiritualisation in which humans are involved. Art promotes human freedom and self-determination through greater

---

285   Hegel, Georg Wilhelm Friedrich: *Aesthetics: Lectures on Fine Art*. Vol. I, translated by T.M. Knox, Oxford (Oxford University Press), 1975, p. 94.

detachment from material attachment and necessity. Artistic creation and reception as an end in itself promote the spirit as the essence of humans. Art is therefore a very specific form of outstanding significance at a specific phase of the historical development process.

Hegel's hypothesis of the end of art refers to the necessity of transcending the 'art' stage in the developmental process of the absolute mind. It no longer represents the most important realisation of the spiritual; it does not imply a de facto termination of the preoccupation with art. The tendency towards meta-reflection on art and towards the conceptualisation and theorisation of art in art itself and in the theory or philosophy of art, which in Hegel's work also includes a history of art, reflects the increasing detachment from the sensual-material in the realm of art. It documents the transition to philosophical thought, which is more strongly related to the spiritual, as the most adequate form of self-awareness of the spiritual. Hegel's aesthetics as a philosophy of art reflect this development and can themselves be considered part of the process of increasing philosophical abstraction with regard to art. In his aesthetics, Hegel also adequately describes the self-reflexive tendency of modern and contemporary art, so that it is possible to continue using Hegel's precepts, which transcend him.[286] The connections which Hegel makes between art, on the one

---

286   Robert Pippin, for example, pursues this idea in his work *After the Beautiful*. Cf. Pippin, Robert: *After the Beautiful. Hegel and the Philosophy of Pictorial Modernism*. Chicago, London (University of Chicago Press), 2014. In this context, Gethmann-Siefert distinguishes between three different ways of updating Hegel's aesthetics: "Firstly, the reactualisation of Hegelian aesthetics as a theory of modernity, then the rescue of at least some remnants of the Hegelian conception as the background of post-modern deconstruction, and finally the identification of the Hegelian concept with the project of art of the present." In: Gethmann-Siefert, Annemarie: "Danto und Hegel zum Ende der Kunst – Ein Wettstreit um die Modernität der Kunst und Kunsttheorie". In: Gethmann-Siefert, Annemarie; Nagl-Docekal, Herta; Rózsa, Erzébet; Weisser-Lohmann, Elisabeth (Eds.): *Hegels Ästhetik als Theorie der Moderne*. Berlin (Akademie), 2013, p. 17. (Own translation) In contrast to the theories which she addresses and especially in her critique of Danto's recourse to Hegel, an aesthetic theory of the avant-garde in its own world of art connoisseurs and art critics, Gethmann-Siefert emphasises the significance of art for the everyday human world in Hegel's aesthetics, especially with regard to its function of interpreting the world with an action-orientated intention in a communicative overall context, its 'aboutness'. (Cf. Gethmann-Siefert 2013: 26, 33) "Through the perception [of art] reasonableness, responsibility and freedom are to be conveyed." (Gethmann-Siefert 2013: 33; own translation) Today, art no longer has the task of creating identification through mediated content, but offers a 'formal education' through a reflected engagement with proposals for viewing the world. (Cf. Ibid.) This concerns the con-

hand, and anthropology and philosophy, on the other, remain relevant to theoretical reflections on art, albeit mostly from a critical point of view.

2.2.1.3   'Know yourself' and 'care of the self'. Anthropological perspectives in Foucault's aesthetics and ethics

Similarly to Hegel, Foucault criticises the overemphasis placed on the preoccupation with humans and humanity in philosophy and other sciences. In his book *The Order of Things*, Foucault identifies the episteme 'human being' as the knowledge-structuring principle of the modern era.[287] Foucault takes the historical transcendence of this focus and structuring with regard to the time-specific knowledge of modernity as his starting point. He also vehemently rejects the Christian form of 'know yourself' as a renunciation of oneself and refers to the Platonic and Stoic form of care of the self (*epimeleia heauton*). Self-awareness is linked to care of the self by using the technologies of the self and is thus related to human action. Self-awareness is primarily connected to the subject's development in aesthetic-ethical terms and to responsible action in the interpersonal sphere and the general social framework – also in political terms. Foucault investigates the relationship between 'care of the self' (*epimeleia heautou*) as an attitude towards oneself, the others and the world, which results in non-egoist ethics,[288] and 'know yourself' (*gnothi seauton*). He combines this with a perspective which moves from the outside to the inside,[289] observing that in antiquity 'know yourself' primarily only refers to becoming aware of one's own boundaries and should thus be thought of as being integrated into care of the self. "There is a dynamic entanglement, a reciprocal call for the *gnothi seauton* and for the *epimeleia heautou* (knowledge

---

frontation "with interpretations of the world and proposals for orientation from the past and present". (Gethmann-Siefert 2013: 32; own translation) She emphasises the "reflection-promoting (i.e. formally educating) relevance" of art in general and, in her critique of Danto, speaks out decidedly against the idea of a special artistic world which does not conform to Hegel's concept. (Gethmann-Siefert 2013: 34; own translation)

287   Foucault uses the episteme 'man' to describe modernity as opposed to the epistemes 'similarity' and 'representation' used for the Renaissance and the Classical age. (Cf. Foucault 1971)

288   Cf. Foucault, Michel: *The Hermeneutics of the Subject: Lectures at the Collège De France, 1981–1982*. New York (Palgrave-Macmillan), 2005b, p. 14. Further he states "Taking care of oneself and being concerned with justice amount to the same thing." (Foucault 2005b: 72)

289   Cf. Foucault 2005b: 18–19.

of the self and care of the self)."[290] Foucault disqualifies the principle of care of the self and rehabilitates the principle of 'knowing yourself' in accordance with an ancient culture of care of the self which lasted for almost a millennium, generally referring to this as a "Cartesian moment"[291] of "recogniz[ing] the truth and hav[ing] access to it [...] solely through his [man's] activity of knowing".[292] Foucault rehabilitates self-practice in the form of the application of technologies of the self as "the fullness of the self's relationship to the self",[293] as an ethics of the self.[294] Foucault explains that "although the theory of political power as an institution usually refers to a juridical conception of the subject of right, it seems to me that the analysis of governmentality—that is to say, of power as a set of reversible relationships—must refer to an ethics of the subject defined by the relationship of self to self".[295] For Foucault, it is also part of the art of living in the sense of creating a way of life, in which he understands life as a work of art. Self-awareness and ethical-aesthetic care of the self should be considered together. In this context, Foucault combines

---

290 Foucault 2005b: 69. In the Platonic model of recollection, the identification of care of the self and knowledge of the self are interwoven, while the Hellenistic model of the ethics of the self, interlinks self-care and self-knowledge. Only in the Christian model of self-exegesis are knowledge of the self and renunciation of the self intertwined. In this context, Foucault engages in a genealogy of the subject: "Généalogie veut dire que je mène l'analyse à partir d'une question présente." In: Foucault, Michel: "Le souci de la vérité". In: Foucault, Michel: "Le souci de la vérité". In: Foucault, Michel: *Dits et Écrits II. 1976–1988*. Paris (Gallimard), 2001b, p. 1493.

291 Cf. Foucault 2005b: 14.

292 Foucault 2005b: 17.

293 Foucault 2005b: 129.

294 "And in this series of undertakings [he refers to Stirner, Schopenhauer, Nietzsche und Baudelaire in particular] to reconstitute an ethic of the self, in this series of more or less blocked and ossified efforts, and in the movement we now make to refer ourselves constantly to this ethics of the self without ever giving it any content, I think we may have to suspect that we find it impossible today to constitute an ethics of the self, even though it may be an urgent, fundamental, and politically indispensable task, if it is true after all that there is no first or final point of resistance to political power other than in the relationship one has to oneself." (Foucault 2005b: 251–252)

295 Foucault 2005b: 252. Foucault writes "Putting it schematically, we could say that classical antiquity's moral reflection concerning the pleasures was not directed toward a codification of acts, nor toward a hermeneutics of the subject, but toward a stylization of attitudes and an aesthetics of existence." In: Foucault, Michel: *The History of Sexuality. Volume II: The Use of Pleasure*. New York (Vintage Books), 1990, p. 92.

ethics, aesthetics and politics. Habermas' theory that Foucault, like Hegel,[296] is primarily oriented towards the past and thus neglects the possible critical-utopian view of the future cannot be upheld. Unlike Hegel, who systematises the particular and places it within a process of the deprivation of the absolute spirit and its return to itself, Foucault's consideration of the historically particular is primarily concerned with the shaping of future life. It takes as its starting point the formation of the self and the shaping of specific living conditions in the socio-historical context of a time, in which self-knowledge is part of care of the self. According to Foucault, aesthetics is more than a special field of human cultural activity; it encompasses the creative process of shaping human life from an ethical-political point of view and thus represents the key to a practical-heterotopic change of self and society.

The principle of 'know yourself' is historicised, relativised and criticised by Foucault. In Hegel's work it remains the fundamental principle of the subject, world and historical process. Hegel's and Foucault's analysis of aesthetic reasoning illustrates this in a specific way. For both philosophers, 'know yourself' is also of central importance in the aesthetic field. For Foucault, in contrast to Hegel, it is subordinated to care of the self; detaches itself from the tendency to disregard itself and is given an ethical orientation. The forming of the self is oriented towards artistic creation, individual life should become a work of art. For Hegel, art is not the objective of human action, rather its importance is located in the context of a certain stage of human development with regard to the materialisation and dematerialisation of the mind in the world – as an expression and return to oneself. Foucault adopts Hegel's reservations about anthropology, decentralises them and regards them as outdated in historical development – albeit in very different ways. Hegel's reservations about anthropology are particularly important from a systematic aspect. In Hegel's system of philosophy, humans are neither the starting point nor the end point of philosophical reasoning. Anthropology in a broader sense is absorbed into Hegel's

---

296   "Hegel was unable to free himself from the demands of his systematization to employ the appropriate elements of his system as critical instruments." (Gallagher 1997: 146)

philosophy of mind and in his philosophy[297] as a whole.[298] In Hegel's work, the "concept of the mind must be regarded as the basic concept of a critically reformulated anthropology".[299] In Foucault's work, the human being is first and foremost an element of the history of knowledge and as such, as an episteme of modernity, marks a historical stage in the organisation, structuring and thematic focusing of knowledge. Foucault emphasises that new formation rules of knowledge discourses will replace the paradigm of 'man'. Conversely, the other two areas of Foucault's philosophy, which can be more specifically defined using the theorems of power and aesthetics/ethics, allow human beings to return to the centre as the starting point of power and resistance and as the subject of the application of technologies of the self. The human being thus evolves into the bearer of an ethos, a critical attitude, in ethical or aesthetic terms and as an individual subject returns to the focus of thinking. Hence, human action is a presupposition for socio-political changes. For Foucault, aesthetics based on 'know yourself' in the sense of care of the self are a field in which human autonomy becomes conceivable. Despite the constructedness of the subject, self-determination and a potential for transformative action remain possible. Humans can expand their scope of action to form themselves and society through the use of the aesthetic.

Both philosophers combine self-awareness and aesthetics. However, in Hegel's work the importance of aesthetics diminishes in relation to religion and philosophy as areas more adequate for the mind, while in Foucault's work aesthetics gain importance. For Foucault, the combination of aesthetics and ethics is the guarantor of the expansion of human freedom. For Hegel it is the end of art and the transition to philosophical reasoning which makes freedom conceivable in relation to humans and beyond them. For Foucault,

---

297 "All in all we can speak of Hegel consistently immanentising (secularising) the traditional conceptions [...] by critically analysing the logical, ontological-metaphysical, consciousness-philosophical interpretations of reason in terms of their conditions of meaning. It is this comprehensive sense which I understand when I assert that for Hegel, philosophy in general is anthropology and philosophy specifically is the science of reason." (Lomar 1997: 131; own translation) According to Lomar, considerations which are critical of reason are simultaneously anthropological considerations. (Cf. Lomar 1997: 132) Within the scope of his remarks, Lomar attempts to introduce Hegel's concept of the spirit as the basic concept of his anthropological philosophy. (Cf. Lomar 1997: 219)

298 Cf. Lomar 1997: 22.

299 Lomar 1997: 25. (Own translation)

aesthetics as ethics remains the primary means of practical self-discovery in terms of care of the self as an aesthetic/ethical self-forming of the subject and is located in the context of the philosophical attitude of ethos. In Hegel's work, the anthropological is transformed into the speculative-metaphysical, which is an appropriate form of understanding the human being, with aesthetics representing only one phase in the process of human spiritualisation. Hegel thus determines the essence of humans in a specific manner. Although Foucault, like Hegel, historicises the forms of self-knowledge, they are not dissolved into the absolute, but instead remain attached to the pragmatic. In Foucault's work, the anthropological takes the form of the aesthetic-ethical as the work of the subject on themself in the historical context of adaptability and malleability, and detaches itself from the super-temporal determination of human nature. The focus on the human being, which Hegel transcends, takes on a new, modified form in Foucault's work, with an emancipatory potential for the self and society.[300]

2.2.2   The empty form of salvation. The ethics of the good life in Michel Foucault

2.2.2.1   The ethics of the good life and human happiness

There is a conspicuous absence of a preoccupation with the question of human happiness in Foucault's ethics, although he studied ancient forms of living and their techniques of the self in depth and, in the final phase of his philosophy, developed aesthetics and ethics of the self on this basis. A question can also be posed regarding the status of the subject-theoretical element of his philosophy. Should his ethics or aesthetics be understood in the sense of a contemporary socio-political analysis with regard to the given possibilities for the partial emancipation of the individual by means of the liberation from heteronomous determinations through technologies of the self, or is his concept more general, so that only the respective techniques of the self vary according to the given socio-historical conditions, and the basic orientation remains the same? This question will be explored within the context of the concept of salvation in Foucault's work. In *The Hermeneutics of the Subject* (1982) Foucault identifies an

---

300   By making this claim I am consciously contradicting Gallagher's theory that Hegel and Foucault are primarily focused on the past and thus neglect a possible critical-utopian view of the future.

"empty form of salvation"[301] in connection with his analysis of Hellenistic philosophy and speaks of salvation as the "form"[302] and the "content"[303] of this philosophy. Does the concept of salvation (*salut*) as a teleological orientation of human action replace the concept of happiness (*bonheur*) in Foucault's work? How can the two concepts be distinguished from each other and why does Foucault prefer the concept of salvation? Can we have salvation, feel salvation or identify a lack of salvation in Foucault's work, or does the posited emptiness remain? What function does the term have within the framework of the related philosophical theory?

While philosophical anthropology in the classical sense and the imposition of humans as an absolute within formation of knowledge are indeed obsolete, reflection on human conduct of life and thus the question of human well-being, salvation and happiness are not. In this context, Foucault strengthens the significance of the aesthetic, which presupposes a self-development of the subject combined with liberation from heteronomy. He speaks of being governed, whereby the aesthetic enters into a close relation with the ethical, which is attributed a political relevance. Moments such as autonomy; exploring possibilities in self-formation; life style and an ethical attitude towards the other constitute human well-being. How can the relationship between ethics and aesthetics be understood with regard to the question of what is a good life in Michel Foucault's work?

2.2.2.2   The empty form of salvation and the question of happiness

Foucault considers the ancient techniques of the self to be an example of the process of partial liberation from heteronomy. "[The philosophy of the art of living] is the project of the self-managing and governing human being who, despite all imponderables and external influences, possesses autonomous control over his life."[304] The concepts of the good life and objective criteria for the good life as understood in ancient models are not incorporated. In my opinion, this is where Foucault's theorem of the empty form of salvation should be located. Foucault writes

---

301   Foucault 2005b: 127.
302   Ibid.
303   Ibid.
304   Heidbrink, Ludger: "Autonomie und Lebenskunst: Über die Grenzen der Selbstbestimmung". In: Kersting, Wolfgang; Langbehn, Claus (Eds.): *Kritik der Lebenskunst*. Frankfurt a.M. (Suhrkamp), 2007, p. 267. (Own translation)

"This interplay between a universal principle which can only be heard by a few, and this rare salvation from which no one is excluded *a priori*, will be at the very heart of most of the theological, spiritual, social, and political problems of Christianity. Now this form is very clearly articulated in this technology of the self. Or rather, since we should no longer speak just of technology, Greek, Hellenistic, and Roman civilization gave rise to a veritable culture of the self that, I believe, assumed major dimensions in the first and second centuries A.D. It is within this culture of the self that we can see the full extent and function of this form, once again so fundamental to our culture, between universal appeal and rarity of salvation. Moreover, this notion of salvation (of being saved, of earning one's salvation) is absolutely central to this."[305]

In this context, Foucault refers in particular to Epictetus: "So you see that all this leads us to a theme of salvation, the form of which is clearly defined in the text of Epictetus I quoted a while ago. A salvation, once again, which must answer to a universal appeal but which in fact can only be reserved for some."[306] This way of life is therefore not accessible to everyone "It is the final aim of life for every man, but a rare form of existence for a few and only a few: we have here, if you like, the empty form of that major transhistorical category of salvation."[307]

According to Foucault, the imbuing of this empty form of salvation results in the importance of the Other from a historical perspective "The question of the Other, of other people, of the relationship to the Other as mediator between this form of salvation and the content it will have to be given."[308] Further he remarks "in the practice of the self, someone else, the other, is an indispensable condition for the form that defines this practice to effectively attain and be filled by its object, that is to say, by the self. The other is indispensable for the practice of the self to arrive at the self at which it aims."[309] Foucault continues to argue that "The practice of the self links up with social practice or, if you

---

305   Foucault 2005b: 120.
306   Foucault 2005b: 120–121.
307   Foucault 2005b: 127. "You see that this empty form of salvation appears within ancient culture, certainly as an echo of, or in correlation and connection with, religious movements, which will of course have to be defined more precisely, but it should also be said that to a certain extent it appears by and for itself and not merely as a phenomenon or aspect of religious thought or experience." (Ibid.)
308   Ibid.
309   Ibid.

like, the formation of a relationship of the self to the self quite clearly connects up with the relationships of the self to the Other."[310] He suggests that this can already be identified in Plato's works "Throughout this text [Plato's Alcibiades], care of the self is therefore instrumental with regard to the care of others."[311]

The concept of salvation is generally perceived as Christian and is linked to the transition from life to death, from mortality to immortality, from good to evil, from impure to pure. "It is always on the boundary, therefore, and is something that brings about passage."[312] Furthermore, salvation is structured in a dramatic fashion "Salvation, then, is linked to the dramatic force of an event."[313] According to Foucault, however, salvation can also be found outside of religion

> "However, and I think this is fundamental for what I want to say, I would like to emphasize that whatever the origin of this notion of salvation, and whatever reinforcement it may have received from the religious theme in the Hellenistic and Roman period, it is not a notion that is heterogeneous to philosophy, and it functions effectively as a philosophical notion within the field of philosophy itself. Salvation developed and appeared as an objective of philosophical practice and of the philosophical life."[314]

Foucault evokes the broad meaning of the term

---

310   Foucault 2005b: 155.

311   Foucault 2005b: 175. "Conversely, however, the cathartic and the political are not differentiated in Plato." (Ibid.) This can be seen in the following statement: "I practice this art of the cathartic precisely so that I can become a political subject." (Ibid.) And he continues "The care of the self therefore finds its reward and guarantee in the city's salvation." (Foucault 2005b: 176) And "[t]his is, very roughly if you like, the link Plato establishes between care of the self and care of others, and establishes in such a way that it is very difficult to separate them." (Ibid.) This separation becomes increasingly apparent and according to Foucault was already well advanced in the first and second centuries A.D. The care of the self-gradually emerges as a self-sufficient end. (Cf. Foucault 2005b: 177) "The self is the definitive and sole aim of the care of the self." (Ibid.) This can be observed among the Cynics as well as the Epicureans and Stoics. According to Foucault this was the origin of Christian spirituality which extends the art of oneself through ascetic, monastic life. (Cf. Foucault 2005b: 178)

312   Foucault 2005b: 181.

313   Ibid.

314   Foucault 2005b: 181–182.

> "In what I will call this Hellenistic and Roman salvation, this salvation of Hellenistic and Roman philosophy, the self is the agent, object, instrument, and end of salvation. You can see that we are a long way from the salvation in Plato that is mediated by the city-state. We are also a long way from the religious form of salvation linked to a binary system, to a drama of events, to a relationship to the Other, and which in Christianity involves self-renunciation. Rather, salvation ensures an access to the self that is inseparable from the work one carries out on oneself within the time of one's life and in life itself."[315]

Salvation is thus located in a relation to the Other and does not have purely religious connotations. The pursuit of salvation is localised in Foucault's theorem of the historical a priori at the moment of working with the self. In Foucault's work, the empty form of salvation is thought of as a generalisable form based on a Kantian figure of thought, but should be understood through the historical a priori in the sense of his theorem. At this point, it becomes apparent that the figure of thought of the apriority structuring knowledge has been transferred to the realm of subjectivation with its assigned domain of self-practices, i.e. from the philosophy of knowledge to the subject-philosophical element of its thinking in the narrower sense. Foucault therefore poses the question of happiness in a more indirect manner, concealing it in his reflections on human salvation. In the context of salvation, happiness appears as a concretely fulfilling experience in the current course of life. Salvation, argues Foucault, is, on the other hand, a philosophical concept in its emptiness, focusing on historical openness and simultaneously falling out of the dimension of chance and pure receptivity. For Foucault, salvation is a central analytical concept of his historical reconstruction of the hermeneutics of the subject and, unlike the concept of happiness, enables him to develop various forms of subject constitution beyond the aspect of a fulfilled individual life. The question of salvation is tied to historically changing modes of the subject which encompass the question of happiness in different historical forms. Life as art or ethics as aesthetics can be regarded as a contemporary form of human salvation. This is connected to the conception of work on oneself within the framework of the idea of life as art and can be regarded as a form of 20th or 21st century salvation. This conception is based on the creative potential of the individual, which, according to Foucault, also includes a socio-political dimension including the formation

---

315   Foucault 2005b: 185.

of the self and thus also the possibility of realising the heterotopic moment of his philosophy.

The question of salvation thus manifests itself today more as a personal task of self-development with consequences for the forming of human relationships and personal coexistence, as well as of a general political nature. Salvation has the status of an episteme which, in a historical analysis, allows a dissection of society to identify the underlying ideas of salvation, which also include various ideas concerning human happiness. In Foucault's work, the ethics or aesthetics of the self appear as a historical a priori, as a contemporary form of human salvation. Within the scope of historical development new forms of human salvation emerge,[316] which, as becomes clear, incorporate moments of past forms and are linked to the struggle for human autonomy under changed socio-historical conditions – as specific manifestations of the empty form of salvation.

2.2.3 Aesthetics of play and techniques of the self. The relationship between ethics and aesthetics in Michel Foucault's work[317]

2.2.3.1 Subject between heteronomy and autonomy

At the centre of Foucault's philosophy is the question of the subject. In this context, Foucault analyses "different modes by which, in our culture, human beings are made subjects."[318] Foucault distinguishes three areas of subject constitution procedures of knowledge, power practices and technologies of the self. The subject is thus the target of both heteronomy and self-determination. The thesis of the death of the subject in critical theory uses rationalist or teleological approaches which draw on the basic anthropological assumptions of philosophy to explore what a human being is. In contrast, Foucault regards the

---

316 Foucault describes health as one of the historical forms of salvation. According to Foucault, the doctor succeeded the priest in the 19th century.

317 This section has been previously published in German with minor changes. Cf. Rainsborough, Marita: "Ästhetik des Spiels und Techniken des Selbst. Der Zusammenhang von Ethik und Ästhetik bei Michel Foucault". In: Recki, Birgit (Ed.): *Kongress-Akten der deutschen Gesellschaft für Ästhetik, Band 3: Techne – poiesis – aisthesis. Technik und Techniken in Kunst und ästhetischer Praxis*, IX. Kongress der Deutschen Gesellschaft für Ästhetik 2015, pp. 1–24; retrieved from: www.dgae.de/kongresse/techne-poiesis-aisthes is- technik-und-techniken-in-kunst-und-aesthetischer-praxis/.

318 Dreyfus, Herbert L.; Rabinow, Paul (Eds.): *Michel Foucault: Beyond Structuralism and Hermeneutics*. Chicago (University of Chicago Press), 1983, p. 208.

human being as an 'animal of experience', whose openness is exposed to so-cio-historical formations, but who also has the possibility of self-forming. Ac-cording to Foucault, the subject is heteronomous, but also characterised by its autonomy. Heteronomy, the constitution of the subject, is the starting point for this. Autonomy must be fought for and obtained over and over again in a process of detachment from the existing, the self-design of the subject, and social influence. Technologies of the self are of vital importance in this regard. Foucault argues that self-formation makes it possible to turn oneself into a work of art. The paradigm of life as art simultaneously understands the eth-ical as an individual task of the creative composition of the self; the aesthet-ics of the self become the ethics of the self. The Greek and Hellenistic concep-tion of concern for oneself, which according to Foucault provides a stimulat-ing repertoire of technologies of the self[319] functions as the basis for this. The application of the technologies of the self does not fundamentally detach the subject from existing power structures. This process is particularly aimed at constituting oneself as a moral subject. With regard to the contemporary so-cial situation, Foucault comments on the lack of morality and demands "And to this absence of morality corresponds, must correspond, the search for an aes-

---

319   When referring to Foucault's analysis of ancient texts Wolfgang Detel speaks of a "cre-ative theoretical work" which does not fully measure up to the ancient texts, e.g. Fou-cault represents a false model of the regulation of sexual desire. It is a model of lim-itation, not control, a "model of self-controlled integration of sexual desire into the overall complex of higher and lower desires." Detel also speaks of Foucault's ascetic understanding of Plato. According to Detel, these misinterpretations result in an "in-appropriate exaggeration of the part played by aesthetic stylisation" by suppressing epistemological and power-analytical aspects. In: Detel, Wolfgang: *Foucault and Classi-cal Antiquity. Power, Ethics and Knowledge.* Cambridge UK (Cambridge University Press), 2005, pp. 3–5. Even if Detel's interpretation is partially correct, Foucault's overall argu-mentation is not affected by this, since Foucault does not use the ancient models in an exemplary manner for contemporary solutions to problems, but merely draws on them as the starting point for his ethical considerations and to provide impulses in terms of content. Furthermore, Detel does not question the fundamental ethical approach of care of the self in antiquity, to which Foucault primarily refers. In addition to this, I be-lieve that Foucault's understanding of the control of desires in the sense of his concept of governmentality would ultimately be compatible with a model of limitation.

thetics of existence."[320] Should the term art, on which Foucault's orientation towards aesthetics is based, be understood as rule-driven action in the sense of a *techne* or *poiesis* or as creative artistic design as in *ars*? Does the term self-technology refer to a model of the art of living as a technology or craft? Can a cathartic function of technologies of the self also be discerned in this context? In the context of dealing with these questions, it is important to outline the connection between ethics and aesthetics in Foucault's work, which undermines "Kierkegaard's Either-Or";[321] to investigate the question of "the unity and difference of the aesthetic and the ethical";[322] and to examine Foucault's aesthetics of play in terms of their ethical implications.

2.2.3.2 Technologies of the self and the question of the subject

The technologies of the self considered by Foucault in the context of ethics include asceticism, ataraxy, truth speaking, dietetics, meditation, silence, reading and writing. In his history of morality, Foucault distinguishes between moral codes, deeds and relation to oneself. "In what we call morals there is the effective behavior of people, there are the codes and there is this kind of relationship to oneself with the above four aspects."[323] These are, according to Foucault, on the one hand ethical substance, the proportion of the self such as the feelings affected, the intention or the moral matter, and on the other the mode of subjectivation, such as divine law, natural law, reasonable law or an aesthetic principle of existence. The third aspect refers to the practice of the self such as asceticism; the fourth to moral teleology, which determines the nature of being which should be achieved through moral action. "For instance, shall we become pure, or immortal, or free, or masters of ourselves,

320 Foucault, Michel: "An Aesthetics of Existence" (An Interview with Alessandro Fontana, 1984). In: Foucault, Michel: *Politics, Philosophy, Culture: Interviews and Other Writings 1977–1984*. Kritzman, Lawrence D. (Ed.), London, New York (Routledge), 1988a, pp. 47–53.

321 Gamm, Gerhard; Kimmerle, Gerd (Eds.): *Ethik und Ästhetik: Nachmetaphysische Perspektiven*. Tübingen (edition discord), 1990, p. 7. (Own translation)

322 Gamm/Kimmerle 1990: 10. (Own translation)

323 Cf. Dreyfus/Rabinow 1983: 239. Foucault continues "I think, very important: the kind of relationship you ought to have with yourself, *rapport a soi*, which I call ethics, and which determines how the individual is supposed to constitute himself as a moral subject of his own actions. This relationship to oneself has four major aspects." (Dreyfus/Rabinow 1983: 238)

and so on."[324] These aspects must be considered independently of each other, although they are also interconnected.[325] Foucault observes that there is great similarity between Greek and Christian morality with regard to the history of moral codes and themes, but significant differences in the relationship with the self which he calls *ethics*.[326] His research focuses on the field of ethics, while his philosophical explanations are primarily concerned with the ethical-moral subject. In this context, the concept of the self often takes the place of the concept of the subject.[327]

> "Stylisation occurs where the focus is on production of the self and not the subject in the traditional sense. In contrast to the subject, the self exists as a circular movement, which the person who cares for himself describes starting from oneself via another and then returning to oneself modifies the initial status. In the relationship to oneself there is no rehabilitation of a soul substance (no more than there is one of the body), but 'only' the creation of an arc which is stretched over an emptiness, which as such would have nothing to say. [...] This is the interface at which a constantly changing self-relation originates; it is not assigned its unchanging shape by the structures of power and knowledge formations."[328]

Technologies of the self represent practices of freedom, which, however, do not imply a detachment from power contexts. The ethical/aesthetic subject represents a revision of Descartes' concept of the subject "This is obvious for the aesthetics of existence, which is explicitly understood as a revision of Descartes' attempt to 'substitut[e] a subject as founder of practices of knowledge, for a subject constituted through practices of the self.' Thus 'evidence

---

324   Dreyfus/Rabinow 1983: 239.

325   Cf. Dreyfus/Rabinow 1983: 240.

326   Cf. Ibid.

327   "In the first place, I do indeed believe that there is no sovereign, founding subject, a universal form of subject to be found everywhere. I am very sceptical of this view of the subject and very hostile to it. I believe, on the contrary, that the subject is constituted through practices of subjection, or, in a more autonomous way, through practices of liberation, of liberty, as in Antiquity, on the basis, of course, of a number of rules, styles, inventions to be found in the cultural environment." (Foucault 1988a: 50–51)

328   Hebel, Kirsten: "Dezentrierung des Subjekts in der Selbstsorge: Zum ästhetischen Aspekt einer nicht-normativen Ethik bei Foucault". In: Gamm, Gerhard; Kimmerle, Gerd (Eds.): *Ethik und Ästhetik: Nachmetaphysische Perspektiven.* Tübingen (edition discord), 1990, p. 230. (Own translation)

is substituted for ascesis' by Descartes, the theoretical self-relation replaces the practical one."[329] Menke characterizes Foucault's understanding of subjectivity as follows "Subjectivity is then the self-relation of and to powers. And this self-relation is the power to do something by one's own powers."[330] Here, as in the context of his concept of power in the area of disciplinary power, how this power is exercised is particularly significant. Menke attributes this commonality to the underlying concepts of the subject, which presuppose that they are practical and active. This concept of the subject opposes the "equivalence of subjectivity and self-consciousness."[331] The theoretical justification for Foucault's interest in the ancient technologies of the self within the framework of the *epimeleia heautou*, the concern for himself, and his preoccupation with the *technê tou biou*, the art of living, is grounded in this. The objective of practicing these technologies is to acquire skills and abilities, and this includes "an ability to carry something out [Ausführen] and an ability to direct oneself."[332] Menke's explanations are based on the thesis that "Foucault understood the practices of an aesthetics of existence as a normative alternative to disciplinary practices."[333] He continues "The aesthetics of existence

---

329 Menke, Christoph: "Two Kinds of Practice: On the Relation between Social Discipline and the Aesthetics of Existence." In: *Constellations*, 10 (2), 2003, p. 201.

330 Ibid. He continues "Subjectivity means power to act, and power to act is two-fold: carrying something out and self-direction. Subjectivity consists in this two-fold power." (Menke 2003: 202)

331 Ibid.

332 Ibid. Further Menke remarks "The primary self-relation is not one of knowledge, but rather of self-direction in actively carrying something out." (Ibid.) And "This is at the same time connected to a second insight, on which the conception of the subject of disciplinary power and that of an aesthetics of existence also agree: the insight into the primacy of ability not only with respect to knowledge, but also with respect to will." (Menke 2003: 201–202) Menke further observes "The conceptions of the aesthetic-existential and the disciplinary subject thus agree not only in the critique of theoreticism and its primacy of transparent self-consciousness, but also of voluntarism and its primacy of free will: I can only want what I can do – what I have the power, the ability, and the possibility to carry out and toward which or according to which I direct myself. The ability to act therefore entails that power comes not only before knowledge; power also comes before freedom." (Menke 2003: 202) Here Menke mentions not only criticism of Descartes, but also criticism of Sartre: "By the same token, the double critique of the theoreticism of the model of self-consciousness and the voluntarism of the model of self-determination – Foucault's double critique of Descartes and Sartre – shows that this is the fundamental way in which we refer to ourselves." (Ibid.)

333 Menke 2003: 200.

must not only be a convincing model for a non-disciplinary, free form of sub-jectivity; it must also be in a position to allow for a reformulation of Foucault's critique of discipline."[334] Foucault's ethics and aesthetics are concerned with an increase in the individual's autonomy. Menke identifies an opposition between the disciplinary and the ethical/aesthetic subject which is based less on content than on form; they cannot be regarded as mutual complements.[335] "The aesthetics of existence must be understood and performed such that it presupposes a concept of subjective power, capacity, and freedom that stands in direct opposition to normalization, not in its content and aim, but rather in its form, which is bound up with the constitution of the subject through social discipline."[336]

Self-determination should thus not be misunderstood in a teleological transformation as submission to a life plan; it should not degenerate into self-submission. Correspondingly, the art of living does not refer to life as a product, but as a process. The art of living must be understood in a pluralistic way.[337] Menke argues that it is within this conception of a personal lifestyle that normative guidelines such as the orientation towards the idea of a suc-cessful unity of life, goodness and beauty, which Foucault regards as a 'strong

---

334   Ibid. And "The disciplinary and the aesthetic-existential subject form a duck-rabbit fig-ure, the two faces of one Janus head." (Ibid.)

335   "That the relation between the disciplinary and the aesthetic-existential subject is not simply one of addition but rather of opposition can first of all be explained in contrast to its understanding as two phases of the process of subjectification." (Menke 2003: 206) He continues "Autonomy does not only consist in the self-determination of the good of my life in view of possibilities and capacities acquired through processes of discipline. Rather, autonomy first begins where the subject concerned with the good of his life attempts to transform these possibilities and capacities, particularly at their most elementary level, the direction of one's own body." (Ibid.) The experimental char-acter of this process is described as follows: "In this way are they 'experimental'; they test other – other than those by which we were disciplined and normalized – possibil-ities and capacities for self-direction in view not of carrying out social practices well or better, but rather of leading a good life." (Ibid.)

336   Cf. Menke 2003: 207.

337   Nehemas remarks on this: "Which is to say that the art of living has no rules, that there is no such thing as the art of living. There are only arts of living—many arts." In: Ne-hamas, Alexander: The Art of Living: Socratic Reflections from Plato to Foucault. Berkeley (University of California Press), 1998, p. 184.

structure' can be discerned.[338] Foucault speaks of the "will to live a beautiful life, and to leave to others memories of a beautiful existence".[339] For Foucault, aesthetics become a general model for an individual lifestyle in the "movement of self-overcoming".[340] There are no predefined norms and objectives for this practice. "Personally leading a life in accordance with an 'ethics of an aesthetic kind' is characterized by the aesthetic freedom of transformations and processes that do not obey any teleological order."[341] This involves an attitude in life, an "attitude of aesthetic freedom", a "freedom of self-overcoming".[342]

2.2.3.3 The aesthetics of play for Foucault

In Foucault's work, the concept of play is simultaneously at the centre of literary, artistic and subject theory, aesthetics and ethics. For Foucault, play as a lifeworld, literary-artistic and aesthetic/ethical theorem determines both the specificity of the aesthetic and the link between the aesthetic and the lifeworld, as formed by the connection of ethics and aesthetics in the subject's transformation process as their ethical/aesthetic self-design. Foucault's conception of the concept of play thus transcends Derrida's autonomisation in the aesthetic,[343] laying claim to ethical relevance in the process of subjectivation, whose central core is concerned with processes of power and the connection between power and knowledge. In contrast to Schiller, Foucault's concept of play is not conceived of as an instinct to play – the disparate, the material instinct and the creative instinct of the human being – and thus bringing sensuality and reason into harmony in order to make the human being's ethical perfection conceivable in the pedagogical/political process, but instead is an enabling space for something new, an experimental field. In this

---

338 Refer to footnote 21 in Menke 2003: 210. Menke points out that Foucault makes the judgement of this life dependent on others.

339 Menke 2003: 204.

340 Menke 2003: 208.

341 Ibid.

342 Menke 2003: 209. Further Menke states "In it, in this attitude of aesthetic freedom alone, lies what distinguishes the practices of an aesthetics of existence from the normalizing practices of disciplinary power – and so what can guard against the practices of an aesthetics of existence becoming a further, perhaps ultimate and most subtle, form of disciplinary subjection." (Ibid.)

343 Sonderegger, Ruth: *Für die Ästhetik des Spiels: Hermeneutik, Dekonstruktion und der Eigensinn der Kunst.* Frankfurt a.M. (Suhrkamp), 2000.

context Foucault refers to Nietzsche, who assigns the playful dimension to the childlike.

"Rather, this includes an instinct for play which is still animated by the child – according to Zarathustra. In 1944, Georges Bataille called this child, who echoes in the superhuman, who drives the individual and who sometimes risks being lost when the individual becomes a mother or father, the will to chance and not the will to power. Ultimately the child always represents a new beginning. Similarly, Hannah Arendt interprets humans from a Christmas perspective as new-borns and beginners, not from an Easter perspective as mortals. [...] But such playful inspiration is crucial for the individual to transcend themselves."[344]

The new beginning is not ethically and morally bound, but instead should be understood in the sense of transgression, which can certainly display traits of madness, intoxication and ecstasy. "After all, turning one's life into a work of art cannot be rationally planned, but is like playing with desires, dreams, delusions, intoxication, discourses and power."[345] This process recognises both re-iteration and the Other, the not-yet. Values are thereby also modified or new values are created. The aesthetics of play, which strive to transform the subject, in particular also with regard to the ethical, focus on detachment, self-forming and dealing with the other, in addition to a connection to the delusional, in particular on the basis of the idea of governmentality. The concern is no longer to expand experience in the ecstatic, but instead "the possibility of forming oneself as a subject in control of his conduct [...] a skillful and prudent guide of himself."[346] For Foucault, the concept of governmentality links epistemology, aesthetics and ethics with politics. Governmentality not only entails being governed – inferiority in the processes of the microphysics of power[347] – but also 'govern[ing] oneself'[348] to not be governed in the struggle for autonomy and, moreover, primarily to govern well in the sense of appropriate

---

344   Schönherr-Mann: *Der Übermensch als Lebenskünstlerin: Nietzsche, Foucault und die Ethik.* Berlin (Matthes & Seitz), 2009, p. 97. (Own translation)

345   Schönherr-Mann 2009: 131. (Own translation)

346   Foucault 1990: 138–139.

347   Cf. Foucault, Michel: *Psychiatric Power: Lectures at the Collège de France, 1973–1974.* New York (Palgrave Macmillan), 2006.

348   Cf. Foucault, Michel: *Ethics, Subjectivity and Truth: The essential works of Michel Foucault 1954–1984.* Rabinow, Paul (Ed.), New York (New Press), 1997, p. 87.

leading of the other, which presupposes a conscious contact with oneself – the leading of the self. At this point, Foucault becomes eminently political – the general worldly, artistic and ethical aspects of the concept of aesthetics change into the political. It thus becomes the central form of shaping the future in political terms. When carrying out experimental testing, the concept of the game therefore not only emphasises the possibility of transgressing and expanding experience, but also self-forming in an ethical/political dimension which requires discipline and asceticism.

2.2.3.4 Life as a work of art

Foucault generally attributes vital importance to aesthetics in his philosophy. He asks "But couldn't everyone's life become a work of art? Why should the lamp or the house be an art object, but not our life?"[349] According to Hesse, Foucault can only ask himself this question because he does not refer to the distinction between action and production, *techne* and *phronesis*. His technological-strategic choice of words conceals the hermeneutic achievement underlying an ethical way of life, which Foucault intends when speaking of a philosophical exercise of self-transformation. This should be regarded as embedded in a practical context. He understands life in particular as creative forming based on the model of artistic activities, but at the same time also as technology and craftsmanship. Foucault strives for the transgression of the existing, which presupposes imaginative trial and error; re-conceptualisation and experimentation; and, in the broadest sense, the idea of life as a work of art. When combining this with the playful he is also aware that there is a proximity to madness and ecstasy, in which a cathartic moment of cleansing or liberation could be inher-

---

349   Hesse, Heidrun: "'Ästhetik der Existenz': Foucaults Entdeckung des ethischen Selbstverhältnisses". In: Honneth, Axel; Saar, Martin: *Zwischenbilanz einer Rezeption: Frankfurter Foucault-Konferenz 2001*. Frankfurt a.M. (Suhrkamp), 2003, pp. 305–306. (Own translation) Hesse quotes here from "Genealogy of Ethics". (Cf. Foucault 1984: 350) Foucault says "What strikes me is the fact that in our society, art has become something which is related only to objects and not to individuals, or to life. That art is something which is specialized or which is done by experts who are artists. But couldn't everyone's life become a work of art? Why should the lamp or the house be an art object, but not our life?" In: Foucault, Michel: "On the Genealogy of Ethics: An Owerview of Work in Progress". In: Rabinow, Paul (Ed.): *The Foucault Reader*. New York (Pantheon Books), 1984, p. 350.

ent.[350] When discussing the phenomenon of catharsis from Plato to Christianity in historical terms, Foucault does not, however, take a current view of the situation. It can thus only be assumed that the cathartic element in a modified historical form has significance for the present.

Nehamas points out that this process of shaping life in the sense of a work of art is not about self-discovery, which would presuppose a self as a given, but about self-invention "More important, he believed that the care of the self was not a process of discovering who one truly is but of inventing and improvising who one can be. Foucault's model for the care of the self was the creation of art."[351] Further Nehamas explains "Only in this form does the ethical recommendation acquire a specific aesthetic meaning, and its most consequential and – to no philosopher does this attribute apply better – most eloquent proclaimer (herald) is Nietzsche."[352] Foucault refers to his ethical concept derived from *The Gay Science* as his aesthetics or ethics of the self. Art can thus be understood as "artificiality" and "culture", as self-control with the aim of perfection and, beyond that, as aesthetic pleasure. Asceticism plays an important role here. The practice of asceticism is intended to help avoid excess "Asceticism is not the repression but the regulation of pleasure. Its objective is not denial but satisfaction. The conventional ascetic ideal of denying pleasure altogether is not a fact of nature but the product of centuries of Christian theorizing."[353] He continues "But ascesis is something else it's the work that one performs on oneself in order to transform oneself or make the self appear which, happily,

350   Foucault examines the history of catharsis from Plato to Christianity. While Katharsis' initial aim was constitution into a political subject, in the case of the Neoplatonists it detaches itself from the political context and generally becomes the transformation of the self through itself. In Christianity it finally becomes primarily "a decipherment of interiority, the subject's exegesis of himself." (Foucault 2005b: 301) In his reflections, Foucault follows in the footsteps of Freud, but in a different form, freeing the concept of catharsis from its narrow interpretation as an aesthetic or dramatic category of literary studies which references Aristotle's theory of drama (e.g. Lessing, Goethe, Lukács).
351   Nehamas 1998: 178. Foucault writes "Maybe the target nowadays is not to discover what we are but to refuse what we are. We have to imagine and to build up what we could be to get rid of this kind of political 'double bind', which is the simultaneous individualization and totalization of modern power structures." (Foucault 2002b: 336)
352   Früchtl, Josef: *Ästhetische Erfahrung und moralisches Urteil: Eine Rehabilitierung*. Frankfurt a.M. (Suhrkamp), 1996, p. 157. (Own translation)
353   Nehamas 1998: 179.

one never attains."[354] Foucault draws on Nietzsche when asserting that there is a link between autonomy and perfection. Früchtl discovers a certain resemblance to Kant in the works of both philosophers

"He [in this case Nietzsche and therefore also Foucault] concludes the thought, in which Kant discovers the principle of ethics, namely that freedom is obedience to the self-given law. He completes this thought because he conceives it not only from the perspective of the general public, but also from that of the individual; because he conceives it, more sharply accentuated, not primarily from the perspective of the general public, but conversely from that of the individual. Nietzsche's ethics formulate an 'individualistic moral of autonomy'".[355]

Nietzsche's work, and with him Foucault, posits an individualistic and perfectionist meaning of the concept of art. Früchtl summarizes "the individualistic moral of autonomy is an aesthetic moral of autonomy".[356] The objective is to give style to one's character, i.e. unity, harmony in tension, order and distinctiveness. Philosophy becomes the theory and practice of the good life and has a proximity to art.

"Talk of artistic creation always provokes thoughts of genius, unlimited freedom, absolute spontaneity—the very ideas of which Foucault remained resolutely suspicious throughout his life. But in the end there is no contradiction. For creativity, too, is always historically situated. Not everything is possible at every time. Like everyone else, artists have to work within the limitations of their traditions. Creation demands rearranging the given; innovation requires manipulating the dated. Lives, seen aesthetically, are no different."[357]

Furthermore, Kant with his concepts of Enlightenment and critique, his call for an 'exit' from self-incurred immaturity and his assumption of the necessity to produce publicity is of crucial importance for Foucault in this process. Kant propagates an attitude of courage, a specific ethos of self-legislation. Foucault

---

354 Foucault, Michel: "Friendship as a Way of Life". In: Foucault, Michel: *Ethics: Subjectivity and Truth (Essential Works of Foucault, 1954–1984, Vol. 1)*. Rabinow, Paul (Ed.), New York (The New Press), 1997, p. 137.
355 Früchtl 1996: 159. (Own translation)
356 Früchtl 1996: 161. (Own translation)
357 Nehamas 1998: 178.

combines this Kantian attitude of courage with the Greek courage of speaking the truth (parrhêsia), of 'saying everything', which can be associated with the risk of death. Socrates not only demands this in the political framework, but also understands it as a general philosophical activity which wishes to change individuals' lives with a view to achieving a good life.[358] In addition, for Foucault Baudelaire's remarks about the dandy which, with their emphasis on rebellion, courage, self-discipline and the desired originality in a cult of the self, represent an example of the desired ethics or aesthetics of the self, which, however, should not degenerate into egocentrism. In Früchtl's essay on this, it is stated that "Foucault argues specifically in favour of ethics of perfection aesthetics in the sense of perfecting autonomy. Foucault develops his conception through an idiosyncratic but not unconventional combination of Kant and Baudelaire and in the tradition of Nietzsche's individualistic moral of autonomy."[359]

Foucault thus combines Nietzsche's concept of style with Baudelaire's concept of the dandy and Kant's striving for maturity and autonomy as well as his critical ethos. Foucault advocates a "socially responsible individualism".[360] He does not strive for hedonism "In the same way that he hardly references Kierkegaard, he also hardly has a life of unreflected enjoyment in mind as an ethical ideal."[361] Früchtl, however, argues that Foucault is also suspicious of an unreflected anti-hedonism which is hostile to physical pleasure and individualism. "Hedonism in this form can be considered a possible variation of the 'aesthetics of existence'."[362] With his concept of friendship, which represents a relationship shaped by the structure of reciprocity, he tries to establish an antithesis to the self-centredness of the aesthetic concept. Foucault thinks in terms of maximalism and perfectionist aesthetics.[363] Früchtl explains that "philosophically, this tension is personalised in Kant and Nietzsche [but] in Foucault's own work it remains unresolved, so it is possible to speak of a Kantian and Nietzschean, a liberal and an anarchist [...] Foucault."[364] With dis-

---

358   "Courage is central to Foucault's image of Socrates" (Nehamas 1998: 168) Nehamas speaks of a public and a private practice in relation to telling the truth. (Cf. Nehamas 1998: 166)

359   Früchtl 1996: 27. (Own translation)

360   Früchtl 1996: 148. (Own translation)

361   Ibid. (Own translation)

362   Ibid. (Own translation)

363   Cf. Früchtl 1996: 182.

364   Früchtl 1996: 184. (Own translation)

cussing Foucault's reception of Nietzsche, Früchtl observes the danger of a totalised concept of maturity which results in a fundamentally aesthetic ethic. However, Foucault is always aware of this danger; it is banished in particular by the Kantian elements of his philosophy.

2.2.3.5 On the relationship between ethics, aesthetics and politics

According to Davidson, Foucault shifts from *You* to *Me* and criticises "it is agreed by all that our duties to others are far greater in number, complexity, and even interest than our duties to ourselves".[365] Nevertheless, the *You* does not lose meaning for him. Socrates, to whom Foucault refers in particular with regard to his concept of care of the self, was, according to Nehamas, also collectively oriented by means of his dialogical procedure; although his primary goal was care of the self, this only became significant in the context of the polis. Davidson says "Foucault wanted to shift the emphasis to 'how the individual is supposed to constitute himself as a moral subject of his own actions', without, however, denying the importance of either the moral code or the actual behaviour of people".[366] In this context, Foucault raises the question of the objective of moral behaviour "What is the goal to which our self-forming activity should be directed?"[367] According to him, the art of life is inconceivable without the shaping of the ethical dimension into a political orientation in which it constitutes the goal of moral behaviour. He states,

> "quite simply, this means that in the type of analysis I have been trying to advance for some time you can see that power relations, governmentality, the government of the self and of others, and the relationship of self to self constitute a chain, a thread, and I think it is around these notions that we should be able to connect together the question of politics and the question of ethics."[368]

Within the scope of this political orientation, ethics are both bound to the self-forming of the individual and, beyond that, integrated into a context of society as a whole which must take the Other into account in a unique way.

---

365 Davidson, Arnold I.: "Archaeology, Genealogy, Ethics". In: Hoy, David Couzens: *Foucault: A Critical Reader.* Oxford, Cambridge (Blackwell), 1996, p. 232.

366 Davidson 1996: 228. Davidson refers here to Rabinow, Paul (Ed.): *Foucault Reader.* London (Penguin Books), 1991, p. 337.

367 Davidson 1996: 229.

368 Foucault 2005b: 252.

Seel describes Foucault's ethics as a form of agonal ethics, stating "His ethics remain a semi-agonal ethics – it remains without analysis of the dispute between the conflicting components".[369] He criticizes that "without a positive concept of social morality, without an eye for the problem of the correct (just or solidary) limitation of one's own and others' interests and claims, the renaissance of individual ethics remains an infertile gesture."[370] Seel lacks the consideration of the "equal interests of the other individuals".[371] He summarises that "an agonal ethics must not only be the ethics of existence, it must at the same time be the ethics of consideration for others."[372] According to Seel, "an agonal ethics is only possible in the form of an agonal moral theory",[373] otherwise "every dimension of the conflict is missing in which the individual (or also a collective) stands by his own, at the same time ego- and altocentric orientations."[374] In his criticism of Foucault, Seel, however, neglects the aspect that concern for the other also has an important significance in concern for oneself. This becomes clear in Foucault's analysis of ancient or late antique ethics "Care for self is ethical in itself, but it implies complex relations with others, in the measure where this ethos of freedom is also a way of caring for others."[375] Respect for others is anchored in concern for oneself. Conflicting negotiation processes are involved in this process. Seel also overlooks the fact that Foucault, despite his model of the historical openness of 'code-oriented' morality, presents a positive conception which is less moral in the narrower sense but rather, as a socio-political concept, includes moral components and has a moral orientation. With the model of friendship, Foucault's philosophy envisages the inclusion of the interests of others and their claim to an equally

---

369   Seel, Martin: *Versuch über die Form des Glücks*. Frankfurt a.M. (Suhrkamp), 1999, p. 37. (Own translation)

370   Ibid. (Own translation)

371   Ibid. (Own translation)

372   Ibid. (Own translation) Based on this critique, Seel emphasises the superiority of the ethical concepts of Martha Nussbaum, Thomas Nagel, and Bernhard Williams.

373   Seel 1999: 46. (Own translation)

374   Seel 1999: 47. (Own translation)

375   Foucault, Michel: "The ethic of care for the self as a practice of freedom". An interview conducted with Fornet-Betancourt, Raúl; Becker, Helmut; Gomez-Müller, Alfredo with Michel Foucault on January 20, 1984, transl. by Gauthier J. D. In: *Philosophy & Social Criticism*. 12(2-3), 1987a, p. 118. Christianity envisages a renunciation of the self, which was denounced as "a form of self-love, a form of egoism or individual interest". Whereby Foucault notes a "paradox of concern for oneself", since refraining from oneself was supposed to realise the salvation of the self. (Foucault 1987a: 115–116)

fulfilled life. He asserts that individual ideas can also conflict with the ideas of
life which others have and thus require individual and collective negotiation.
For Foucault, the conflict does not arise from the moral code, but from the
position of the other and their moral orientation which is integral to their
personal lifestyle. According to Foucault, the way in which given conflicts are
dealt with is a component of personal ethical/aesthetic style but at the same
time has an eminently political character. Foucault's respect for others is based
on his conception of human autonomy, which must be seen in the context of
his relational, strategic concept of power, in which freedom is logically rooted
and which constitutes the core of his theory of resistance. This argues that it is
necessary to grant others the same freedom to form their own selves. Freedom
of ethical/aesthetic self-design thus reaches its limits, which are determined
by the freedom of the other. The corresponding political implications must be
integrated into the individual's ethical and aesthetic striving and into a common task of creative and resistive behaviour, resulting in a social constitution
which guarantees individual freedom and presupposes, includes and requires
the self-forming of the individual. The *ego-ethics* imply the *us*.

2.2.3.6 Ethics and aesthetics in relation to the subject

Foucault's recourse to the ancient philosophy of Greek classicism and the Stoa
forms the main starting point, but is deliberately not understood as a recipe.
The individualisation and contextualisation of ethics are the key reason for the
referencing of aesthetics. In his idea of life as a work of art, Foucault draws
parallels to the independence of art. Distance, alienation and difference with
the freedom of denying norms and self-referentiality are specific characteristics of both. It is precisely in this quality of the aesthetic that Foucault seeks to
locate his alliance between the aesthetic and the ethical. He refers primarily to
autonomous modernism and, to a lesser extent, to late 20th century contemporary art. Foucault emphasises the playful, creative and experimental aspects
of art.[376] He favours a concept of art which is oriented towards the innovative,
towards the disruption and transgression of the existing, and not towards the
traditions of social-functional or mimetic art which can be observed in art history, and thus has a normative orientation. When discussing Foucault's concept of beauty and work, Kersting erroneously speaks of a "subjectivism of ro-

---

376   Cf. Welsch, Wolfgang: "Ästhet/hik: Ethische Implikationen und Konsequenzen der Äs-
      thetik". In: Wulf, Christoph; Kamper, Dietmar; Gumbrecht, Hans U. (Eds.): *Ethik der Äs-
      thetik*. Berlin (Akademie), 1994, p. 12. (Own translation)

mantic aesthetics".[377] Foucault's concept of beauty, which he does not, however, define sufficiently, must be historically adaptable in the sense of the work concept developed in his essay *What is an Author?*, which Foucault strengthens with regard to life as a personal work of art.[378] He defines the concept of work as being of a historical-functional nature, like the concept of author.[379]

Foucault's philosophical remarks concern neither a moral theory nor a theory of aesthetics in the narrower sense. His preoccupation with the relationship between ethics and aesthetics is of theoretical significance in terms of subject and power and is located in the context of his overall philosophical orientation with its political dimension of wishing to change the individual and society. "Ethics and politics are henceforth no longer separate domains".[380] For Foucault, aesthetics primarily determine human autonomy. Aesthetics can defy heteronomy and show that self-determination is possible. However, Seel explains "the fact that aesthetics are an element of the ethics of good life, does not mean that either should merge into the other."[381] With regard to Foucault's aesthetics, Hebel speaks of creating a balance. He writes "perhaps, however, closer examination will show that only an aesthetic value can maintain the balance between order and freedom without drifting into the consolidation of power into domination and standardisation on the one hand or into a dissolution of boundaries into chaos and the inhumane on the other".[382]

The aesthetics of play, which strive to transform the subject, focus on the aspect of detachment, of self-forming and dealing with the other, particularly on the basis of the idea of governmentality, which encompasses the art of governing the self in addition to leading others. Foucault calls on his readers to face

---

377   Kersting, Wolfgang: "Einleitung: Die Gegenwart der Lebenskunst". In: Kersting, Wolfgang; Langbehn, Claus (Eds.): *Kritik der Lebenskunst*. Frankfurt a.M. (Suhrkamp), 2007a, p. 28. (Own translation)

378   Cf. Foucault n.y.: 135.

379   Cf. Foucault, Michel: "What is an Author?". In: Foucault, Michel: *Ethics: Subjectivity and Truth (Essential Works of Foucault, 1954–1984, Vol. 1)*. Rabinow, Paul (Ed.), New York (The New Press), 1997, pp. 205–222. In accordance with the tendency observed in Foucault to transfer concepts gained in certain theoretical contexts to other areas, I would like to claim the same for the concept of work.

380   Jambet, Christian: "The constitution of the subject and spiritual practice". In: Armstrong, Timothy J. (Ed.): *Michel Foucault, Philosopher. Essays translated from the French and German*. New York, London (Harvester Wheatsheaf), 1992, p. 240.

381   Seel, Martin: *Ethisch-ästhetische Studien*. Frankfurt (Suhrkamp), 1996, p. 12. (Own translation)

382   Hebel 1990: 234. (Own translation)

up to the task of shaping their individual lives in the sense of Kant's ethos of critique, while at the same time shaping themselves and living up to their human and political responsibilities. Foucault says "Yes, for what is ethics, if not the practice of freedom, the conscious [*réfléchie*] practice of freedom?",[383] continuing "Freedom is the ontological condition of ethics. But ethics is the considered form that freedom takes when it is informed by reflection".[384] He also notes that "Freedom is thus inherently political".[385] Foucault's ethics or aesthetics thus prove to be a pillar of his political conception, which strives for a society which enables a greater autonomy of the self. Foucault's programme of self-formation has a challenging and demanding character in its openness; in its call for self-reflexivity and for the application of techniques and practices of forming the self; in its conception of life as a work in aesthetic and ethical terms; and in its search for a committed, critical way of life encompassing individual and social responsibility.

2.2.4 Economy, art and emotion. The emotional economy and its boundaries in the philosophical concept of Michel Foucault[386]

2.2.4.1 Economy and emotion in Foucault's work

Foucault's interest in the economy is a continuous theme in his work, even if there are some longer interruptions. In his book *The Order of Things*, for instance, he examines knowledge of riches in order to present the underlying epistemes of the 17th and 18th centuries in detail, while the concept expounded in his lecture *The Birth of Bio-Politics*, which deals with the history of governmentality, focuses on the economy. Foucault argues that in liberal and neoliberal governance the question of the legitimacy or illegitimacy of government is replaced by the question of its success or failure. The rise of the political economy has

---

383 Foucault, Michel: "The Ethics of the Concern for Self as a Practice of Freedom". In: Foucault, Michel: *Ethics: Subjectivity and Truth (Essential Works of Foucault, 1954–1984, Vol. 1)*. Rabinow, Paul (Ed.), New York (The New Press), 1997, p. 284.

384 Ibid.

385 Foucault 1997: 286.

386 Cf. Rainsborough, Marita: "Economy, art and emotion. The emotional economy and its boundaries in the philosophical concept of Michel Foucault". In: Justo, José Miranda; Lima, Paulo Alexandre; Silva, Fernando M. F. (Eds.): *Experimentation and Dissidence: From Heidegger to Badiou*. (Centre for Philosophy at the University of Lisbon), 2018, pp. 209–223.

given birth to liberalism, the new form of rationality of governance, which focuses on maximising the limitation of governmental action and governmental practices in a minimal state – Foucault writes of a "principle of self-limitation"[387] – in order to create a free market which, in accordance with the principle of free competition respectively of rivalry, conceals the truth of prices,
resulting in mutual enrichment.[388]

> "In other words, it is the natural mechanism of the market and the formation
> of a natural price that enables us to falsify and verify governmental practice
> when, on the basis of these elements, we examine what government does,
> the measures it takes, and the rules it imposes."[389]

He continues, "The market determines that a good government is no longer
quite simply one that is just. The market now means that, to be a good government, government has to function according to the truth."[390] He describes the

---

387   Cf. Foucault, Michel: *The Birth of Biopolitics. Lectures at the Collège de France, 1978–79*. London, New York (Palgrave Macmillan), 2008a, p. 20. Elsewhere Foucault refers to a "regulative principle [...] of a frugal government". (Foucault 2008a: 29)

388   Foucault points to a Europe of collective enrichment. (Cf. Foucault 2008a: 54) He continues "This idea of a progress, of a European progress, is a fundamental theme in liberalism and completely overturns the themes of European equilibrium". (Foucault 2008a:
54) A further consequence of the free market as a governmental practice is, asserts
Foucault, an extension of the market; a world market and, in the end, globalisation.
(Cf. Foucault 2008a: 55) "I mean simply that this may be the first time Europe appears
as an economic unit, as an economic subject in the world, or considers the world as
able to be and having to be its economic domain. It seems to me that it is the first
time that Europe appears in its own eyes as having to have the world for its unlimited
market. Europe is no longer merely covetous of all the world's riches that sparkle in its
dreams or perceptions." (Foucault 2008a: 55) He continues "That is to say, there will be
Europe on one side with Europeans as the players, and then the world on the other,
which will be the stake. The game is in Europe, but the stake is the world." (Foucault
2008a: 55–56) Foucault believes that what he sees here is neither the beginnings of
colonialism, which must be viewed as having started earlier, nor the imperialism which
first commenced in the 19th century, "but let's say that we have the start of a new type
of global calculation in European governmental practice. I think that there are many
signs of this appearance of a new form of global rationality, of a new calculation on the
scale of the world." (Foucault 2008a: 56)

389   Foucault 2008a: 32.

390   Ibid.

market as a "principle of veridiction".[391] When considering the task of public law under such conditions he poses the question of "how to set juridical limits to the exercise of power by a public authority?"[392] These changes lead to shifts in two directions; firstly towards natural rights – Foucault calls this the revolutionary approach – and secondly towards the principle of utilitarianism, the radical approach. "Government's limit of competence will be bounded by the utility of governmental intervention."[393] In this context Foucault asserts that "Utilitarianism is a technology of government".[394] Taking this as his starting point, he distinguishes between two different kinds of freedom – freedom to exercise basic rights and freedom as the independence of the governed with regard to the government.[395] The political and socio-economic systems are heterogeneous and disparate, resulting in the ambiguity of the European liberalism of the 19th and 20th centuries, since the logic of the strategy requires a connection to the heterogeneous.[396] In this context it becomes apparent that the radical approach has been more powerful than the revolutionary approach to human rights and has prevailed to a greater extent: "Since the beginning of the nineteenth century we have been living in an age in which the problem of utility increasingly encompasses all the traditional problems of law."[397] Foucault defines exchange and utilitarianism as the two points which anchor liberal governmental technology: "Exchange for wealth and utility for the public authorities: this is how governmental reason articulates the fundamental principle of its self-limitation. Exchange on one side and utility on the other."[398] He continues, "Government is only interested in interests."[399] Foucault asserts "that the limitation of its power is not given by respect for the freedom of individuals, but simply by the evidence of economic analysis".[400]

---

391 Cf. Foucault 2008a: 33. The market before this was 'a market of jurisprudence'. (Cf. Foucault 2008a: 34)

392 Foucault 2008a: 39.

393 Foucault 2008a: 40. He continues "The question addressed to government [...] is: Is it useful? For what is it useful? Within what limits is it useful? When does it become harmful?" (Ibid.)

394 Foucault 2008a: 41.

395 Cf. Foucault 2008a: 42.

396 Cf. Foucault 2008a: 42–43.

397 Foucault 2008a: 44.

398 Ibid.

399 Foucault 2008a: 45.

400 Foucault 2008a: 62.

Parallel to the establishment of freedom, this form of governmentality is simultaneously concerned with its limitation. The problem of security is closely interlinked to liberal governmental skill – protection of individual interests as well as the protection of collective interests over individual interests, thus resulting in a "game of freedom and security".[401] These tendencies have become even more pronounced in the late 20th and early 21st centuries; the security dispositive has thus established itself as one of the most important phenomena behind social structures; stimuli which Foucault analyses in his work *Security, Territory, Population*. In this context, the 19th century saw the rise of a 'culture of danger', comprising an invasion of 'everyday dangers' and a 'stimulation of the fear of danger'.[402] It also becomes apparent that forms of government constitute the subject formation in specific ways, also in terms of emotionality and affectivity, such as feelings of fear, of being threatened and of uncertainty. These characteristics are further reinforced and disseminated by neoliberalism.

> "Neoliberalism, according to Foucault, extends the process of making economic activity a general matrix of social and political relations, but it takes as its focus not exchange but competition (Foucault, 2008: 12). What the two forms of liberalism, the 'classical' and 'neo' share, according to Foucault, is a general idea of *homo economicus*, that is, the way in which they place a particular 'anthropology' of man as an economic subject at the basis of politics."[403]

As *homo economicus* the neoliberal subject is focused on competition, increasingly becoming the entrepreneur of his own self. "As neoliberalism takes root as a widespread cultural discourse, the market-centric economic calculation – and all its attendant profit-seeking epistemologies and individualist social ontologies – becomes the mode of rationality for self-reflection and the barome-

---

401   Foucault 2008a: 65. He continues "The second consequence of this liberalism and liberal art of government is the considerable extension of procedures of control, constraint, and coercion which are something like the counterpart and counterweights of different freedoms." (Foucault 2008a: 67)

402   Cf. Foucault 2008a: 67–68. In this context Foucault alludes to the emergence of crime novels. He also writes, "There is no liberalism without the culture of danger." (Foucault 2008a: 67)

403   Binkley/Capetillo 2009: 4.

ter for individual success."[404] Foucault defines formation of the neoliberal subject as the 'subject of interests'.

> "Foucault characterizes these 'interests' as the bedrock for all decisions:
> '[the] principle of an irreducible, non-transferable, atomistic individual
> choice which is unconditionally referred to the subject himself' (C-BB, 272).
> Interests are those irrational and sometimes ineffable connections, whether
> positive or negative, that we have to experience; they are the reasons we
> care about things; they are what psychoanalysis calls cathexes."[405]

This choice is related to the desire for self-enhancement; neoliberalism is thus
also linked to excess, "too much is never enough".[406] Commenting on this, Winnubst writes, "It lays claim to excess as its central social value – and thus kills
it."[407] She continues, "it also tells us the truth of neoliberalism: the excess is
not, finally, what it claims to be. Indeed, as both Bataille and Foucault see so
lucidly, forms of human living in the twentieth century know nothing of real
pleasure, nothing of jouissance."[408] The proliferation of emotions is not of a
satisfying nature, but rather binds the subject to the existing power structures
of being governed. Foucault sees the conclusions derived from these observations as being, among others, the concept of aesthetics respectively the ethics
of the self, in which the self converts its formation into a topic to counter its
economising within the scope of the subjectification process. "Particularly in
the rise of the neoliberalism that we are currently witnessing across the globe,
this examination of economics is central to the shared Bataillean-Foucauldian

---

404 Winnubst, Shannon: "The Missing Link: Homo Economicus (Reading Foucault and
     Bataille Together)". In: Falzon, Christopher; O'Leary, Timothy; Sawicki, Jana (Eds.): *A
     Companion to Foucault.* Malden, Oxford, Chichester (Wiley-Blackwell), 2013, p. 466. She
     continues "The fundamental values of work and utility that are sanctified in the in-
     famous Protestant work ethic are thus fading from prominence in the contemporary
     milieu of neoliberalism. While we may still express allegiance to them, particularly, as
     in the US, as well worn vehicles for xenophobic nationalism, we reserve our true ad-
     miration for those who achieve economic success with the smallest effort of labour:
     the great entrepreneurial innovation is great precisely because it grants success with
     minimal effort. 'Maximize interest, minimize labour!' This becomes the slogan of these
     neoliberal times." (Winnubst 2013: 466)
405 Ibid.
406 Winnubst 2013: 467.
407 Ibid.
408 Ibid.

projects of rethinking the possibilities for living meaningful lives – of rethinking ethics."[409] A consideration of economics in all its varying dimensions is indispensable for this purpose.

2.2.4.2 The boundaries of the emotional economy in Foucault's work

On the one hand Foucault defines the term 'economy' in the narrower sense of a doctrine of affluence respectively as business and, on the other, as a mode of socialisation which characterises power structures, including, in particular, disciplining, normalisation and sexualisation; stimuli for the subject's being governed. Foucault argues that we must assume both the 'power of the economy' and also the 'economy of power', whereby there is a "decentralized understanding of the economy and of power";[410] a "micro/macroeconomics of power".[411] It is possible to speak of a "decentralization of the economy"[412] and, simultaneously, of a decentralisation of the concept of power which understands power as being productive, whereby, in line with the principle of rationality, power is exercised either calculatingly or economically.[413] Krämer asserts "He thus decentralizes and 'dethrones' the term 'economy', locating it in the complex arena of balances of power",[414] concluding

> "The assumption of the 'political economy of the body' provides the concept of the economy in Foucault's work, with the crucial addition required to include the dimensions of disciplining and normalization. [...] He 'dethrones' the economy, as it were, by taking it out of its previous framework of meaning, linked to work, production of goods and market events, and placing it in the politically volatile field of complex social balances of force. [...] Foucault

---

409   Winnubst 2013: 468.

410   Krämer, Thomas: *Die Ökonomie der Macht: Zum Ökonomiebegriff in Michel Foucault's Spätwerk (1975–1979).* Marburg (Tectum), 2011, p. 13. (Own translation)

411   Krämer 2011: 13. (Own translation)

412   Krämer 2011: 21; Krämer references William Walters. (Own translation)

413   Seen from the perspective of a power strategy, processes can also prove to be 'uneconomic'. It is thus certainly possible to refer to increased efficiency within the context of the application of power strategies: "The political economy of the body utilizes the microphysics of power and political anatomy in an attempt to optimize and rationalize this relationship of input and output." (Krämer 2011: 37; own translation) In this context one must assume historically differing types of rationality. (Cf. Krämer 2011: 99)

414   Krämer 2011: 77. (Own translation)

thus also simultaneously opposes a centralist view of a capitalist-economic totality as a transcendental, eternally valid entity."[415]

He continues, "'[T]he capitalist economy' [is] itself something which is social engineered [...], whereby it is, nevertheless, able to open up a new field of rationality and operational access to political intervention."[416]

Foucault's interest increasingly focuses on forms of governmentality and processes of subjectification, which are equally concerned with the constitution of affectivity. "The domestication of passions illustrates that early liberal concepts were already primarily focused on the shaping of the subject. The subject experiences impetus towards rationalization."[417] Furthermore, "The first significant innovation of neoliberalism consists of the removal of limits to the market, affecting not only the state but also the subject."[418] And

---

415   Krämer 2011: 20. (Own translation)

416   Krämer 2011: 56. (Own translation)

417   Michalitsch, Gabriele: *Die neoliberale Domestizierung des Subjekts: Von den Leidenschaften zum Kalkül.* Frankfurt, New York (Campus), 2006, p. 63. (Own translation) Elsewhere she writes "The early liberal domestication of passions into interests is now further developed into a reduced consideration of costs and benefits. Rationality now means a market-oriented, utility-maximizing calculation." (Michalitsch 2006: 66; own translation) She continues "Calculation now also determines the self-relationship. Passions appear to have become extinct; they are replaced by the commodity of calculated passion, simulated to facilitate its marketability. The process of domestication thus comes to its temporary end in the form of simulation. The economization of the social culminates in the economized shaping of subjectivity." (Michalitsch 2006: 98; own translation) And "Access to the individual takes place on the cognitive, emotional and social plane." (Michalitsch 2006: 100; own translation) The author describes the emotive consequences as follows: "In the emotional context, it is not possible to make connections between a negative sensitivity and social conditions. This results in uncertainty, fear of the future, indifference and resignation, leading to a lessening of emotions or increased aggressiveness, manifested in the social field as exclusion, competition and the erosion of solidarity (Cf. Gerlach 2001, 173ff.)." (Ibid.; own translation) She continues "Self-alienating identifications, depoliticization and privatization of individual existences, resignation, indifference – in particular with regard to democracy –; development of a real life perceived to be uninfluenceable and de-historicization of social and personal consciousness are the consequence, however ensure the production of utilizable human capital." (Ibid.; own translation) "This domestication of passions is the prerequisite for the autonomization of the economy." (Michalitsch 2006: 148; own translation)

418   Michalitsch 2006: 93. (Own translation)

"This early concept of the domestication of passions, aimed at shaping the subject, is radicalized in the neoliberal context. Reason is reduced to calculation. Passions – the expression of the incalculable, anti-reasonable – are not only tamed, becoming merely interests, but also completely eliminated, since market calculation determines not only all arenas, but also the self-relationship."[419]

On the other hand, passion mutates into a commodity. In this context, neoliberal government presents itself as "a freedom-creating form of the exercise of power."[420] This also includes a tendency to stimulate emotions. Foucault combines this 'having become' of the subject with the aspect of self-formation through the application of technologies of the self. The concept of governmentality allows him to consider these aspects in tandem. In addition to being governed, the governing of the self, self-management, thus increasingly becomes the central focus of Foucault's philosophy.[421] The aspect of self-constitution takes on equal significance to that of the external constitution of the subject – ethics and aesthetics come to the fore. The boundaries of the emotional economy in Foucault's philosophical concept are clearly delineated. Art is particularly significant in this context.

2.2.4.3 Emotion, literature and art in the work of Michel Foucault

In its murmuring of language, literature exhibits a proximity to madness which represents the otherness of reason. The otherness of literature, which characterises its specificity, allows it to become a counter-discourse. Literature and philosophy are thus partners in thought. Foucault's preoccupation with literature takes as its starting point the ontology of language; the self-referentiality of language which he demonstrates on the basis of Raymond Roussel's literature and its potential for transgression. In this context, Foucault references Bataille, de Sade, Artaud, Blanchot, etc., discussing each from a specific perspective. What is the significance, what is the function and what is the position of literature in the overall context of Foucault's philosophy? What link can be identified between emotion and literature? The focus of his exploration of various authors proves to be desire as described in fictional

---

419 Michalitsch 2006: 149. (Own translation)

420 Krämer 2011: 116. (Own translation)

421 Krämer writes "Foucault's analysis of transformation processes in our Western episteme demonstrates that neither freedom nor rulership are immutable entities." (Krämer 2011: 129; own translation)

representations of literature. While, in de Sade's work, discipline as a form of power transcending limits of possible experience is integral to the narrative, Bataille displays a desire for self-transgression as a form of ecstasy in both sexual experience and death. Artaud focuses on the experience of physicality in conjunction with the possibilities which the body offers for forms of expression, culminating in the scream; and Klossowski describes a sexual-mythical experience. Literature, asserts Blanchot, moves towards the furthest point, providing the opportunity to experience the impossible; literary language is the embodiment of contradiction, incomprehension and uncertainty. Blanchot's universe of literature is a universe of the 'dispossession' of the self. When considering visual art Foucault references Bosch and Goya. Literature and art should thus be viewed as spheres of the 'experience of the outside', facilitating borderline experiences – also in the sense of the insane/distorted, of madness. Descartes' methodical doubt in his *Meditations*, argues Foucault, already excluded such knowledge from modern thinking. The various concepts of literature presented in Foucault's work demonstrate, on the one hand, the possibility of other, new and excessive forms of affectivity in the literary setting and, on the other, of affective subject constitution by means of involved quasi-discourses which bring with them the shaping and regulation of feelings, thus enhancing the governability of the subject.

Modern art[422] in its various fields such as literature and painting is, argues Foucault, the "Cynicism in culture", a "cynicism of culture turned against itself",[423] and is thus integral to his analysis of parrhesia and therefore "linked to a manifestation of the truth".[424] The objective is "one of laying bare, exposure, stripping, excavation, and violent reduction of existence to its basics."[425] In this context Foucault writes that

---

422   Foucault references here in particular artists of the classical modern movement, such as Manet, Klee and Kandinsky. By analysing their art Foucault demonstrates fractures in the visual which make the invisible visible. Comparable phenomena can also be observed in the visual within the context of the change of epistemes and/or discourse rules. When exploring this topic Foucault wishes to retain its independence, not permitting it to be subsumed in the sphere of the un-speakable. Foucault cites Magritte when discussing the question of the representation of art.

423   Foucault, Michel: *The Courage of the Truth (The Government of Self and Others II). Lectures at the Collège de France, 1983–1984*. London, New York (Palgrave Macmillan), 2011, p. 189.

424   Ibid.

425   Foucault 2011: 188.

"there is an anti-Platonism of modern art which was the great scandal of Manet and which, I think, without characterizing all art possible today, has been a profound tendency which is found from Manet to Francis Bacon, from Baudelaire to Samuel Beckett or Burroughs. Anti-Platonism: art as the site of the interruption of the basic, stripping existence bare."[426]

Foucault posits "And art thereby established a polemical relationship of reduction, refusal, and aggression to culture, social norms, values, and aesthetic canons."[427] He continues, "And if this is not just in art, in the modern world, in our world, it is especially in the art that the most intense forms of a truth-telling with the courage to take the risk of offending are concentrated."[428] 'Aggression' and 'vulnerability' point to emotionality in the creative and receptive process which is mobilised by artistic truth-telling; linked to an experimental critique in a fundamental manner and facilitates a breaking open of the emotional economy. The concept of the parrhesia of modern art can be understood as a resumption and contextual intensification of Foucault's reflections on the ontology of language and his concept of literature as a counter-discourse. Art, in this context, increasingly becomes a specific form of truth-telling. Here also, Foucault's tendency to return to a topic in a procedural, extending, shifting, refining manner which locates the topic in a larger context becomes apparent. For him, the ontology of language is increasingly integrated into the ontology of the subject. Modern literature and art as a form of truth-telling combine the artistic existence; the creation of art and the courage to say everything in the sense of critique, resuming Foucault's concept of art as a counter-discourse within the scope of his subject-theoretical considerations in the shift to a series of self-practices, without wishing to codify art in its function. The genealogical examination of the forms of subjectification linked to truth-telling within the framework of the ethics respectively the aesthetics of the self also illustrates the methodological premise of the historical a priori in the context of a nexus of knowledge, power and subject.

When discussing the photography of Duane Michals Foucault emphasises the significance of thought and feeling in the reception process of visual art. Art should, argues Foucault, facilitate experiences and penetration of new spheres of experience. He thus writes, "Time may bring changes, old age and death, but

---

426   Ibid. Foucault also speaks of an anti-Aristotelianism of modern art.
427   Ibid.
428   Foucault 2011: 189.

thought and feeling are stronger than time. Only they can see and make visible its invisible wrinkles."[429] He continues "He [referring to Duane Michals] invites him to take on the undefined role of the reader or viewer, suggesting thoughts or feeling to him (because feelings move the soul and spread spontaneously from soul to soul)."[430] The purpose of this process is to reveal the invisible. In addition to the significance of thought Foucault unambiguously emphasises feeling as a dimension of the production and reception of art which can heighten awareness. Artistic experience is concerned with the transformation of the subject, focusing in particular on the consideration of perception, feeling and emotion. When discussing film Foucault concentrates on the affective-physical experience; what is seen becomes part of our bodies. This also results in a specific experience of the story which goes beyond knowledge.[431] The particular effect of film on the human body within the scope of the reception process initiated by its presence mode is to establish a comprehensive connection to the individual's relationship to the world and, over and above this, an action-theoretical dimension. The link to what is dreamed and possible is also important; it can thus be concluded that overall Foucault's work views film as having a subject-shaping function – in conjunction with a subject-changing effect. The close relationship between art, physicality and the creation of emotions in Foucault's work thus also becomes clear when considering artistic media.

Foucault gives preference to 'emotion' and 'affectivity' as the overarching terms for differing types and intensities of feeling.[432] While he does not offer any theory of feelings in the narrower sense, affectivity is, nevertheless,

---

429 Foucault, Michel: "Denken, Fühlen". In: Foucault, Michel: *Dits et Écrits: Schriften in vier Bänden: Dits et Écrits IV: 1980-1988*. Defert, Daniel; Ewald, François (Eds.), Frankfurt a.M. (Suhrkamp), 2005d, p. 302. (Own translation)

430 Foucault 2005d ": 300. (Own translation)

431 Foucault writes, "and she [referring to the grandmother seen in the film] is not part of what we know but instead part of our bodies, our way of acting, doing, thinking, dreaming and suddenly we have removed the sand which concealed these small, enigmatic gems inside us." In: Foucault, Michel: "Die Rückkehr des Pierre Rivière". In: Foucault, Michel: *Dits et Écrits: Schriften in vier Bänden: Dits et Écrits III: 1976-1979*. Defert, Daniel; Ewald, François (Eds.), Frankfurt a.M. (Suhrkamp), 2003c, p. 161. (Own translation) He continues "One cannot pose the question of knowledge to the cinema; this would be a completely pointless undertaking." (Foucault 2003c: 16; own translation)

432 This preference places Foucault in the philosophical tradition stretching from antiquity to the 17th century. See on this subject Hübsch, Stefan: "Vom Affekt zum Gefühl". In: Hübsch, Stefan; Kaegi, Dominic (Eds.): *Philosophische Beiträge zur Theorie der Emotionen*. Heidelberg (Universitätsverlag C. Winter), 1999, pp. 137–150.

of key significance to his philosophical concept. Subjectification and the construction of emotionality must be viewed in a narrower relationship and are located in a social and political context. Emotions implement subject positions linked to the use of practices of power, in particular in institutional contexts, anchoring them in the individual's body.[433] Feelings are subject to continual 'pacification', as Foucault illustrates using the example of rage and resentment. When considering desire he refers to "the normalisation and domestication of pleasure".[434] Nevertheless, emotions remain connected to a potential for resistance, which Foucault associates in particular with the self-shaping of affectivity by means of technologies of the self – also including reading and writing – within the framework of his ethics respectively aesthetics of the self. Despite their tendency to be fixed, emotions are thus changeable and capable of elaboration. An example of this self-shaping in the sense of a *de-subjectification* and *de-subjugation* can be found in Baudelaire's dandyism as a form of self-stylisation in both the real and the literary world. Foucault thus understands affectivity as, on the one hand, constructed, subject to discursive and dispositive shaping, as well as, on the other, as self-shaped. This also applies to the relationship between the shaping of emotions and the economy. While the emotional economy can also be found in the fields of literature and visual art; art can, over and above this, be viewed as a special area of the boundaries of the emotional economy – as an area which facilitates the transgression of boundaries and the transformation of the subject.

Overall it is possible to speak of a "historically enlightened potential of Foucauldian governmentality studies".[435] Foucault consistently links the term 'economy' with "forms of the political rationality of practices", exploring "fields of the rationality of the exercise of power",[436] whereby the specific rationality of neoliberalism takes the form of a proliferation of emotions. The metaphor of the emotional economy refers to subjectification processes, e.g. means of disciplining and bio-politics which also involve the formation of perceptions, moods, feelings and emotions. The shaping of the subject by micro-and macro-physical forms of power makes it appear to be heteronomously determined, because of, among other things, the related processes of creating emotions.

---

433   Cf. Foucault, Michel: "Pouvoir et corps". In: Foucault, Michel: *Dits et Écrits I. 1954–1975.* Paris (Gallimard), 2001a, pp. 1622–1628.

434   Winnubst 2013: 467.

435   Krämer 2011: 129. (Own translation)

436   Krämer 2011: 123. (Own translation)

In this context, the discursive respectively quasi-discursive disposition of literature and visual art also contributes to the emotional economy and the emotion-creating economy. The discursive and dispositive constitution of the subject also takes place by means of the quasi-discourses in literature and visual art and by means of cultural dispositions, however, these arenas also have a high potential to release possibilities for disengagement from emotional economies and for their restructuring. In Foucault's work art even becomes the benchmark for lifestyle and the model for a liberal self-determined life of ethical responsibility. This examination of literature and visual arts is related to Foucault's ethical-aesthetic viewpoint, whereby life should be based on the role model of art.

> "What strikes me is the fact that, in our society, art has become something that is related only to objects and not to individuals or to life. That art is something that is specialized or done by experts who are artists. But couldn't everyone's life become a work of art? Why should the lamp or the house be an art object, but not our life?"[437]

In the analogy to, and referencing of, art, the self becomes, with the aid of technologies of the self, an autonomous ethical subject – also in the political context. In this way, Foucault attempts to move closer to a political desideratum. He asserts that "'There is a science of governing but none of not-wanting-to-be-governed.'"[438] His objective is to develop such a science. To this end, knowledge of the emotional economy's methods and of boundaries is essential. In this context, art and aesthetics play a key role in an ethical-political turnaround with regard to subjectification.

2.2.5 Affect. Body. Desire. Emotionality in the philosophical concepts of Foucault and Butler

2.2.5.1 Subject and the construction of affect

The constitution of the subject is, as has become clear, to a large extent linked to the construction of affectivity. It plays a decisive role both for the heteronomous formation of the subject and for the application of liberation

---

437   Foucault, Michel: "On the Genealogy of Ethics". In: Foucault, Michel: *Ethics: Subjectivity and Truth (Essential Works of Foucault, 1954–1984, Vol. 1)*. Rabinow, Paul (Ed.), New York (The New Press), 1997, p. 261.
438   Krämer 2011: 121; Krämer quotes Bröckling 2007: 287. (Own translation)

techniques which promote its autonomy and lead to a change in the manner of subject. The terms emotion, feeling, affect, mood and perception cannot always be clearly separated from one another and, in certain theoretical contexts, are also defined differently and/or delimited from one another. The current general view is that, in contrast to perceptions, feelings are more subjective and/or more closely related to the subject, while perceptions are linked more to circumstances within the context of absorbing sensory data. In contrast to this, moods primarily describe long-term nuances in the human attitude to life. Emotions are generally considered to be states of excitement, while affective responses represent intense states of agitation within the context of the human attitude to life. They are transitory intense states of agitation which usually occur in conjunction with a narrowing of consciousness and physical phenomena such as, e.g., clenching of the fists, reddening and crying, and are linked to varying stages in the progressive process. Foucault and Butler display a preference for the terms 'affect' and 'affectivity' as the umbrella term for a variety of types and intensity of feelings.[439] While they may not develop any theory of feelings in the narrower sense, affectivity is, nevertheless, of key importance in their philosophical concepts. Subjectivity and the construction of emotionality must, for both authors, be seen as closely related and located within a social and political context. The constitution of the subject by means of discourses concerning their dispositive constitution and by means of power strategy-related operations, which also represents constructive performance on the part of the individual, is, simultaneously, related to the shaping of affective responses and emotions; to their changeability; to the form of affect regulation and the presentation of feelings. "Feelings are not only 'subjective' but rather are also deciding factors in the constitution of subjectivity".[440] The process of subjectivity is generated, among other things, by the shaping of affects and feelings. For the purposes of the implementation process, in which specific subject positions, generated by discourses, are absorbed in conjunction with the application of power practices, in particular in institutional

---

439   This preference places them in the philosophical tradition spanning the era from the ancient world to the 17th century. Cf. in this context Hübsch, Stefan: "Vom Affekt zum Gefühl". In: Hübsch, Stefan; Kaegi, Dominic (Eds.): *Philosophische Beiträge zur Theorie der Emotionen.* Heidelberg (Universitätsverlag C. Winter), 1999, pp. 137–150.

440   Henckmann, Wolfhart: "Über das Verstehen von Gefühlen". In: Herding, Klaus; Stumpfhaus, Bernhard (Eds.): *Pathos, Affekt, Gefühl.* Berlin, New York (de Gruyter), 2004, p. 56. (Own translation)

contexts which usually also involve the individual's body, they are interlinked and facilitate the anchoring of the process within the individual. Parallel to this, they define interaction with the other to a high degree and are the basis for the rejection, admiration, disregard or glorification of the other or for the projection of desire, revulsion, fear, etc. onto the other. Classification categories regarding gender; race; ethnic background; social status; professional class; age; etc. are of an affective nature, thus making them significant to the individual as well as also above and beyond the individual. These categories, with their associated positive or negative feelings, are also the basis for the individual's self-perception; thus have an influence on self-esteem, self-doubt or self-hate. According to Butler the overlaying of certain names, categories etc., which are accepted or rejected within the scope of the process of invocation, is linked to the shaping of emotions and results in the establishment of a web of feelings accompanying the formation of the subject, creating a specific range of emotions, within which certain affects are preferred; certain intensities of emotions and also the interaction of feelings are based. Foucault assumes that discourses provide empty spaces for the subject, which the latter fills and which are linked to the constitution of affects. Discourses should be viewed as being embedded in the dispositive so that the formation of the subject and the constitution of affective responses also take place by means of non-verbal practices. The theory of affect constitution serves to make the process of consolidation or, where applicable, change when adopting subject positions more comprehensible. In this context the works of Foucault and Butler see a close relationship between the theory of the constitution of emotion, affect and desire as well as also perception and thought – Foucault speaks in this context of historical apriority – and the new interpretation of the concept of the subject which focuses in particular on the physical and the question of subject constitution. Here, the distinctiveness of Foucault's interpretation of Kant's concept of critique, enlightenment and his theorem of desubjugation is highly evident. He emphasises the affective and physical side of the process.

2.2.5.2 Affect, body and desire in the work of Foucault

In Foucault's work, affective responses as the primary modalities of the body and the expression of mental affects and the physical-mental state should not be understood as a natural endowment but rather as taking specific, social, historically influenced forms, in particular, corresponding to discursive constitutions and physical practices within the scope of power strategic formalities.

Within the scope of this relationship, the body assumes special importance in Foucault's theory.

> "In reality, bodies are shaped by society: they are used and experienced in many different ways and their characteristics vary according to cultural practices. They are moulded by rhythms of work, eating habits and changing norms of beauty. They are concretely shaped by diet, exercise and medical interventions."[441]

Foucault is interested in "the essential intertwinement of body and power", examining "how power operates through the manipulation of bodies".[442] The body is "an important anchorage point for power."[443] The analysis of the relationship between 'body and power' is a central focus of his work: "he wants to bring the body into the focus of history and study history through it."[444] Desire is thus also not of a fixed nature but rather must be considered as constituted. "Foucault challenges this view by showing how our conceptions and experiences of sexuality are in fact always the result of specific cultural conventions and mechanisms of power and could not exist independently of them."[445] The constitution of desire subjects depends on a thought process based on categories such as, for e.g., man and woman; the gendering of behavioural patterns and their emotional connotations and the coupling of emotions to sexual practices. It is, according to Foucault, the dispositive of sexuality which constitutes sexuality as desirable. In this context his analysis is particularly concerned with the exploitation of eroticisation; he speaks of a 'contrôle-stimulation'.[446]

---

441   Oksala, Johanna: "Freedom and bodies". In: Taylor, Dianna (Ed.): *Michel Foucault: Key Concepts.* Durham (Acumen), reprinted 2013, p. 85. Oksala says "the body is completely shaped by history and culture." (Oksala 2013: 86) In this way Foucault overcomes the dichotomy of nature and culture. His concept of the relationship between power and the body references Nietzsche. In order to examine historical shaping he employs genealogical methods based on Nietzsche's work. Oksala continues "Foucault aims to bring the body into focus of history by studying its connections with techniques and deployments of power." (Oksala 2013: 86) Although Foucault views the body as shaped by socio-historical influences he emphasises the possibility of transgressive change, particularly via technologies of the self.

442   Oksala 2013: 87.

443   Oksala 2013: 92.

444   Oksala 2013: 87.

445   Oksala 2013: 90.

446   Cf. Foucault 2001a: 1623.

Affect situations have a tendency to be fixed; are, however, on the other hand without doubt expandable, changeable and capable of elaboration. It is thus possible for, among other things, changes in intimacy and sexuality to occur.[447] Desire is constituted within changing discursive practices and, over and above this, by the application of technologies of the self. Foucault rejects the repression theory of sexuality, as represented by, for e.g., Freud and Marcuse, emphasising the productive character of shaping by means of practices of power. The basis for this is his conception of the subject, according to which the subject should not be viewed as substance but rather as form, with subject forms taking various shapes depending upon the socio-historical context. "Les hommes s'engagent perpétuellement dans un processus qui, en constituant des objets, le déplace en même temps, le déforme, le transforme et le transfigure comme sujet."[448] Practices of the self enable the subject to also form itself by using historically variable technologies of the self – Foucault speaks in this context of an aesthetic and/or ethics of the self. "We constitute ourselves as subjects (we are enabled) by way of various 'practices of the self', which include activities of writing, diet, exercise and truth-telling."[449] In this context Foucault is concerned with practices of liberation which are also related to the body: "In order how the body is implicated in resistance and the practices of freedom".[450] In Foucault's words

---

447 In a monogamous, heterosexual constitution of desire the predominant culture of feelings is defined by jealousy, inter-gender violence and deviating practices. Male desire is, for e.g., generally linked to the wish for dominance and activity; the female to being subjugated and passivity. These desires substantially define the feelings of individuals and influence yearning and satisfaction. This form of desire cannot, of course, be understood as natural.

448 Foucault, Michel: "Entretien avec Michel Foucault". In: Foucault, Michel: *Dits et Écrits II. 1976–1988*. Paris (Gallimard), 2001b, p. 894.

449 Taylor, Dianna: "Practices of the self". In: Taylor, Dianna (Ed.): *Michel Foucault: Key Concepts*. Durham (Acumen), reprinted 2013, p. 173. She continues "We therefore find ourselves confronted with the task of figuring out when and how we are enabled and when and how we are constrained, of determining ways in which existing practices have the potential to loosen constraints and thus resist normalization, and of employing those practices not only for that purpose, but also in order to develop new and different ways – new and different ways of relating to ourselves and others. We need, in other words, to be able to reflect critically on the very process of becoming a subject." (Taylor 2013: 173)

450 Oksala 2013: 86.

"We must not think that by saying yes to sex, one says no to power; on the contrary, one tracks along the course laid out by the general deployment of sexuality. It is the agency of sex that we must break away from, if we aim – through a tactical reversal of the various mechanisms of sexuality – to counter the grip of power with the claims of bodies, pleasures and knowledges, in their multiplicity and their possibility of resistance. The rallying point for the counterattack against the deployment of sexuality ought not be sex-desire, but bodies and pleasures."[451]

Foucault differentiates between the experiences of desire facilitated by the body and sexuality in the narrower sense. "The body represents a dimension of freedom in the sense that its experiences are never wholly reducible to the discursive order."[452] He continues "Bodies are capable of multiplying, distorting and overflowing their discursive determinants and of opening up new and surprising possibilities that can be articulated in new ways."[453] Foucault thus views the body as being at one and the same time the effect of power and the source of freedom: "Foucault's conception of the body provides fruitful tools for theorizing the body *both* as an effect of power *and* as locus of resistance and freedom."[454]

2.2.5.3   Affectivity in the work of Judith Butler

Butler believes that Foucault fails to sufficiently substantiate this position, developing her own theory of performance, which provides a new theoretical basis for the transgressive, resistive potential of the body and desire and other affects. While in Foucault's work desire is the focus of his discussion of affective responses, Judith Butler widens her horizons by examining the social production of affectivity in general, using the theory of invocation and the concept of vulnerability as the basis for this. In this context, she combines the Foucauldian approach with the psychoanalytical methods of Freud and Melanie Klein.

"We are already social beings, working within elaborate social interpretations both when we feel horror and when we fail to feel it at all. Our affect is never merely our own: affect is from the start, communicated from else-

---

451   Foucault in Oksala 2013: 93.
452   Oksala 2013: 94.
453   Ibid.
454   Oksala 2013: 97.

where. It disposes us to perceive the world in a certain way, to let certain dimensions of the world in and to resist others."[455]

She thus creates a relationship between affectivity and power, since *framing*, the creation of a frame[456] around what can be perceived, as she terms the visible aspect of the discursive, constructs an inside and an outside, which has a regulating effect on affect. Taking up Foucault's conception of an inside and outside by using the term 'framing' Butler, in contrast to Foucault, emphasises imagery and mediality. Butler also speaks in this regard of an interpretation framework or of a pattern of interpretation, thus establishing a closer relationship with the cognitive theory of feelings in this context.[457] Feeling in her work does not, however, quite add up within the scope of this theoretical framework, as indicated by the qualificatory adverb 'partially'. "Feelings, as an element of the mental state, [may] structure the situation from the subject's perspective",[458] are in this context, however, simultaneously shaped by socio-historical influences. Butler is, in this regard, particularly interested in the relationship between affect and morals – moral reactions are, according to Butler, first expressed in the form of affective responses.

The barrier to the perceptibility of endangered life should be lifted – a problem which, logically, also has a medial aspect for Butler – in order to be able to view every life as worthy of being grieved for, instead of only specific lives. In this context, her concern is to become conscious of mutual dependency and vulnerability and to give up the attempt to immunise ourselves against vulnerability by means of a specific method of forming the subject

---

455 Butler, Judith: *Frames of War: When Is Life Grievable?* London, New York (Verso), 2010, p. 50.

456 "If, as I have argued, norms are enacted through visual and narrative frames, and framing presupposes decisions or practices that leave substantial losses outside the frame, then we have to consider that full inclusion and full exclusion are not the only options. Indeed, there are deaths that are partially eclipsed and partially marked, and that instability may well activate the frame, making the frame itself unstable. So the point would not be to locate what is 'in' or 'outside' the frame, but what vacillates between those two locations, and what, foreclosed, becomes encrypted in the frame itself." (Butler 2010: 75)

457 "[N]amely, that what we feel is in part conditioned by how we interpret the world around us; that how we interpret what we feel actually can and does alter the feeling itself." (Butler 2010: 41)

458 Landweer 2007: 251. (Own translation)

as a sovereign and/or national subject.[459] Wils comments as follows on this aspect: "The fear of danger, injury and pain [is] an emotion which is as basic as it is immoral [...], by means of which we are also able to directly perceive the vulnerability of the other."[460] Vulnerability can thus become morally significant. The process of neutralising feeling in the sense of creating moral competence to judge is not the central element of Butler's ethics but rather the emotional components of morals, a moral perception. Due to the interdependency of perception and emotionality, perception processes, including their medial aspect, play a major role as do thought structures, which co-determine moral judgements. In accordance with her balance model, which concerns differing human abilities, morals are equally defined by affectivity, perception and rationality and the interdependency of these components, whereby all impulses are subject to socio-historical shaping[461] by processes of power – the creation of norms should be viewed as integrated into this process – however, which also possess an emancipatory potential within the process of their performativity. For Butler, emotions have a global, self-realisatory function. This is demonstrated, among other things, by the significance of melancholy in the process of subject constitution, which indicates the painful processes of

---

459   Butler comments as follows on this: "It cannot be that the other is destructible while I am not; nor vice versa. It can only be that life, conceived as precarious life, is a generalized condition, and that under certain political conditions it becomes radically exacerbated or radically disavowed. This is a schism in which the subject asserts its own righteous deconstructiveness at the same time as it seeks to immunize itself against the thought of its own precariousness." (Butler 2010: 48)

460   Wils, Jean-Pierre: "Emotionen in ethischen Begründungsverfahren". In: Landweer, Hilge (Ed.): *Gefühle – Struktur und Funktion*. Berlin (Akademie), 2007, Deutsche Zeitschrift für Philosophie, Special Edition 14, p. 229. (Own translation)

461   Wils comments on this: "Emotions are by no means just *private* states. Precisely because they have a representative function, they are affected by the changes in the culturally shaped environment." (Wils 2007: 231; own translation) Landweer says on this subject: "The assumption that feelings are highly individual is a romantic idea that fails to recognise the character of moral feelings – to speak only of these for the time being. A legal culture is held together above all by the large area of naturally shared legal and moral feelings, even if there may also be very different emotional evidences and correspondingly different norms in relation to many individual legal issues." (Landweer 2007: 244; own translation) Landweer speaks of a 'communication with emotions' which points to a broad consensus of emotions. According to Landweer shame and indignation in particular are relevant indicators in a moral context. These feelings point to the anchoring of norms in habit and their perceived binding nature. (Cf. Landweer 2007: 244–245)

limitation and forbearance within the scope of subjectivity and thus indirectly also possibilities and potentials. Melancholy as an emotional state is always also located in the interpersonal arena, indicating on the one hand relationship deficits and, on the other, also desiderata. In Butler's work emotionality thus fulfils an orientational and judgemental function, also in moral terms; can, however also have a destabilising effect. "The stabilizing function which emotions obviously possess *because they are of a representational nature, simultaneously* also has the unpleasant consequence that their representation is also the gateway for culturally determined destabilization."[462] For Butler feelings also have an additional motivational character; Landweer speaks of a 'motivation theory'[463] with regard to this function of feelings in a general context. In Butler's work, it becomes clear that the fundamental model of knowledge is based on the idea of perception as the 'mode of recognition' and intelligibility as "the general historical schema or schemas that establish domains of the knowable. This would constitute a dynamic field understood, at least initially, as a historical *a priori*."[464] In this context, she references Foucault's epistemological theories. According to Butler, these changeable schemes generate the norms for acceptability. In contrast to Foucault, who speaks of boundary, break, passage and transgression in order to illustrate the changeable character of perception and recognition on the basis of historical apriority, Butler emphasises displacement as an element of iterability, working on the basis of assumptions grounded in speech act theory. This process incorporates the constitution of affectivity: "The conditions are set for astonishment, outrage, revulsion, admiration, and discovery, depending on how the content is framed by shifting time and place."[465] The framework or pattern of perception and intelligible recognition are formed by interpretations of reality, which are linked to affectivity. Butler continues by posing the question "How is affect produced by this structure of the frame? And what is the relation of affect to ethical and political judgment and practice?"[466]

---

462   Wils 2007: 232. (Own translation)
463   "For any action, but also for moral action and the indispensable recognition of norms, feelings are required as motivation, according to the thesis presented here. This can be described as the 'motivational thesis'." (Landweer 2007: 243; own translation)
464   Butler 2010: 6.
465   Butler 2010: 11.
466   Butler 2010: 13.

According to Butler *grief* and *mourning* demonstrate "the interdependent nature of human existence."[467] Lloyd continues "She is interested in them only because they expose the precariousness of life and our vulnerability to the Other."[468] And

> "for Butler the body is central to her conceptualisation of vulnerability since it is the body that exposes us or opens us up to the other: to their gaze, their touch, their violence (Butler 2004b: 21) – that human existence is explicitly exposed as one of interdependence. Vitally, it is this porosity to the other (a corporeal porosity) that is also the source of an ethical connection with the other."[469]

The conception of the body[470] as open; existing outside of itself and dependent implies affective responses which must be viewed as basically communicated and brings into play specific interpretation frameworks.[471] Loss, suffering and vulnerability result in ethical responsibility. When discussing human vulnerability Ben-Ze'ev points to the possibility of self-deception, to which he also assigns a positive function as regards the maintenance of a positive self-image.

> "Emotions may be viewed not merely as an expression of our profound vulnerability but also as *a way to cope* with it. By attaching significance to specific, local changes in our current situation, we ignore, in a way, the more profound type of change underlying our vulnerability; this is a type of self-deception. A certain measure of such self-deception is highly advantageous from an evolutionary point of view, as it enables us to protect our positive self-image and mobilize the required resources of facing daily changes. We deal with such changes as if our profound vulnerability is insignificant. This seemingly reduces our vulnerability, but it does not significantly change it."[472]

---

467   Lloyd, Moya: "Towards a cultural politics of vulnerability: Precarious lives and ungrievable deaths". In: Carver, Terrell; Chambers, Samuel A. (Eds.): *Judith Butler's Precarious Politics: Critical encounters*. London, New York (Routledge), 2008, p. 93.

468   Ibid.

469   Lloyd 2008: 94.

470   Butler derives a social ontology from her conception of the body.

471   Cf. Butler 2010: 40.

472   Ben-Ze'ev, Aaron: *The Subtlety of Emotions*. Cambridge, London (MIT Press), 2001, p. 17.

In Butler's work self-deception plays a different role in the creation of the sovereign subject, in which the subject's own vulnerability is largely negated; she views self-deception as negative. The chief concern within the scope of negation of the self's vulnerability is to form a sovereign or national subject which rises above other subjects. As a result, relationship quality in the moral and political sense within the national and international contexts is impaired and reduced. Butler thus refers to the eminently important role of feelings in the political arena. In Butler's work, the basis of the theoretical grounding of affectivity is a social ontology, within the scope of which the general vulnerability of life predisposes a fundamental interdependence.[473] In this context, Butler propounds "a rethinking of the subject as a dynamic set of social relations".[474] In contrast to Foucault, she views the term 'performativity of the subject' as more useful than that of construction.[475]

Overall Butler ascribes a special power to the affect, which should be steered, reduced or used by means of regulating the affective response. "Whether we are speaking about open grief or outrage, we are talking about affective responses that are highly regulated by regimes of power and sometimes subject to explicit censorship."[476] Foucault speaks in this regard of "tout ce lent travail d'apaisement qu'assure au jour le jour le discours 'vrai'."[477] His concern in this context is the appeasement of the affects anger, rage, irritated sensitivity and intolerance which are generated against the "grande machine théorique à produire des rationalités dominantes".[478] While Foucault places the focus more on containment attempts by means of discourses and dispositives, e.g. the economic discourse; spatiality and architecture, Butler emphasises, in particular, the significance of visual management or the field

---

473   Butler rejects anthropocentrism in this context, referring to the fact that the 'ontology' of the human is no different to that of the animal. Life is always co-joined to systematic relationships of interdependency.

474   Butler 2010: 162.

475   "The idea of iterability is crucial for understanding why norms do not act in deterministic ways. And it may also be the reason why performativity is finally a more useful term than 'construction'." (Butler 2010: 168) She continues "The 'break' is nothing other than a series of significant shifts that follow from the iterable structure of the norm." (Butler 2010: 156)

476   Butler 2010: 9.

477   Foucault, Michel: "La grande colère des faits". In: Michel Foucault: *Dits et Écrits II. 1976–1988*. Paris (Gallimard), 2001b, p. 277.

478   Ibid.

of perception steering in general. "The tacit interpretive scheme that divides worthy from unworthy lives works fundamentally through the senses, differentiating the cries we can hear from those we cannot, the sights we can see from those we cannot, and likewise at the level of touch and even smell."[479] In this context, she once again emphasises the medial aspect. It is this which also provides the location for racist perception and the shaping of affective responses as well as the regulation of affective responses in the field of racism. Viewed overall, asserts Butler, the attempt to regulate affective responses by means of power indirectly illustrates the latent explosive force of the affect and thus also the power of the affect.[480]

2.2.5.4   Subjectivity and affectivity in Foucault and Butler

Foucault's conception of subjectivity has, on the one hand, a theoretical focus; on the other it is practical – he develops a 'theory and practice of subjectivity'.[481] In Foucault's work the ethical/aesthetic lifestyle allies itself to a critical ethos of the ad-hoc reconfiguration of the social/historical situation and individual lifestyles. Foucault views the changing of our own desire and affectivity within the scope of the process of self-design using technologies of the self as the starting point for emancipatory changes of key significance. While Foucault locates the shaping of the subject in the institutional, discursive and dispositive arenas, Butler views interactions within the scope of invocation as being at the heart of the process of subjectivity, which simultaneously also incorporates the constitution of affectivity. While Foucault emphasises individual self-formation, *de-subjugation*, as an individual task, as *ethos*, Butler focuses on social interaction and the interdependence of human life. The starting point for ethics and politics is the theory of the vulnerability of life. Experiences of pain and melancholy are closely interlinked to rage and indignation, motivating ethical and political action. Butler favours taking influ-

479   Butler 2010: 51.
480   "Responsiveness – and thus, ultimately, responsibility – is located in the affective responses to a sustaining and impinging world. Because such affective responses are invariably mediated, they call upon and enact certain interpretive frames; they can also call into question the taken-for-granted character of those frames, and in that way provide the affective conditions for social critique. As I have argued elsewhere, moral theory has to become social critique if it is to know its object and act upon it." (Butler 2010: 34–35)
481   McGushin, Edward: "Foucault's theory and practice of subjectivity". In: Taylor, Dianna (Ed.): *Michel Foucault: Key Concepts*. Durham (Acumen), reprinted 2013, pp. 127–142.

ence on the steering and increasing of perception of others and our own suffering, taking mediality into special consideration when doing so – an aspect
which Foucault views as being summarised under the terms 'discourse' and
'dispositive' as an ethical/political task. Foucault and Butler provide themselves
with supplementary conceptions of the body, of physicality, desire and affectivity. Both reject the dichotomy of emotion and cognition, entirely in keeping with Wils' theory which paraphrases Kant's maximum, stating that "without emotions cognitions are empty, without cognitions emotions are blind."[482]
Both Butler and also Foucault argue that affectivity includes cognitive, motiva-
tional-voluntative and physical elements and should be viewed as fundamentally constructed. Patterns of interpretation not only have consequences for affective responses but can also take on the form of affective responses.[483] They
are not only defined and structured by interpretations but rather also have consequences for interpretations.[484] The issue at hand in this context is "to query
the conditions of responsiveness by offering interpretive matrices".[485] Despite
the constructed nature of the subject in general and their affectivity in particular, both authors emphasise the emancipatory potential of affective responses
within the scope of formation of the subject. Butler states, similarly to Foucault, "[o]pen grieving is bound up with outrage in the face of injustice or indeed of unbearable loss has enormous political potential."[486] In this context,
Taylor speaks of "the development of new, emancipatory forms of subjectivity."[487] She argues that Foucault's work incorporates "refusal, curiosity and innovation"[488] as technologies of the self, which have the capacity to facilitate
change. Foucault demonstrates "how engaging in refusal, curiosity and innovation facilitates new modes of self-constitution".[489] As also in Butler's work,

---

482 Wils 2007: 232. (Own translation) Wils refers to Kant's statement "Thoughts without
     content are empty, intuitions without concepts are blind." (Kant, KrV B 76, 77/A 52) He
     simultaneously draws attention to the limited character of his theory.
483 Cf. Butler 2010: 56.
484 Cf. Butler 2010: 73.
485 Butler 2010: 52.
486 Butler 2010: 39. She continues "Whether we are speaking about open grief or outrage,
     we are talking about affective responses that are highly regulated by regimes of power
     and sometimes subject to explicit censorship." (Butler 2010: 39) According to Butler
     moral reactions initially take the form of an affective response. (Cf. Butler 2010: 41)
487 Taylor 2013: 174.
488 Taylor 2013: 182.
489 Taylor 2013: 183.

the practise of criticism is of key significance. Butler attributes emancipatory potential to the recurring, shifting practice of performativity and the practices of 'speaking out'. These processes impact on the human dispositions of perception, affectivity and intelligibility, which are shaped by the processes of power. Both philosophers consider emotions as the foundation of ethical action and of socio-political relevance due to their cognition-inducing, self-and world-understanding[490] and also their motivating function. Both Foucault and also Butler argue that any emancipatory practice in the ethical and political sense which fails to take human affectivity into account is doomed to failure.

---

490   Landweer also speaks of the *Erschließungsfunktion* of feelings. "This accessing function applies to feelings not only in cases in which rationality is not possible or fails; they do not function merely as a substitute for a rational view of things. [...] rathermore I would like to argue that this sensitivity accompanies every situational perception and interpretation." (Landweer 2007: 251; own translation) Rational distancing does remove us from physical-affective dependence: "Such a distancing, however, does not fully remove us from our physical-affective attachment to the situation; we remain situated, physical beings with specific sensitivities and the convictions and values anchored in them. Rationality can thus actually be understood as a distancing resulting from direct, physical-affective sensitivity and so also from emotions; this is, however, a distancing which behaves derivatively as a quasi-theoretical attitude to the entanglement of the situation. Distanced rationality is not located in a placeless no man's land; it is, necessarily, attached to the situation and thus to the implicitness based on it – in other words, it is attached to the cultural context." (Landweer 2007: 252; own translation) She continues "Rationality cannot, however, ever completely break loose from its anchoring in sensitivity." (Landweer 2007: 253; own translation) According to Landweer emotionality and rationality are located on one continuum: "In this model feelings and rationality are communicated via the term 'explication'; rational judgements are directly dependent on it." (Landweer 2007: 253; own translation) Landweer speaks of 'integrative common sense' which "is also able to integrate those feelings which at first sight seem to contradict each other." (Landweer 2007: 252; own translation)

2.3 Subject and power. Foucault's concept of power and resistance in a global context

2.3.1 Power and limits of power. Resistance and autonomy in Michel Foucault's work

2.3.1.1 Foucault and the question of power

The topic of power is at the heart of Foucault's philosophy: "In the end, I had only produced a history of power."[491] Power is one of the three central theorems of his philosophy, which he defines as knowledge, power and the subject. His theory of power emphasises the strategic character of power, which can take very different forms: "That which was ill-tolerated and continuously questioned, which produced that sort of discomfort, was 'power'. And not only state power, but also that which was exercised within the social body through extremely different channels, forms, and institutions."[492] Foucault examines these different forms – combined with discursive and dispositive determinacy and associated specific strategies – in socio-historical contexts. He distances himself from traditional concepts of power, such as Freud's repressive theory of power, which assumes a repressive character of culture.[493] According to Foucault, power should not be understood as a form of prohibition, as an instance of 'you must not', to which the individual is subjected in Freud's concept and which, as a result of power processes, is internalised in the conscience. Foucault also criticises Durkheim's sociological theory of power and other concepts based on Durkheim such as Lévi-Strauss' works. Social facts, collective goals, beliefs, norms, duties and customs which are regarded as something *supra-individual* are regarded as emergent characteristics of social systems and, like laws or doctrines, have an oppressive and coercive character.

---

491   Foucault, Michel: *Remarks on Marx: Conversations with Duccio Trombardori.* New York (Semiotext(e)), 1991, p. 145.

492   Foucault 1991: 144.

493   Foucault remarks "I am not the first, far from it, to bypass the Freudian schema that opposes instinct to repression, instinct and culture." In: Foucault, Michel: "The Meshes of Power". In: Crampton, Jeremy W.; Elden, Stuart (Eds.): *Space, Knowledge and Power. Foucault and Geography.* London (Routledge), 2007a, p. 153. Further he says "We must therefore think instinct not as a natural given, but already as a whole development, a wholly complex game between the body and the law, between the body and the cultural mechanisms that ensure the control of people." (Foucault 2007a: 153) Desire is not a constant human basic instinct, but instead is constituted in socio-historical processes.

"We are thus always doing a juridical sociology of power for our society and, when we study societies different from our own, we do an ethnology that is essentially an ethnology of rules, an ethnology of prohibition. See, for example, in ethnological studies from Durkheim to Lévi-Strauss, what was the problem that would always reappear, perpetually re-worked: a problem of prohibition, essentially the prohibition of incest."[494]

According to Foucault, Rousseau's social body as the *sovereign* already emerged from the transfer or abolition of individual rights and from the establishment of legal prohibitions.

"[T]he West never had a system for the representation, the formulation and the analysis of power other than law and the system of law. And I believe that this is the reason for which, when it comes down to it, we have not had, until recently, other possibilities of analyzing power besides utilizing these elementary, fundamental, etc., notions that are those of law, of rules, of the sovereign, of the delegation of power, etc. I believe that it is this juridical conception of power, this conception of power derived from law and the sovereign, from rule and prohibition, of which we must now rid ourselves if we want to proceed to an analysis not just of the representation of power, but of the real functioning of power."[495]

Unlike Max Weber,[496] who also explores other forms of power in addition to the juridical understanding, Foucault does not primarily focus on the aspect of

---

494   Foucault 2007a: 154.

495   Foucault 2007a: 155–156.

496   According to Weber, however, power is "the probability that one actor within a social relationship will be in a position to carry out his own will despite resistance, regardless of the basis on which this probability rests." In: Weber, Max: *Economy and Society. An Outline of Interpretive Sociology*. Berkeley (University of California Press), 1978, p. 53. Rule as a special form of power implies the possibility of obedience. Max Weber distinguishes between three forms of rule: legal, traditional and charismatic rule, each of which has a different legitimation strategy. Legal rule – the democratic constitutional state and bureaucracy (considered to be the purest form of legal rule) are cited here as examples – is impersonal and promises equal opportunities and equal burden sharing, while traditional rule legitimates itself through, for example, faith and the 'sanctity' of orders. Patriarchal rule and monarchies are provided as examples of traditional rule. Charismatic rule is bound to a person with charisma, sects and religious groups are examples of this. The general principle of rule is to guarantee survival and/or well-being through subjugation.

authority and its legitimation, but instead conceives power in the sense of historical power practices, diverse power relations and strategic situations. Power should be regarded as a function of the construction of the world and the subject, of the foundation of individuality and identity, shaping knowledge, discourses, body and desire. Power acts productively, there is *no outside of power* in these processes. The philosophical concepts of Marx and Nietzsche can be considered as precursors of Foucault's theory of power. For Foucault, Marx's concept of power is also inspiring in particular due to its assumption of local and regional forms of power.

> "In sum, what we can find in Volume II of *Capital* is, in the first place, that there exists no single power, but several powers. [...] Powers, which means to say forms of domination, forms of subjugation, which function locally, for example in the workshop, in the army, in slave-ownership or in a property where there are servile relations. All these are local, regional forms of power, which have their own way of functioning, their own procedure and technique. All these forms of power are heterogeneous."[497]

Foucault also remarks "Marx gave, for example, superb analyses of the problem of discipline in the army and in the workshops."[498] Foucault continues these investigations into the disciplinary form of power. In addition to this, his genealogy, which is based on Nietzsche, investigates the emergence of forms of power. Nietzsche's essay *On the Genealogy of Morality*[499] in particular deals with the origin and emergence of moral ways of thinking, distinguishing between 'master morality' as the attitude of the rulers and 'slave morality' as the attitude of the miserable, poor and powerless. He speaks of a hatred of *nobility* which leads to moral development. In his critique of morality in general and Christian morality in particular, Nietzsche calls for the revaluation of all values. His theorem of power establishes the will or the multiple wills to power. Foucault takes up Nietzsche's thoughts on the decentralisation and historicization of power. Foucault's analysis of power produces a repertoire

---

497   Foucault 2007a: 156.

498   Foucault 2007a: 157.

499   Cf. Nietzsche, Friedrich: "On the Genealogy of Morality". In: Ansell-Pearson, Keith (Ed.): *'On the Genealogy of Morality' and Other Writings: Revised Student Edition (Cambridge Texts in the History of Political Thought).* Cambridge (Cambridge University Press), 2006.

of different forms of power in different socio-historical contexts, such as sovereign power,[500] pastoral power,[501] juridical power,[502] biopower,[503] disci-

---

500   Sovereign power is characterised by its tendency to demonstrate power over life and death. Foucault gives the following example: "On 2 March 1757 Damiens the regicide was condemned 'to make the *amende honorable* before the main door of the Church of Paris', where he was to be 'taken and conveyed in a cart, wearing nothing but a shirt, holding a torch of burning wax weighing two pounds'; then, 'in the said cart, to the Place de Grève, where, on a scaffold, that will be erected there, the flesh will be torn from his breasts, arms, thighs and calves with red-hot pincers, his right hand, holding the knife with which he committed the said parricide, burnt with sulphur, and, on those places where the flesh will be torn away, poured molten lead, boiling oil, burning resin, wax and sulphur melted together and then his body drawn and quartered by four horses [...]'." In: Foucault, Michel: *Discipline and Punish: The Birth of the Prison*. London (Penguin Books), 1995, p. 3.

501   Pastoral power can be characterised by the ability to serve others as a shepherd; by sacrificing oneself for the life and mental welfare of the flock; by permanent concern for the individual and by being focused on spiritual salvation. This process is about exploring the most intimate secrets of the individual.

502   According to Foucault's analysis, law as an instrument of monarchic power is directed against feudal powers and, in terms of its origin, is primarily the power of the state. Roman law is regarded as the source of law. It increasingly constitutes a common system for representing the power of the bourgeoisie and the monarchy. In certain historical situations, the bourgeoisie disposes of monarchical power with the help of legal discourse. Prohibition is at the centre of legal power.

503   Biopower is a normalising power, its effect is homogenising, mass-constituting and the norm play a more important role than law. It uses regulative techniques of biopolitics; statistical surveys and demographic surveys such as birth rates, death rates, frequencies of diseases, public hygiene and age curves (i.e. Gaussian normal distribution), often appearing as care of the self. "And what does population mean? It does not simply mean to say a numerous group of humans, but living beings, traversed, commanded, ruled by processes and biological laws. A population has a birth rate, a rate of mortality, a population has an age curve, a generation pyramid, a life-expectancy, a state of health, a population can perish or, on the contrary, grow." (Foucault 2007a: 161) Foucault also speaks of the politics of life: "Sex is the hinge between anatomo-politics and biopolitics; it is at the intersection of disciplines and regulations, and it is in this function that it has become, at the end of the 19th century, a political drama of first importance for making society a machine of production." (Foucault 2007a: 162)

plinary power[504] and test[505] at the level of microphysics and, starting from the concept of domination and *dispositives*, also macrophysics. He remarks "Il n'est pas vrai que dans une société il y a des gens qui ont *le* pouvoir, et en dessous des gens qui n'ont pas *de* pouvoir du tout. Le pouvoir est à analyser en termes de relations stratégiques complexes et mobiles, où tout le monde n'occupe pas la même position, et ne garde pas toujours la même."[506] Domination results from relatively stable power relations, which, however, have an unstable character and are constantly threatened in their existence, causing permanent shifts. Based on an analysis of the society of his time, Foucault observes the interaction of normalising power and pastoral power in the final decades of the 20th century – the latter refers to the actions of the state in a modified form. He also examines neoliberalism in economics and politics as a specific form of power with present-day relevance. His analyses retain their significance for today's society.

---

504   "On one hand, there is this technology that I would call 'discipline'. Discipline is basically the mechanism of power through which we come to control the social body in its finest elements, through which we arrive at the very atoms of society, which is to say individuals. Techniques of the individualization of power. How to oversee someone, how to control their conduct, their behaviour, their aptitudes, how to intensify their performance, multiply their capacities, how to put them in the place where they will be most useful: this is what discipline is, in my sense." (Foucault 2007a: 159) "What is to be understood by the disciplining of societies in Europe since the eighteenth century is not, of course, that the individuals become more and more obedient, nor that all societies become like barracks, schools, or prisons; rather, it is that an increasingly controlled, more rational, and economic process of adjustment has been sought between productive activities, communications networks, and the play of power relations." In: Foucault, Michel: "The Subject and Power". In: Foucault Michel: *Power: Essential Works of Foucault 1954–1984. Vol. 3.* Faubion, James D. (Ed.), London (Penguin Books), 2002b, p. 339.

505   The test is similar to a duel and was a form of power prevalent in archaic Greek society and the Middle Ages. It was also the basis of legal structures in historic Germanic law. The legal dispute resembles a battle, a ritualised continuation of conflict and war, without interest in the determination of true facts or real obligations and without mediating entities. Remnants can be found in feudal jurisdiction. It represents a trial of strength and considers prevailing differences in power as a criterion for decision-making. The prerogative of the more powerful applies.

506   Foucault, Michel: "Le style de l'histoire". In: Foucault, Michel: *Dits et Écrits II. 1976–1988.* Paris (Gallimard), 2001b, p. 1475.

2.3.1.2   Freedom and power in Foucault's works

Foucault's concept of freedom within the framework of the subject-knowl-edge-power complex can be understood as an ad-hoc theory of freedom, in which freedom is not contradictory to power, but is closely connected to it – as the other facet of power. In his relational concept of power, the power of all participants to act is always presupposed.

> "It's clear that power should not be defined as a constraining act of violence that represses individuals, forcing them to do something or preventing them from doing some other thing. But it takes place when there is a relation be-tween two free subjects, and this relation is unbalanced, so that one can act upon the other, and the other is acted upon, or allows himself to be acted upon."[507]

In Foucault's productive, non-repressive theory, freedom to change one's ac-tions is always designed "in order to not to be governed thusly, like that, in this way".[508] Foucault calls this process, which always also has a political dimen-sion, *desubjugation*.

In Foucault's view, the concept of freedom can be understood negatively in the sense of 'liberating from', as the removal of restrictions, and positively as the exercise of freedom, with the act of liberation possibly being regarded as a prerequisite for the exercise of freedom. In this process the task is always to identify the fault lines which permit transformations; there are no precon-ceived concepts or processes. This also entails the concept of the ethics or aes-thetics of the self with varying forms of self-formation in the historical process, according to which the subject has the possibility of self-design. The technolo-gies of the self allow the subject to form themself in an area of conflict between power and freedom. The subject does not detach themself from historically variable relations of knowledge and power, but instead tries to create them-selves based on these relations, in a partial liberation from the procedures of submission. In addition to the development of a lifestyle, Foucault is also con-cerned with the subject's development of a moral attitude. He believes that all three modes of the subject must be considered within the context of this pro-cess – the subject of knowledge, of power and of the ethics/aesthetics of the self.

---

507   Taylor, Dianna (Ed.): *Michel Foucault: Key Concepts*. Durham (Acumen), 2011, p. 5.
508   Foucault 2007b: 76.

Foucault embeds his theory of governmentality in his concept of power as the art of domination, which also refers to how one deals with oneself. In his works, the concept of governmentality links epistemology, political philosophy, aesthetics and ethics. Governmentality not only entails being governed – being subjected to processes of microphysics – but in particular governing oneself and, moreover, primarily governing well – meaning appropriate leadership of the other. The latter presupposes a conscious relationship with oneself, leadership of the self. "This *techne* created the possibility of forming oneself as a subject in control of his conduct [...] – a skilful and prudent guide of himself."[509] This is where Foucault begins his investigation of the technologies of the self of ancient times and Christianity, which can be regarded as concrete examples of socio-historical manifestations of self-technique. These primarily aesthetic manifestations of lifestyle also have an ethical and political character.

Byung-Chul Han[510] criticises Foucault's theorem of care of the self as an ethical principle: "Foucault raises care of the self to the status of an ethical principle and awards it preference over care for others".[511] For Han this *beyond the self* represents friendliness, a detachment of the self, as "an *extrinsic* quality that cannot be attributed to power".[512] According to Han's understanding of Nietzsche, this represents a type of *supra-power*, a giving oneself away in friendliness.[513] He asserts that Foucault formulates "a concept of power *in which, to a certain extent, a critique of power is already contained.*"[514] He also remarks "Foucault's revised concept of power results from an ethos of freedom."[515] And "Thus, an ethos of freedom stops power from solidifying into domination and makes sure that it remains an open game."[516] Han admits that power relations require a minimal degree of freedom for power-logical reasons, but accuses Foucault

---

509   Foucault 1990: 138–139.

510   Byung-Chul Han develops his theory of power in the following publications: Han, Byung-Chul: *What is power?* Cambridge (Polity Press), 2019; Han, Byung-Chul: *Hegel und die Macht: Ein Versuch über die Freundlichkeit.* Munich (Wilhelm Fink), 2005; Han, Byung-Chul: *Topology of Violence.* Cambridge (The MIT Press), 2018.

511   Han 2019: 89.

512   Han 2019: 91.

513   According to Han, this relationship of friendliness to the *other* stands in contrast to Levinas' ethics of the 'for-the-other'. (Cf. footnote 70 in Han 2019: 122)

514   Han 2019: 86.

515   Ibid.

516   Ibid.

of using "the concept of 'freedom' in an emphatic sense".[517] He accuses Foucault of distancing himself from real occurrences of power.[518]

2.3.1.3   Autonomy and resistance

In his philosophy, Foucault always assumes the existence of the possibility of resistance, based on his concept of power and his idea of freedom; the subject as the focal point of transforming behaviour always remains conceivable for him. Despite his critique of the subject, his socially and historically based concept of freedom enables him to maintain the emancipatory potential of human action. "Freedom for Foucault is not a state we occupy, but rather a practice that we undertake. Specifically, it is the practice of navigating power relations in ways that keep them open and dynamic and which, in doing so, allow for the development of new, alternative modes of thought and existence."[519] In his concept of freedom he defines "freedom as 'ongoing work'".[520] "This leads us to reexamine more or less entirely the postulate according to which the development of knowledge is undoubtedly the guarantee of liberation."[521] Freedom must always be attained in specific situations.

Foucault's conception of the political, autonomy as self-determined decision-making based on freedom and resistance linked with the concept of the construction of the subject in discursive and dispositive configurations. Resistance manifests at edges, in gaps and at thresholds, where new rules are brought into play. On the other hand, an important element of the motivation behind his philosophical work is to constantly demonstrate this possibility to the individual.[522] Foucault's definition of resistance must be regarded as very broad

"Foucault's pathos formula of the omnipresence of resistance, however, (still) includes no reference to domination, legitimacy or even normativity, and

---

517   Ibid.

518   Cf. ibid.

519   Taylor 2011: 4.

520   Taylor 2011: 6.

521   Foucault 1991: 165–166.

522   "In Foucault's understanding, subjects are formed by the discourse and power relations of their time and yet are self-reflexive as well as capable of action and are thus able to partially evade their heteronomous constitutional conditions." In: Hauskeller, Christine: *Das paradoxe Subjekt: Unterwerfung und Widerstand bei Judith Butler und Michel Foucault.* Tübingen (edition diskord), 2000, p. 21. (Own translation)

thus seems to move beyond even the final stopping points of a broad concept of resistance. The initial question remains: What qualifies one power among powers; one power against another; a counter-power to resistance? How does Foucault define resistance?"[523]

Hechler/Philipps describe various forms of resistance in the Foucauldian sense: "Resistance and freedom practices aimed at preventing states of domination can thus be identified both in confrontational, warlike conflicts, in flight, refusal and withdrawal, as well as in attempts to carry out autonomous self-design."[524] Foucault remarks on this aspect: "Instead there is a plurality of resistances, each of them a special case: resistances that are possible, necessary, improbable; others that are spontaneous, savage, solitary, concerted, rampant, or violent; still others that are quick to compromise, interested, or sacrificial".[525] Various forms of resistance develop in different socio-historical situations; Kastner speaks of a "flexibility of counter-behaviour".[526] They also include political revolts and resistance struggles.

"I have tried to show that, based on Foucault, there is certainly a possibility of thinking political resistance, precisely out of the immanence of discourse, i.e. on the basis of a discursive separation between two fields. The immanent field of an expressible relationship of binary, but in reality overlapping, poles (e.g. rulers and governed, autonomy and heteronomy) which is determined in a certain way in the discourse, in the body of society, in the power structure, and the field which transcends this immanence, an unspeakable *beyond* of this determination, which, however, in the immanent field always emerges and asserts itself as the possibility of another determination, a complete restructuring or even the dissolution of the binary relationship."[527]

---

523   Hechler, Daniel; Philipps, Axel (Eds.): *Widerstand denken: Michel Foucault und die Grenzen der Macht.* Bielefeld (transcript), 2008, p. 10. (Own translation)

524   Hechler/Philipps 2008: 11. (Own translation)

525   Foucault, Michel: *The Will to Knowledge: The History of Sexuality: Vol. 1.* London (Penguin Books), 1998, p. 96.

526   Kastner, Jens in Hechler/Philipps 2008: 49. (Own translation)

527   Kupke, Christian: "Widerstand und Widerstandsrecht. Ein politik-philosophischer Versuch im Ausgang von Foucault". In: Hechler, Daniel; Philipps, Axel (Eds.): *Widerstand denken: Michel Foucault und die Grenzen der Macht.* Bielefeld (transcript), 2008, p. 80. (Own translation)

The author uses the idea of immanent transcendence, "an unsayable implemented in the sayable", which is incorporated in the concept of transgression to justify this.[528] Han criticizes Foucault's omnipresence of resistance in his concept of resistance,[529] claiming that power relations are not fundamentally linked to possibilities of resistance "There is no resistance not only in the case of infinite violence but also in the case of infinite power. Thus, there may well be a power relation without any resistance. Foucault apparently does not notice this constellation. He takes cue from the paradigm of struggle."[530] For Han, profound tiredness is the opposite of power.[531] Consequently, all resistance has a weakening effect. However, Han's idea of an infinite power must be understood as an abstract construct based on Foucault's historical-concrete orientation for the analysis of the phenomenon of power and thus cannot refute Foucault's theory. Klass also carries out an intensive, in-depth analysis of Foucault's concept of resistance, which culminates in the formula "Where there is power, there is resistance".[532] Klass offers a series of paraphrases of this formula: "Where there is power, there are possibilities of resistance",[533] "Where there is domination, there should be resistance",[534] "Where there is 'domination' as a form of power, then indeed resistance is

---

528   Ibid. (Own translation)

529   According to Han, resistance, like power, is attributed to the principle of the living, which always has the "capacity to give an independent response", and he references Nietzsche in this context. (Han 2019: 3) Foucault's concept of resistance completely omits recourse to the metaphor of the organism, which occupies a central position in Han's reasoning, whereas Foucault's arguments are functional and can, instead, be compared to the second point of Han's derivation of resistance. According to Han the complexity of the processes of power, which are based on interdependencies and reciprocity, results in the dependence of the person exercising power on the inferior, thus "even the very weakest can turn their powerlessness into power". (Han 2019: 4)

530   Han 2019: 85.

531   Han 2019: 59; Han is referring to Handke, Peter: *Versuch über die Müdigkeit*. Frankfurt am Main (Suhrkamp), 1992, p. 75.

532   Foucault, Michel: *The History of Sexuality. Vol. I: An Introduction*. New York (Pantheon Books), 1978, p. 95.

533   Klass, Tobias N.: "Foucault und der Widerstand: Anmerkungen zu einem Missverständnis". In: Hechler, Daniel; Philipps, Axel (Eds.): *Widerstand denken: Michel Foucault und die Grenzen der Macht*. Bielefeld (transcript), 2008, p. 158. (Own translation)

534   Klass 2008: 160. (Own translation) Similarly, Klass writes on p. 165: "Where there is dominion, there should be resistance." (Own translation)

made more difficult, but never impossible";[535] "When you encounter 'domination' as a form of power, please do not forget to use your 'enlightenment
ethos' to oppose this form of power resistance!".[536] In this context, resistance
is understood as a counter-power which opposes domination and, in some
cases, assumes a normative character. Klass' criticism of Foucault's thesis of
the omnipresence of power and resistance, however, neglects the complexity
of the concept of resistance in Foucault's work, which encompasses a socio-
historical oscillation ranging from simple counter-power as power reflected
in power – an identical but never fully identical form of power – to other
forms of power and resistance in the sense of revolt and its pathos formula.
Walzer says "Foucault's political theory is a 'tool kit' not for revolution but
for local resistance".[537] Resistance is initially only a power opposing power
where one has an active and the other a reactive character. As Klass correctly
assumes, this was preceded by a decision between giving in and confronting
one another. Resistance therefore begins with the opposing of power, but does
not end with it.[538] Furthermore, Klass claims that Foucault rejects domination
or wishes to prevent states of domination, since they contradict his concept
of power. Foucault, however, is not concerned with a general rejection of
domination, but instead only with a distinctive interpretation of domination,
understood as the art of appropriate governance. For Foucault, therefore, the
concept of resistance should not be seen merely in the sense of the struggle
against domination. He argues that power, in contrast to force, can generally

---

535   Klass 2008: 164. (Own translation)

536   Klass 2008: 165. (Own translation)

537   Walzer, Michael: "The Politics of Michel Foucault". In: Hoy, David Couzens (Ed.): *Foucault: A Critical Reader*. Oxford UK, Cambridge USA (Blackwell), 1996, p. 55. Foucault expresses a deep distrust of all comprehensive social change programmes when he states
that they have "led only to the return of the most dangerous traditions." (Foucault 1997:
316)

538   Also in this process power itself changes, perhaps demonstrating forms of counter-
power or becoming counter-power. This point of view emerges when the relational,
agonal and dynamic, historically variable character of power and counter-power is genuinely accepted. The positions of power and counter-power change repeatedly, also in
contexts of domination, in which counter-power can therefore always take the form
of selective and solidifying resistance – conceived individually or in cooperation with
others.

be understood as a confrontation with a counterforce.[539] In this context Klass' reference to Foucault's problem of the imperceptible, undeclared transition from the descriptive to the normative, from the descriptive formula to the pathos formula of resistance is of interest, and, as became clear above, is also criticised by Han. Since Hume this has been referred to as the *is-ought problem*. This aspect raises the fundamental question of how the normative is conceived in Foucault's theory. It becomes apparent that Foucault's normative is based on power theory. "This inquiry, however, is never neutral. The price of Foucauldian methodology is that there is no objective, transcendental, capital-T Truth out there that adjudicates between warring forces. [...] There is no neutrality or universality."[540] Further Stone writes "Unlike the disinterested observer with 'a view from nowhere', the modern historico-political thinker cannot, and is in fact not trying to, occupy the position ... of a universal, totalizing, or neutral subject [...] the person who is speaking [...] is inevitably on one side or the other (C-SMD, 52)."[541] What is noteworthy in Foucault's work in this context is usually the absence of different levels of description and prescription; due to his assumption of the constructedness of knowledge in power contexts in which *ought-statements* arise both levels coincide.[542] In the conceptual grid, the interests and intentions of the speakers, the authorisation of the speakers, which form statements on the basis of formation rules, the performance of normative operations is already concealed on the descriptive level. In most cases, judgements remain hidden but are accessible for analysis by means of archaeological and genealogical procedures.[543]

When discussing the ethos of critique as the basis of the pathos formula of resistance Foucault employs a strictly historical approach, claiming that the

---

539   Klass' interpretation of Foucault's variably conceived notion of resistance forms the basis for a concept which encompasses historically diverse forms and keeps possible future forms open.

540   Stone, Brad Elliott: "Power, Politics, Racism". In: Falzon, Christopher; O'Leary, Timothy; Sawicki, Jana (Eds.): *A Companion to Foucault*. Chichester (Wiley-Blackwell), 2013, p. 357.

541   Ibid. Stone cites Foucault, Michel: *Society Must Be Defended. Lectures at the Collège de France, 1975–1976*. Davidson, Arnold I. (Ed.), New York (Picador), 2003a.

542   According to Foucault, the descriptions already contain judgements; he asserts that there are no value-free descriptions. In a struggle of power relations, what should be is decisive, determining the being; it appears in a naturalised way as natural or real. In this process orders become norms.

543   However, judgements can also be clearly visible. In such cases they include a more or less direct reference to their discourse- and power-theoretical foundations.

Enlightenment ethos originated as a moral and political way of thinking in the 18th century and is therefore not universal. For this reason, critique should in no way assume the role of law in his work. His commitment to the preservation of the critical ethos can therefore only be seen as a philosophical position which he locates in the struggle for power and resistance. "Even if Foucault does not place himself as explicitly and polemically 'beyond good and evil' as Nietzsche does, it is nevertheless clear that for him too a supra-historical, universally valid morality, which should be given precedence over the phenomenon of power, no longer exists."[544] According to Foucault, the outcome of the emancipatory struggle remains uncertain.

2.3.1.4 Comparing contemporary concepts of power – Byung Chul Han and Michel Foucault

Han's concept of power, which is primarily based on Hegel's theory of power, is certainly similar to Foucault's position when he says that "For a superior power is one that forms the future of the other, not one that blocks it."[545] Han also understands power as productive and relational, not primarily in the sense of coercion. Han and Foucault also associate the ideas of reciprocity of power,[546] relationality[547] and the compatibility of power with freedom: "There is an obstinate belief that power excludes freedom. But this is not the case."[548] According to Han, to have power means to make use of the freedom of others: "Whoever wants to achieve absolute power will have to make *use* not of violence but of the freedom of the other. Absolute power is achieved at the point at which freedom and submission coincide completely."[549]

---

544 Klass 2008: 159. (Own translation)
545 Han 2019: 2.
546 "And complex interdependencies mean that there is reciprocity of power." (Han 2019: 4)
547 "But power is a relation." (Han 2019: 19)
548 Han 2019: 5.
549 Ibid.

Despite the similarities,[550] Han profoundly criticises Foucault's concept of power, which he regards as being heavily oriented towards the paradigm of struggle[551] and preventing Foucault from being able to fully describe the phenomenon of power. Han, on the other hand, bases his work on the idea of dialectical mediation in the sense of Hegel, whereby his theoretical model can subsume both power as coercion and power as freedom.[552] Moreover, the diffusion of power "apparently misleads Foucault to define power itself as 'non-subjective', that is, as a purely structural 'multiplicity of force relations immanent in the sphere in which they operate and which constitute their own organization.'"[553] Han defines power from the starting point of the idea that the ego exercising power creates continuity: "Power allows the *ego to be with him- or herself in the other*. It creates *continuity of the self*. The *ego* turns *his or her* decisions into reality in the *alter*."[554] According to Han, the desire for power goes back to this feeling of the continuity of the self, arguing that the increase of space[555] and time is constitutive for power. In addition to this, Han remarks "But it is utterly impossible to think of power outside any relation of domination or hierarchical social order. Furthermore, power necessarily requires *subjectivity*, a subjective intentionality."[556] Han's recourse to Hegel leads him to regard power as a mechanism of externalisation and re-internalisation in the sense of incorporation. In this context he employs the metaphor of devouring and digestion. He interprets power relations as the occupation of space and time by the subject exercising power, with voluntary submission proving to be more powerful

---

550   Han criticises Hannah Arendt's concept of power even more vehemently than Foucault's theory, with which, despite all criticism, he still has many things in common. He states that her concept is very formal and abstract when she attributes power to acting together and thus, like Habermas, presents a communicative model of power. (Cf. Han 2019: 69–71) Further, Han observes internal inconsistencies in her theory, especially with regard to the strategic-polemical dimension of power. (Cf. Han 2019: 71) Habermas neglects the struggle-based model of power in favour of the consensus-based model. According to Han, however, these are different forms of power. (Cf. Han 2019: 76)

551   Han 2019: 27.

552   Han 2019: 17.

553   Han 2018: 85.

554   Han 2019: 5.

555   In the tradition of Carl Schmitt, Han also assumes that there are *side rooms* of power. (Cf. Han 2019: 65) According to Han, power spaces can be both territorial and digital. (Cf. Han 2019: 82)

556   Han 2018: 85.

than violent oppression. In his critique, however, Han neglects Foucault's theory of governmentality, which examines the art of governing the *other* and the *self*. In this regard, Foucault, like Han, understands power specifically from the perspective of the person exercising power, as leading and guiding through intentionality. While Han perceives this relationship as overwhelming, expanding and incorporating, Foucault understands it as art. He consciously incorporates a *self-relation* which contains potential for change with regard to thinking and acting in power processes into this process. According to Foucault, relations of power are simultaneously theoretically anchored as relatively stable power relations by temporarily stabilising the art of ruling people.

Han also criticises Foucault's concept of power for neglecting the aspect of meaningfulness[557] of power through symbols and the significance of the social aspects. In this context he refers to Bourdieu's concept of habitus. Han, however, overlooks the fact that it is precisely the symbolic impact of power which is at the heart of Foucault's thinking when he (Foucault) discusses the epistemes and forms of historical *a priori* which determine thinking in combination with the subject positions of discourse and the practices as well as institutions provided by *dispositives*. These hidden, truth-structuring forms, which shape the imaginable, the sayable and the visible, act as codes at the symbolic level, exhibiting a naturalising effect. It is precisely here that hidden power strategies can be identified. In this context, Foucault refers to power-knowledge complexes. He does not ignore the social level either; on the contrary, it is anchored in the social, especially by the concept of the *dispositive*. However, and here Han must be agreed with, the application of Bourdieu's concept of habitus reveals the densification of individual social behaviour in the social space.

Furthermore, Han also criticises the hedonistic concept of power in Foucault's later works, in which power is given a playful character. "Power may be part of playing. And it may itself have playful elements. Play may even be considered as opposed to power."[558] Han's emphasis on this point does not, however, make clear that Foucault demonstrates another aspect of power and that

---

557   "In order for the positivity and productivity of power to become visible, he would have
       needed to analyse it with regard to its semantic potential". (Han 2019: 27) Han remarks
       regarding this: "Power founds sense." (Han 2019: 24) Han cites national culture with its
       symbols and narratives as an example of this. (Cf. Han 2019: 36) Sense can also be found
       in forms. Han remarks for example that there is "a way for power to achieve eloquence
       through form". (Han 2019: 25)
558   Han 2019: 42.

he is not making the claim to understand the entire character of power. Foucault argues that power can have a playful quality in specific contexts, e.g. in the sexual/erotic domain. Furthermore, in the context of Foucault's conception of power, play is primarily conceived in an agonal sense as competition or warlike confrontation. Han acknowledges this with regard to Foucault's conception of power but does not refer to it when discussing Foucault's concept of play. It should not be equated exclusively with lightness, which Han implies is the detachment from existing things. Han also urges that the creation of pleasure be neglected as a mechanism of power. Since, according to Foucault, knowledge-power complexes however also shape the individual's emotions and construct subjectivity both physically and mentally, his inscription in desire can certainly be associated with hedonistic power and perceived as 'natural' through the self-evidence of these processes, which are not usually apparent. Comparison with Han's concept of power specifically demonstrates the theoretical benefits of Foucault's complex theory of power for contemporary debate on the question of power. Overall, it can be concluded that Han's new interpretation of the phenomenon of power cannot diminish the relevance and significance of Foucault's philosophy of power.

2.3.1.5 The complexity of Foucault's concept of power

The limits of power in Foucault's productive, relational and strategy-oriented concept of power are already theoretically established. The exercise of power is not conceived as static but as based on the application of strategies of action, which must be understood as a permanent reciprocal process of mutual strategic application on the basis of discursive and dispositive possibilities. Each individual is thus perceived as the starting point of power. While the individuals involved are constituted by power practices, they should also be understood as capacities for action, exercising power themselves. Though the individual cannot completely detach himself from the determining knowledge-power complexes in which subjects are constituted, there is, however, the possibility of critique and *desubjugation*. "To become such an autonomous being is an enormous political act, indeed perhaps it is the political act itself, since it constitutes democracy as a political association of responsible citizens."[559] Based on the analysis of the emergence of subjects and the elaboration of *a priori* forms of knowledge in the discursive; the specific power structures of a time and the application of technologies of the self, the individual is able to expand their

---

559 Brieler, Ulrich in Hechler/Philipps 2008: 33. (Own translation)

horizons of thought, feeling and action. In these processes, modifications of the self and society are conceived as possible and founded on theory.

The underlying concept of freedom should not be understood in the sense of complete detachment from the constituent determinations of the subjects, but as freedom on the basis of existing constitutions in the given socio-historical context. Freedom is on the one hand connected to processes of liberation, reinterpretation and transformation of existing forms of knowledge and power and, on the other, to a transformation of the self – processes which intertwine – and is thus also the basis for possible resistance. The concept of freedom represents not absolute autonomy, but an autonomy conceptualised as relative. Foucault's concept of freedom comprises both the aspect of the 'freedom of' the existing and the 'freedom to' possible change in the emancipatory sense – a change of the self, of the relationship to others and of society. In Foucault's philosophy, the concepts of freedom and power are closely linked. Foucault's concept of power itself determines the limits of power. Power and limitations of power are logically incorporated in a strategic game. Foucault's shift from the descriptive to the normative, which can often be observed in this context, must be regarded in the context of his conception of the fundamental transition from description to prescription.

The multi-faceted nature of Foucault's concept of power is particularly convincing, revealing the different aspects of power. Foucault illustrates the character of power as a system of relationally conceived power balances; of naturalisation through epistemologically significant forms of historical *a priori*, practices and dispositive framework conditions such as institutions, architecture, etc.; the hedonistic character of power; its forms and power relations and their possible paraphrases, self-relations and relations to the other, various social levels such as religion, economy and politics. His philosophical concept offers a convincing opportunity for political theory to arrive at a theoretical understanding of the phenomena of power and the limits of power and, in addition, to examine them in concrete social contexts. "The systemic and the personal, the heteronomous and the autonomous must be questioned in the historical dimension of their contradictory symbiosis."[560] His concept of the specific intellectual,[561] of the politicisation of subjectivity and of ethos as an attitude of

---

560   Brieler, Ulrich in Hechler/Philipps 2008: 33. (Own translation)
561   Foucault uses the character of the *specific intellectual* to criticize Sartre's idea of the *universal intellectual*, which Sartre had conceptualized as a writer. The *specific intellectual* is not a spokesperson for all people, but a spokesperson for specific problems in the

critique ensures that his theory does not imply an ethics-free concept of power. The theorems of autonomy and resistance in particular reveal the connection between power and ethics in Foucault's philosophy – his ethics are politics[562] and his politics are ethics. Foucault introduces us to an ethics of power within his theory of power.[563]

2.3.2   Foucault's concept of power from the perspective of the postcolonial and decolonial theories of Mbembe and Mignolo

2.3.2.1   Foucault's theory of power and post-/decolonial thought

The African philosopher Mbembe points out that Foucault has a blind spot – his focus on Western thought, an omission which causes Foucault to overlook the colonial plantation as an origin of, and experimental field for, disciplinary techniques. In addition to Mbembe's critique of the neglect of post-colonialism in Foucault's concept of power – in particular with regard to disciplinary power – it becomes apparent that he also expresses a radical critique of Foucault's power-theoretical thinking, calling for an extending and supplementing of the latter's theory of power. Mbembe asserts that discipline, biopolitics and necropolitics are combined in the postcolonial environment. In response to this, he develops the concept of necropower to provide a theoretical expla-

---

political arena, thus Foucault professionalizes the intellectual. Spivak, on the other hand, focuses on subversive listening by intellectuals who would prevent subalterns from speaking.

562   Cf. Brieler, Ulrich in Hechler/Philipps 2008: 24. (Own translation) The author remarks "His ethics are therefore politics." Jens Kastner also speaks of an "ethical dimension of the political" when referring to Foucault. (Cf. Jens Kastner in Hechler/Philipps 2008: 49; own translation) Han, on the other hand states: "Thus, politics is a practice of *power and decision*." (Han 2019: 79) This is not a matter of consensus, but of a "*compromise* as the act of *balancing power*". (Ibid.)

563   I adopt the term *ethics of power* in relation to Foucault's theory of power from Han: "Foucault's ethics of power are based on ethics of self-care." (Han 2005: 131; own translation) This results in a clear position with regard to the alternative expressed by Hechler/Philipps: "Two points of view emerge: One sees Foucault's concept of resistance as purged of all moral implications and thus close to a Nietzschean affirmation of power, while the other seeks to demonstrate the legitimacy of resistance in Foucault's recourse to critique and Enlightenment." (Hechler/Philipps 2008: 11–12; own translation) According to Foucault, power can take different forms however one can share his view that there is an ethics of power.

nation for the application of current power techniques within the scope of the massacres and forms of terror practiced around the world.

The Argentine decolonial thinker Mignolo also vehemently criticises Foucault's concept of power, calling for the inclusion of geographical constructions of knowledge and power techniques. He speaks of geopolitics and body-politics which consider the body as a racist object. Foucault focuses only on state racism; his view of the phenomenon of racism must be broadened. According to Mignolo, the focus is on decolonial thinking, which is associated with classifications and revaluations and explores identity constructions. Michel Foucault's concept of bio-politics must therefore be extended to include geopolitics and body politics. In connection with this critique, it can be asked if Foucault's concept of power is relevant for postcolonial and decolonial thought and if his theory is still topical. How do the postcolonial or decolonial philosophy and theories of Mbembe and Mignolo engage with Foucault's concept of power? Is it still significant – possibly in modified form – within the framework of postcolonial and decolonial theories, or is it now necessary to redesign forms and strategies of power to take into account postcolonial and decolonial research so that we can adequately understand the current socio-political situation in a global context? What relevance do Foucault's forms of power, such as disciplinary power and bio-power, have in the current environment? And in this context, is the concept of the Panopticon, expounded in Foucault's book *Discipline and Punish*, still of any significance today?

2.3.2.2 Foucault's *Discipline and Punish* and his concept of power

Foucault's book *Discipline and Punishment*, which aims to provide a "history of the present",[564] examines changes in punishment from torture, which is directly focused on the human body and the application of techniques of pain, to a technique of punishment whose objective is to influence the soul,[565] seek-

---

564 Foucault 1995: 31.
565 Foucault explains "Rather than seeing this soul as the reactivated remnants of an ideology, one would see it as the present correlative of a certain technology of power over the body." (Foucault 1995: 29) Further "This is the historical reality of this soul, which, unlike the soul represented by Christian theology, is not born in sin and subject to punishment, but is born rather out of methods of punishment, supervision and constraint." (Foucault 1995: 29) He further explains "A 'soul' inhabits him and brings him to existence, which is itself a factor in the mastery that power exercises over the body. The soul is the effect and instrument of a political anatomy; the soul is the prison of the body." (Foucault 1995: 30)

ing to control the individual by means of panoptical surveillance while still focusing on a "'political economy' of the body".[566] This also has an impact on the question of truth associated with a judicial judgement. The focus is no longer on the question of the act, but on its origin in the perpetrator.[567] Condemnation is associated with 'assessments of normality',[568] which go hand in hand with the development of the humanities. These penalty mechanisms should be regarded as power techniques which can be identified in the context of political tactics and are related to social production systems.[569] They concentrate on the body. Foucault states "[T]he body becomes a useful force only if it is both a productive body and a subjected body".[570] In this respect, Foucault speaks of a "microphysics of power" based on the model of a perpetual struggle.[571] "The

---

566   Foucault 1995: 25.

567   "A whole set of assessing, diagnostic, prognostic, normative judgements concerning the criminal have become lodged in the framework of penal judgement." (Foucault 1995: 19)

568   Cf. Foucault 1995: 23.

569   "From this point of view, Rusche and Kirchheimer relate the different systems of punishment with the systems of production within which they operate: thus, in a slave economy, punitive mechanisms serve to provide an additional labour force – and to constitute a body of 'civil' slaves in addition to those provided by war or trading; with feudalism, at a time when money and production were still at an early stage of development, we find a sudden increase in corporal punishments – the body being in most cases the only property accessible; the penitentiary (the Hôpital Général, the Spinhuis or the Rasphuis), forced labour and the prison factory appear with the development of the mercantile economy. But the industrial system requires a free market in labour and, in the nineteenth century, the role of forced labour in the mechanisms of punishment diminishes accordingly and 'corrective' detention takes its place." (Foucault, 1995: 24–25)

570   Foucault 1995: 26.

571   Ibid. He continues "In short this power is exercised rather than possessed; it is not the 'privilege', acquired or preserved, of the dominant class, but the overall effect of its strategic positions – an effect that is manifested and sometimes extended by the position of those who are dominated. Furthermore, this power is not exercised simply as an obligation or a prohibition on those who 'do not have it'; it invests them, is transmitted by them and through them; it exerts pressure upon them, just as they themselves, in their struggle against it, resist the grip it has on them." (Foucault 1995: 26–27) In his lectures at the Collège de France in 1972–1973, Foucault also refers to the model of civil war to illustrate power processes. He says "One should be able to study the daily exercise of power as a civil war: to exercise power is to conduct civil war in a certain way, and it ought to be possible to analyze all these instruments, tactics, and alliances that

overthrow of these 'micro-powers' does not, then, obey the law of all or noth-ing; it is not acquired once and for all by a new control of the apparatuses nor by a new functioning or a destruction of the institutions; on the other hand, none of its localized episodes may be inscribed in history except by the effects that it induces on the entire network in which it is caught up."[572] According to Foucault, punishment techniques thus always stand in a specific socio-politi-cal context and are situated "in the history of this body politic" as "a chapter of political anatomy".[573] He speaks of a "system of permanent control of individ-uals" in the disciplinary society, characterised by discipline and punishment. He states "It is an inquiry of a general and a priori suspicion of the individual. We can call *examination* this uninterrupted, graduated, and accumulated test that permits a control and pressure at every moment, that makes it possible to follow the individual in each of his steps, to see if he is regular or irregular, or-derly or dissipated, normal or abnormal."[574] This concerns in particular control over time: "We pass from fixing locally to temporal sequestration".[575]

Foucault speaks of a culture of surveillance and, in relation to the 19th century of an "age of panopticism".[576] Panopticism can be regarded as a si-multaneous occupation of space and time, based on an architectural principle of structural surveillance which leads to self-control, and involves an "asym-metrisation of perspectives" and an "inversion of the hierarchy of visibility".[577] Kammerer speaks of a "visibility of the invisibility of power"[578] and the "effect of surveillance" or of the "staging of an unattainable omnipresence".[579] He goes on to say "Coercion becomes invisible, where the means of coercion

---

we can identify in terms of civil war." In: Foucault, Michel: *The Punitive Society. Lectures at the Collège de France, 1972–1973*. London (Palgrave Macmillan), 2015, p. 32.

572   Foucault 1995: 27.

573   Foucault 1995: 28.

574   Foucault 2015: 196.

575   Foucault 2015: 211.

576   Foucault 2015: 258.

577   Kammerer, Dietmar: *Bilder der Überwachung*. Frankfurt a.M. (Suhrkamp), 2008, p. 115. (Own translation)

578   Kammerer 2008: 117. (Own translation)

579   Kammerer 2008: 120. (Own translation) Kammerer also remarks "The panopticon is a machine which incorporates imaginative power into its operations." (Kammerer 2008: 121; own translation)

establish a state of complete visibility".[580] Foucault describes panopticism as a form of society: "Now, this prison-form is much more than an architectural form; it is a social form".[581] According to Foucault, surveillance also leads to a "new type of knowledge".[582] A modified version of these panoptic tendencies can also be observed in the following centuries. Even today, the "surveillance society"[583] is still a common term, carrying out "dataveillance", "social sorting" and "risk management",[584] particularly on the basis of the collection and processing of personal data via electronic media. Terms such as *Superpanopticon*, *Omnicon*, *Banopticon* and *Hyperpanoptics* illustrate the attempt to preserve and transfer Foucault's panoptical form of power in/to the late 20th and early 21st centuries.[585] "The recent 'success story' of the panoptic is astonishing, above all, how easily the principles of a centrally organised power architecture from the 18th century can be transferred to the decentralised network conditions of the late 20th century. [...] Success has exhausted the concept."[586] According to Kammerer, however, "no new paradigm is emerging."[587] In addition, he demands recourse to the concept of the 'societies of control', which Deleuze advocated. "Following Foucault, Gilles Deleuze is about to become the new spokesman for Surveillance Studies. The French philosopher understands the term 'society of control' to mean a series of social and technical (trans-)formations which are in the process of replacing the 'disciplinary society'. Their inclusion settings – prisons, hospitals, schools, barracks and factories – have been disintegrating since the end of the 20th century".[588] Parallel to this, there has also been an increase in the need for security.

---

580 Kammerer 2008: 114. (Own translation) He continues "From now on power was immersed in darkness, while the individual was dragged into the light of the stage". (Kammerer 2008: 118; own translation)

581 Foucault 2015: 227.

582 Ibid.

583 Kammerer 2008: 46. (Own translation) Kammerer refers to David Lyon, i.e. Lyon, David: *Surveillance Society. Monitoring Everyday Life*. Buckingham (Open University Press), 2001. Kammerer primarily applies the term to visual media such as surveillance cameras.

584 Cf. Kammerer 2008: 85–87.

585 Cf. Kammerer 2008: 128. He refers to Haggerty. Cf. Haggerty, Kevin: "Tear down the walls. On demolishing the panopticon". In: Lyon David (Ed.): *Theorizing Surveillance. The panopticon and beyond*. Cullompton (Willan), 2006, p. 23–45.

586 Kammerer 2008: 127. (Own translation)

587 Kammerer 2008: 128. (Own translation)

588 Kammerer 2008: 131. (Own translation) Similarly, a recourse to Deleuze's concept of structure can be observed, e.g. in 'surveillance structure'. (Cf. ibid.)

"Meanwhile, most of us seem to be almost addicted to safety. We have internalised a worldview based on the omnipresence of danger and the inescapable necessity of constant mistrust and suspicion, which can only imagine the social coexistence of a nation under the protection of constant vigilance – and thus we have become dependent on the performance of surveillance measures and the fact that we are aware of them."[589]

In keeping with the principle of "governing by freedom",[590] mobility and mobilisation, which are linked to continuous control,[591] are pivotal in today's societies. Foucault has already presented this type of governance in his analysis of liberalism and neoliberalism. "Surveillance is not (primarily) achieved by coercion, but by seduction".[592] These developments have not, however, made Foucault's conclusions on panopticism obsolete. Kammerer states:

"In an era of high-tech surveillance which employs huge quantities of media, replacing human eyes with algorithms and smart cameras, Bentham's old architectural principle of using the configuration of space to discipline and control access to the subject regains its original significance. In the beginning there was a round tower – now the escalator seems to be the privileged place for the panoptic view."[593]

Buildings and structural layouts which govern spaces to direct and regulate movement "will increase in the future".[594] The 360° cameras and surveillance drones also epitomise the panoptical principle. Kammerer says "In this respect, Bentham's principle is only fully realized in the non-transparent, and panoptical round housings of dome cameras".[595] They "allow the full 360° pan shot".[596] The use of video surveillance as a control technology can be viewed as a gen-

---

589   Baumann, Zygmunt; Lyon, David: *Daten, Drohnen, Disziplin: Ein Gespräch über flüchtige Überwachung.* Berlin (Suhrkamp), 2014, p. 131.
590   Kammerer 2008: 134. (Own translation)
591   Cf. Kammerer 2008: 132.
592   Kammerer 2008: 134. (Own translation). Each surveillance shows the "lynching double aspect of care and control." (Cf. Kammerer 2008: 227; own translation)
593   Kammerer 2008: 210. (Own translation)
594   Ibid. (Own translation)
595   Kammerer 2008: 232. (Own translation)
596   Ibid. (Own translation) Kammerer also refers here to Cusanus. (Cf. Kammerer 2008: 233–234)

eral "cultural phenomenon of our time"[597] which goes beyond the function of surveillance and increasing security, e.g. by taking on an entertainment function. This manifests how the social body as a whole has been penetrated by these power techniques. Baumann also emphasizes the topicality of the panopticon model: "As I see it, the panopticon is enjoying the best of health".[598] He asserts that everyone produces their own "personal panopticon" and drags it along "on their own back".[599] In an era of 'fleeting surveillance', however, it can no longer be regarded as "a universal pattern or strategy of domination, as it was at the time of these two authors [Bentham and Foucault], and not even as their most noble or most frequently practiced means".[600] It experiences specific changes in each case.[601] It can be concluded that Foucault's considerations of monitoring and punishment are still the subject of much discussion today; analysed for their current relevance and modified in various respects. The post/decolonial thinkers Achille Mbembe and Walter Mignolo also engage in a critical examination of Foucault's concept of power. What particular insights have postcolonial and decolonial thinking developed with regard to Foucault's theorems?

2.3.2.3 Mbembe's *Critique of Black Reason* and his concept of power

In his work *Critique of Black Reason* Mbembe discusses the prospect of the world becoming 'black'. "The transnationalisation of the Black condition was therefore a constitutive moment for modernity."[602] *Black reason* can be understood as

---

597   Kammerer 2008: 268. (Own translation)

598   Baumann/Lyon 2014: 74. (Own translation)

599   Baumann/Lyon 2014: 78. (Own translation)

600   Baumann/Lyon 2014: 74. (Own translation) The techniques of coercion are also subject to this process of change. They have increasingly been replaced by temptation and seduction. (Cf. Baumann/Lyon 2014: 76–77)

601   This also includes the "welfare-state panopticism described by Wacquant". (Baumann/ Lyon 2014: 79; own translation) Didier Bigo develops the theory of the 'banoptic', the exclusion of externals in response to security requirements and speaks of a heterogeneous, fragmentary dispositive with regard to panopticism in general. (Cf. Baumann/ Lyon 2014: 81–83.) The creation of transit or refugee camps must also be considered in this context. (Cf. Baumann/Lyon 2014: 84–86) In this context, the term 'synoptic', coined by Mathiesen and describing how many observe a few, can also be regarded as a modification of or supplement to Foucault's concept of the panopticon. (Cf. Baumann/Lyon 2014: 89–91)

602   Mbembe, Achille: *Critique of black reason*. Durham (Duke University Press), 2017, p. 15.

a discourse of exclusion of the racial subject, embedded in a dispositive which is equally concerned with its constitution.

> "In this context 'Black reason' names not only a collection of discourses but also practices—the daily work that consisted in inventing, telling, repeating, and creating variations on the formulas, texts, and rituals whose goal was to produce the Black Man as a racial subject and site of savage exteriority, who was therefore set up for moral disqualification and practical instrumentalization."[603]

The title, provocatively chosen with reference to Kant, refers on the one hand to an analysis of the racial discourses[604] associated with practices, in particular of Western provenance, on the basis of a constructivist epistemology – with moral discourses, socio-political and economic effects – as well as to an analysis of 'black' thinking, exploring the work of the theorists of Pan-Africanism, the Négritude movement and postcolonial theory, who carry out a critical examination of the topic – mostly in connection with a "call to race".[605] According to Mbembe, racial subdivision and the evaluation of the races based on it can be linked to Foucault's observations in *The Order of Things*, which classifies things by genus and species. As Mbembe points out, Foucault views race and racism as "the condition for the acceptance of killing in a normalized society."[606] Referring to Foucault he says "Once the State functions in the biopower mode, racism alone can justify the murderous functions of the State."[607] It becomes apparent that Mbembe is explicitly referencing Foucault's discourse-analytical and historical/genealogical approach in its empirical concreteness and his biopolitical reflections on racism. On the other hand, he expresses strong criticism of Foucault's philosophy, e.g. with regard to his failure to consider the plantation and the colony in his analysis of disciplinary and biopolitical power techniques. Moreover, asserts Mbembe, when analysing the simultaneous pro-

---

603 Mbembe 2017: 28.
604 Mbembe identified the danger of a new variant of racism in the late 20th and early 21st centuries, associated with recourse to genetics, in which molecular biological technologies can be used to transform life according to racial criteria.
605 Mbembe 2017: 33.
606 Ibid.
607 Ibid. Here Mbembe refers to Foucault 2003a: 254–256.

duction and destruction of freedom in liberalism[608] Foucault neglects the fact that "the high point, historically, of the destruction of liberty was the enslavement of Blacks."[609]

According to Mbembe, the plantation economy[610] is the economic and social foundation of modernity. Foucault's analysis of disciplinary power ignores the techniques of punishment and disciplining developed on the plantation, which can be viewed as a kind of experimental field, instead focusing on institutions such as prisons, the military, factories and schools. "The plantation gradually took shape as an economic, disciplinary, and penal institution in which Blacks and their descendants could be bought for life."[611] The experience gained in these areas was transferred to other areas. This process was accompanied by the application of security instruments and legislative work aimed at "establishing [... the] legal incapacity" of slaves.[612] It is linked with the rise and expansion of capitalism.

Contrary to Mbembe's assertion, in his book *Discipline and Punish* Foucault deals with the practice of torturing slaves within the scope of his analysis of torture. He states "It is true that the practice of torture is of ancient origin: it goes back at least as far as the Inquisition, of course, and probably to the torture of slaves."[613] He also assumes a connection between criminal practice and the production system, remarking "In a slave economy, punitive mechanisms serve to provide an additional labour force".[614] Mbembe's accusation that colonialism, slavery and the plantation economy are neglected can therefore not be upheld in such severity. In the foreword to *Madness and Civilization*, Foucault already

---

608   Here Mbembe refers to Foucault, Michel: *The Birth of Biopolitics: Lectures at the Collège de France*, 1978–79. Trans. Graham Burchell, New York (Palgrave Macmillan), 2008, pp. 64–65. "The production of liberty therefore has a cost whose calculating principle is, adds Foucault, security and protection. In other words, the economy of power that defines liberalism, and the democracy of the same name, depends on a tight link between liberty, security, and protection against omnipresent threat, risk, and danger." (Mbembe 2017: 80)

609   Ibid. Further Mbembe establishes "The Black slave represents the danger." (Mbembe 2017: 80)

610   According to Mbembe the "Plantation society as such" which differentiated between colonial masters and multiracial subjugates emerged between 1630 and 1680. (Cf. Mbembe 2017: 19)

611   Ibid.

612   Ibid.

613   Foucault 1995: 39.

614   Foucault 1995: 24–25.

speaks of the colonising reason of the West, which originated in the differentiation from the Orient. He also emphasises the constitution of knowledge associated with colonisation, the relationship of knowledge and power, and the associated exploitation and violence.

> "Maybe could we also say that in order to know other cultures – non-Western cultures, so-called primitive cultures, or American, African, and Chinese cultures etc. – in order to know these cultures, we had not only to marginalize them, not only to look down upon them, but also to exploit them, to conquer them and in some ways through violence to keep them silent?"[615]

It should be noted, however, that Foucault does not explore these phenomena in an all-encompassing and detailed manner, but instead primarily identifies their contextual locations. In this context Mbembe fills an important gap by investigating slavery in association with the "plantation as its core structure",[616] both as a field of experimentation for disciplinary techniques and as an "example of a state exercising the right to kill", whose starting point is the "selection of race".[617]

According to Mbembe, in the current global political situation biopolitics can be combined with the power form of discipline; with the technologies used in the fight against insurgents during the period of decolonisation as well as the 'dirty wars' of the East-West conflict and the 'fight against terror'; and with mass surveillance to obtain data – in addition to biopolitical power[618] there is also a kind of 'digital' power[619] – which results in long-distance warfare and the "unprecedented merging of the civil, police, and military spheres with those of surveillance".[620] In this context, Mbembe also develops the concepts of

---

615   This statement by Foucault originates from a long lost interview dating from 1971, which was recorded in his apartment in Paris. Refer to: Foucault, Michel: *The lost interview*. Paris, 1971. Retrieved August 28, 2024, from: https://www.youtube.com/watch?v=qzoOhhh4aJg.

616   Mbembe 2017: 20.

617   Mbembe 2003: 17. Mbembe further characterises the plantation as a nexus of biopower, state of emergency and state of siege. (Cf. Mbembe 2017: 23)

618   E.g. fingerprints, iris and retina scans and forms of vocal and facial recognition.

619   E.g. digital recordings of telecommunications, internet use and video surveillance.

620   Cf. Mbembe 2015: 23. Mbembe continues "The new systems of security build on various elements of prior regimes (the forms of punishment used within slavery, aspects of the colonial wars of conquest and occupation, legal-juridical techniques used in the creation of states of exception) and incorporate them, on a nanocellular level, into the

necropower, a "terror formation"[621] and necropolitics to arrive at a theoretical understanding of the application of current power techniques in blitzkrieg, massacres and globally practiced forms of terror. Necropower is perceived as the power over life and death. This also includes the staging of public executions, in particular beheadings, "by combining known and identifiable victims with a more gradual and deliberate ceremony of violent death".[622] The terrorist martyr is "instead of being a passive martyr [...] an active, dangerous, exploding martyr, a murderous martyr."[623] In this context, the security dispositive is currently experiencing an increase in importance and differentiation through new biopolitical and digital power techniques. According to Foucault, to whom Mbembe refers here, liberalism and neoliberalism, which presuppose freedom of the market, have historically and politically always been closely linked to the question of security. In this context, Foucault speaks of a 'culture of fear'. Baudrillard provocatively describes the growth of security technology in present-day society as 'security terror'. When discussing the aspect of race Mbembe states "The consequence of fear, as Foucault reminds us, has always been the broad expansion of procedures of control, constraint, and coercion that, far from being aberrations, constitute the counterpart to liberty. Race, and in particular the existence of the Black slave, played a driving role in the historical formation of this counterpart."[624] Expanding on Foucault's remarks, he also refers here to the significance of racism for the formation of control practices, which are related to the constitution of fear, and its psychological

---

techniques of the age of genomics and the war on terror. But they also draw on techniques elaborated during the counterinsurgency wars of the period of decolonization and the 'dirty wars' of the Cold War (in Algeria, Vietnam, Southern Africa, Burma, and Nicaragua), as well as the experiences of predatory dictatorships put into power throughout the world with the direct encouragement, or at least complicity, of the intelligence agencies of the West." (Mbembe 2015: 22)

621   Mbembe 2003: 17.

622   Appadurai, Arjun: *Fear of Small Numbers: An Essay on the Geography of Anger*. Durham, London (Duke University Press), 2006, p. 13. The author speaks of "a return here to the simplest form of religious violence, the sacrifice". (Appadurai 2006: 12) They are "counterparts of the suicide bombers". (Appadurai 2006: 13) "These singular bodies are a desperate effort to bring back a religious element to spaces of death and destruction, that have become unimaginably abstract." (Ibid.)

623   Appadurai 2006: 78.

624   Mbembe 2015: 81.

dimension.[625] Kammerer asserts that racist moments in the sense of a ban-opticon can also be detected, for example, in facial recognition software for the analysis of video footage from surveillance cameras. He says "The result: Algorithms are by no means color-blind. In an initial test sequence, non-whites were identified more easily by the systems than whites. [...] 'Whiteness' [was] 'preferred' by the system in a different way than the researchers had expected."[626] Mbembe also proceeds from the assumption that current forms of state power are still based on racist distinctions, in the sense of the state racism examined by Foucault.[627]

Viewed as a whole, Mbembe's considerations constitute a differentiation, expansion and rearrangement or a different focus with regard to individual power strategies and/or within certain forms of power in Foucault. With regard, for example, to biopolitics and disciplinary power, which he increasingly regards from the point of view of control and has developed into a form of power through control (control-power) which also takes into account, for example, new genetic engineering and digital strategies to become a so-called 'digital' power. These power strategies must be examined in their respective specificity. On the other hand, the 'necro-power' form of power supplements Foucault's power techniques. Although it has similarities to Foucault's power of sovereignty,[628] it has a fundamentally different character due to potential for an attacker to use their own body as a weapon. Appadurai indirectly characterises this type of power as cellular,[629] speaking of new "logics of cellular-

---

625   Foucault refers in this context to Fanon's remarks in: Fanon, Frantz: *Peau noire, masques blancs*. Paris (Éditions Points), 1971.

626   Kammerer 2008: 101. (Own translation) In this context, it becomes clear that Fanon's ideas are still relevant in a modified form.

627   Cf. Mbembe 2017: 33. See also Foucault 2003a: 239–264.

628   Foucault speaks of the terrorising character of sovereign power with regard to its penal practice: "and it is the prince – or at least those to whom he has delegated his force – who seizes upon the body of the condemned man and displays it marked, beaten, broken. The ceremony of punishment, then, is an exercise of 'terror'." (Foucault 1995: 49)

629   Appadurai distinguishes between vertebral systems, among which he counts the nation-state, and cellular systems. (Cf.. Appadurai 2006: 21) According to him, global capitalism is organised both vertebrally and cellularly. Both capital and international terror are characterised by cellularity. (Cf. Appadurai 2006: 26) "Terror organized by cellular networks terrifies the vertebrate structures of the state and blurs the lines between the enemies within and the enemies outside." (Appadurai 2006: 108) In addition, Appadurai refers to colonial history to analyse current political phenomena.

ity".[630] Comparably, but with other emphases, Baudrillard speaks of a power which is 'viral in structure' and relies on rapid spread and infectivity.[631] It can also be observed that Mbembe's remarks ignore the importance of pastoral power as a form of power of care, which asserts Foucault, can be observed in the late 20th century in particular in combination with biological power and disciplinary power. Pastoral power is still of great importance in the 21st century, playing a decisive role particularly in the question of the legitimation of power. It is also reflected in the ambivalence of care and control which can be derived, among other things, from the statement of Baumann/Lyon: "For a long time I have been asserting that supervision often originates from the desire to control – and always involves power – but it does not exclude the possibility that it can be put to the service of care for the other."[632] In addition to a possible moral component, this concern also has a power-theoretical dimension. Taking Foucault as his starting point, Mbembe analyses and criticises the historical, economic and social conditions of the transatlantic slave trade and the plantation economy in relation to the modern and postmodern socio-political situation in the global context. Mbembe's humanist model of *afropolitanism* is an attempt to solve current problems and provide a draft for a target concept for human action.

2.3.2.4 Mignolo's decolonial cosmopolitanism as a concept for the future and the question of power

Like Mbembe, Mignolo repeatedly emphasises the relationship between modernity and coloniality and, with regard to colonialism, speaks of the dark, secretive and repressed side of modernity, which on the other hand constitutes

---

630   Appadurai 2006: 29.

631   Baudrillard, Jean: *The Spirit of Terrorism and Other Essays*. London, New York (Verso), 2012, p. 8. "The fourth stage is viruses [he differentiates between four phases: wolves, rats, beetles and viruses]; to all intents they move in the fourth dimension. It is far more difficult to defend yourself against viruses since they are in the heart of the system." In: Baudrillard, Jean: *Der Geist des Terrorismus*. Peter Engelmann (Ed.), Vienna (Passagen Verlag), [2]2003, p. 86. (Own translation) He also states "Terrorism is not merely the antithesis of the system, it is something different, an otherness which cannot be integrated or assimilated." (Baudrillard [2]2003: 88; own translation)

632   Baumann/Lyon 2014: 122. (Own translation) They continue "The crucial problem is how to live up to our responsibilities to others with whom we interact through the media." (Ibid.; own translation) According to the authors, the problem of adiapherisation also arises in this context. (Cf. Baumann/Lyon 2014: 119)

its basis. The recourse to the theorems of rationality, totality and universalism leads to the exclusion of the other. Mignolo questions the universality of Western knowledge, characterising it as fundamentally regional. On the basis of these considerations, Mignolo develops the concept of trans-modernity.[633] He criticises postmodern thinkers' critique of the aforementioned categories as internal and thus limited. According to Mignolo, decolonial thinking goes far beyond the postmodern and also postcolonial thinking of, for example, Said, Bhabha and Spivak, which in turn builds on poststructuralist conceptions of Foucault, Derrida and Lacan, by presupposing a de-linking of hegemonic references to knowledge associated with the exercise of hegemonic power. When discussing possible changes in the geopolitical situation, Mignolo takes the concept of liberation as his starting point, assigning the idea of emancipation, and thus of a common struggle of the oppressed, to it. It should, furthermore, be accompanied by individual emancipation. According to Castró-Gomez, this is based on a 'we-identity' of the oppressed, whose conception is equally based on the concept of the subject of modernity and represents only a variation of the transcendent subject.[634] Foucault, on the other hand, speaks of *desubjugation* as a concept of emancipation and thus of the necessity of individual self-development through the application of technologies of the self. He regards the success of political upheavals, e.g. by means of revolutions, as endangered if it is not accompanied by a change in the subject mode. According to Mignolo, Foucault is thus trapped in an "ego-logical politics of knowledge and understanding".[635] According to Mignolo, the *decolonial shift* cannot be understood as an epistemic break or paradigm shift in the sense of Foucault or Kuhn, since it belongs to another place; he calls it "another paradigm".[636] As far as Foucault is concerned, this view must, however, be rejected, since it is precisely the shifts in these areas which result in a change in the epistemes or rules of discourses. Equally, this also incorporates geo-political moments within the scope of the inside and outside of knowledge described in his work. Taking his theorems of *border gnoseology*, *epistemic disobedience* and *civil*

633   Mignolo, Walter D.: "Delinking the Rhetoric of Modernity, the Logic of Coloniality and the Grammar of De-coloniality". In: Mignolo, Walter D.; Escobar, Arturo (Eds.): *Globalization and the Decolonial Option*. London, New York (Routledge), 2010, p. 353.

634   Cf. Castró-Gómez in Martin Alcoff, Linda: "Enrique Dussel's Transmodernism". In: *Transmodernity: Journal of Peripheral Cultural Production of the Luso-Hispanic World*, 1(3), 2012, p. 60. Martin Alcoff tries to defend Dussel's philosophy against this accusation.

635   Mignolo 2010: 314.

636   Cf. Mignolo 2010: 339, 347.

disobedience as a basis, Mignolo develops a cosmopolitan concept, *Critical* or *Dialogical* or *Decolonial Cosmopolitanism*.[637] The socio-political process involved includes the formation of "democratic, just, and non-imperial/colonial societies",[638] "decentered networks"[639] and a revaluation of life in general: "[to] place human lives and life in general first".[640] This form of cosmopolitanism can be called *cosmopolitan localism*.[641] In this context Mignolo strives for a "decolonial epistemic shift", a connection to "other epistemologies, other principles of knowledge and understanding"[642] and a different form of universality, which should be understood as a "pluriversality as a universal project"[643] in the sense of a "non-hierarchical and non-dependent pluriversality of all existing civilizations"[644] and "[d]iversality as a universal project",[645] as "universality of the pluriversal".[646] Mignolo emphasises the demanding nature of this project:

---

637   Mignolo says that these forms of cosmopolitanism can be understood as a regulative principle. Cf. Mignolo, Walter: "The Many Faces of Cosmopolis: Border thinking and Critical Cosmopolitanism". In: Beckenridge, Carol A.; Pollock, Sheldon; Bhabha, Homi K.; Chakrabarty, Dipesh (Eds.): *Cosmopolitanism*. Durham, London (Duke University Press), 2002, p. 182.

638   Mignolo, Walter D.: "Epistemic Disobedience, Independent Thought and De-Colonial Freedom". In: *Theory, Culture & Society*. Vol. 26, Los Angeles, London, New Delhi, Singapore (SAGE), 2009, p. 1. He also speaks of cooperative leadership and non material compensations instead of the prevailing competitive thinking and success orientation. Cf. Mignolo, Walter D.: "Border Thinking, Decolonial Cosmopolitanism and Dialogues Among Civilizations". In: Rovisco, Maria; Nowicka, Magdalena (Eds.): *The Ashgate Research Companion to Cosmopolitanism*. Farnham, Burlington (Ashgate), 2011, p. 340.

639   Mignolo 2011: 331.

640   Mignolo 2009: 20.

641   Mignolo 2011: 331. Critical cosmopolitanism should not be cosmopolitanism from above. (Cf. Mignolo 2002: 184) He speaks "from the exteriority of modernity (that is, coloniality)". (Mignolo 2002: 160) Human rights and global citizenship as well as the idea of cosmopolitanism itself and the concept of world history should also be critically reconsidered and questioned with regard to their historical conditions. (Cf. Mignolo 2002: 161–163) According to Mignolo, cosmopolitanism can assume "a benevolent form of control". (Mignolo 2002: 179) Democracy as a form of government should also not simply be seen as a blueprint. (Cf. Mignolo 2002: 182) Other conceptualisations of these phenomena must remain conceivable.

642   Mignolo 2010: 307.

643   Ibid.

644   Mignolo 2011: 335.

645   Mignolo 2002: 181.

646   Mignolo 2010: 354.

"Pluriversality as a universal project is quite demanding."[647] In a global context, the focus is in particular on *decolonial thinking*,[648] which is associated with new classifications as well as revaluations and relates to identity constructions, because "knowledge is also colonized".[649] He replaces the term epistemology with gnoseology, since the latter includes other forms of knowledge which have so far been neglected or suppressed. He characterises Western thinking as structured by "theo-, ego- and organo-logical principles".[650] Overall, Mignolo is concerned with finding a new way for people around the world to deal with each other, a new "inter-cultural communication"[651] and a "dialogue among equals".[652] Michel Foucault's concept of biopolitics must be extended to include the aspects of geopolitics;[653] the context of knowledge and power originating from geopolitical positioning as well as body politics and the connection between knowledge and power with regard to the aspect of ethnicity in order to analyse current forms of power and the orientation of the desired process of change. The inclusion of body politics in the field of bio-power, as demanded by Mignolo, is already laid out in Foucault's theory of disciplining the body in the context of disciplinary power and on the basis of his fundamental conviction different forms of power are interconnected in certain socio-historical situations. Mignolo, however, sensibly develops this further in psychological and sociological regards, incorporating Fanon's considerations, and places it in post-/colonial contexts with regard to power theory. Foucault also integrates body policy into the area of biopolitics, but focuses on the sexuality dispositive. Mignolo's power form of 'body politics' is a recourse to all power forms concerning the body on the basis of colonial and postcolonial experiences connected to ethnicity.

---

647   Ibid.
648   Here he refers to Thiong'o according to his own statement. (Cf. Mignolo 2010: 304)
649   Ibid.
650   Mignolo 2010: 317.
651   Mignolo 2010: 307.
652   Mignolo, Walter D.: "De-colonial cosmopolitanism and dialogues among civilizations". In: Delanty, Gerard (Ed.): *Routledge Handbook of Cosmopolitan Studies*. London, New York (Routledge), 2012, p. 94.
653   In this he refers to Enrique Dussel's *Filosofía de la liberación* of 1977. Refer to the English edition: Dussel, Enrique: *Philosophy of Liberation*. Eugene (Wipf & Stock Publishers), 2003.

"Thus, body-politics is the darker side and the missing half of bio-politics: body-politics describes de-colonial technologies enacted by bodies who realized that they where considered less human at the moment they realized that the very act of describing them as less human was a radical un-human consideration."[654]

It can be observed that in many respects Mignolo remains connected to the very thinking of Foucault which he criticises. His overall theory can be characterised by an indirect attachment to the attempt of compulsive differentiation within the scope of the process of delinking. In addition to this, the aspect of geopolitics ultimately represents a shift in the accentuation of Foucault's basic assumption, emphasising geopolitical classifications, norms and assessments with the associated political, economic and military consequences in the context of post-colonial insights and requirements. This is combined with the demand for political changes which result in a new conception of global connections in geopolitical terms.

This relates in particular to the link between knowledge and power from a geopolitical point of view, e.g. with regard to the notion of centre and periphery. Mignolo, in contrast, speaks of a polycentric world.[655] Contrary to his own assessment, Mignolo's critique of Foucault cannot be regarded as fundamental. Despite the harsh critique of Foucault's work, Mignolo's thinking is based on the former's underlying assumptions, such as his spatial theory of knowledge; the constructiveness of knowledge and the constitution of the subject through knowledge and power. Mignolo, however, focuses more explicitly on the power-theoretical theorems of body and geopolitics and thus the aspects of the ethnic and geopolitical localisation of the connection between knowledge and power shift more explicitly than Foucault. These theorems thus represent an important addition to his observations. This highlighting of the power-theoretical aspects of bio- and geopolitics makes it necessary for Mignolo to expand his explanations in the sense of Mbembe's insights – in particular with regard to digital power and necropolitics – in order to be able to adequately understand current socio-political changes.

---

654   Mignolo 2009: 16. In this context Mignolo uses Frantz Fanon's *Peau noire, masques blancs* in particular.

655   Mignolo 2010: 353. However, the polycentric world should not be understood within the scope of a Western orientation to life but goes beyond it.

2.3.2.5 Relevance of Foucault in postcolonial and decolonial thinking

Mbembe's recourse to Foucault concerns the analytical-historical approach of discourse and dispositive analysis as well as genealogy as the historical analysis of forms of power as methodological instruments and its concept of subject constitution. He expands Foucault's findings, particularly with regard to the processes of the transatlantic slave trade, the plantation economy and the colonial economy in general, by critiquing *black reason* in combination with an analysis of its practices, strategies and institutions, and by linking them to questions of African identity. In his philosophy, Mbembe shifts the focus of his work; explores in more depth the relationships which Foucault has already described and also develops a new set of instruments to assess the current global political situation. The shift in emphasis towards topics such as colonialism and postcolonialism; slavery and racism; and their genealogy together with the referencing of current global political contexts in combination with the concept of digital power and necropower or necropolitics has resulted in new theoretical and conceptual instruments of analysis and new objectives for human action on the basis of a political vision of African humanism which is linked to the concept of *afropolitanism* and the recourse to human hope. The grouping of other power techniques, such as digital power, with disciplinary power when analysing monitoring and punishment and their potential domination, corresponds to Foucault's basic assumption that several power strategies interact with each other and that new forms of power are inserted in a process of shifting, changing the relevance of, hierarchising and renewing power – entirely in in line with his basic idea of power productivity.[656]

In contrast to Mbembe, who locates himself in the theory of postcolonialism and still considers it relevant in today's socio-political situation, Mignolo attempts to use theoretical references from other cultural environments, for example, the South American philosophy of Dussel, as a foundation for his theory. However, in their absolutisation of a we-identity in the sense of a subaltern subject, as has been shown, both also appear to be trapped in Western subject theory. Mignolo does not surpass Foucault's thinking. On the contrary, it becomes clear that in many respects his thinking is based on Foucault's thinking,

---

656   "We must cease once and for all to describe the effects of power in negative terms: it 'excludes', it 'represses', it 'censors', it 'abstracts', it 'masks', it 'conceals'. In fact, power produces; it produces reality; it produces domains of objects and rituals of truth. The individual and the knowledge that may be gained of him belong to this production." (Foucault 1995: 194)

although his theorems of body and geopolitics are useful instruments for social analysis. Mignolo's concept of *Critical Cosmopolitanism* embodies a utopian model of hope for worldwide understanding, attainable through a process of *de-linking* and intercultural communications based on exchange and a diverse coexistence of different models of thought, action and life, in which universal claims to validity, such as those underlying current religious fundamentalisms, are renounced. It becomes clear that Foucault's concept of power – albeit in a modified and expanded form – still remains a decisive theoretical foundation within the framework of postcolonial and decolonial philosophy. Furthermore it continues to be of outstanding importance for the analysis and handling of the current socio-political situation in the global context.

2.3.3   Thinking the resistance. Critique and resistance in the philosophical concept of Foucault and in the theories of Bhabha and Mignolo[657]

2.3.3.1   Critique and resistance in the work of Foucault

While Foucault, in the Kantian tradition, understands critique and resistance as the subject's basic task as an element of transformation of the self and society within the scope of the historical process, that is to say as *de-subjection*, post- and decolonial thinkers have developed theories of resistance and critique which discuss the particular role of the post-/colonial situation, providing both an analytical instrument and also specific models for action. Homi Bhabha's concepts of the *third space*; *hybridity*; *mimicry* and *migration* and Walter Mignolo's theory of *border thinking*; *pluriversality* and *epistemic disobedience* represent attempts to re-think critique and resistance. Do these thinkers succeed in doing greater justice to the specifics of the post-/colonial situation? Foucault's examination of colonialism takes place in various of his works; it can be viewed as the starting point for his analysis of the Occidental concept of reason. However, it is not a key focus of his philosophy. In the foreword to the first edition

---

657   This section has been published in a slightly modified form: Rainsborough, Marita: "Thinking resistance. Critique and resistance in the philosophical concepts of Foucault and in the postcolonial and decolonial theories of Bhabha and Mignolo". In: Beuhausen, Wiebke; Brandel, Miriam; Farquharson, Joseph; Littschwager, Marius; McPherson, Annika; Roth, Julia (Eds.): *Practices of Resistance in the Caribbean; Narratives, Aesthetics and Politics.* London, New York (Routledge), 2018, pp. 264–279.

(1961) of *Madness and Civilization* Foucault emphasises that the Occident's colonizing reason originated from its desire to differentiate itself from the Orient.

> "In the universality of the Western ratio, there is this divide which is the East: the East thought of as the origin, dreamt of as the giddying point which is the place of birth, of nostalgia and promises of return, the East which offers itself to the colonising reason of the West but is indefinitely inaccessible, for it remains always as a boundary: the night of beginning in which the West was formed but where it drew a dividing line, the East is for the West everything which the West is not, yet it is here that it has to seek whatever might be its originating truth. The history of this great divide is something which should be traced, throughout the whole of the West's process of becoming, it should be followed in its continuities and shifts, whilst at the same time its tragically hieratical nature should be allowed to appear."[658]

In his radio lecture *Les Hétérotopies*[659] Foucault discussed the heterotopic character of colonies, where, in addition to the economic benefits they generated, experimental fields for regulatory techniques and population policies were created and the realisation of 'perfect societies' was also aimed for. Foucault emphasises the corresponding exploitation and violence. On the topic of resistance practices in the post-/colonial context, in addition to the significance of liberation practices[660] Foucault emphasises the importance of practices of freedom:

> "When a colonial people tries to free itself of its colonizer, that is truly an act of liberation, in the strict sense of the word. But as we also know, that in

---

658   Jambet, Christian: "The constitution of the subject and spiritual practice". In: Armstrong, Timothy J. (Ed.): *Michel Foucault, Philosopher. Essays translated from the French and German.* New York, London (Harvester Wheatsheaf), 1992, p. 233. Jambet argues that the Orient's experience is comparable to that of unreason. This basic idea is taken from Edward W. Said's work *Orientalism.* See Said, Edward W.: *Orientalism.* London (Penguin Classics), 2003 [1978].

659   Cf. Foucault 2005c.

660   Practices of liberation include revolts. Commenting on their moral validity Foucault says "Is one right to revolt, or not? Let us leave the question open. People do revolt; that is the fact." He continues "A question of ethics? Perhaps. A question of reality, without a doubt." (Foucault 2002b: 452)

this extremely precise example, this act of liberation is not sufficient to establish the practices of liberty that later on will be necessary for this people, this society and these individuals to decide upon receivable and acceptable forms of their existence or political society. That is why I insist on the practices of freedom rather than on the processes which indeed have their place, but which by themselves, do not seem to me to be able to decide all the practical forms of liberty."[661]

For Foucault, the practices of freedom have an ethical dimension and are considered in more detail in the context of his aesthetics respectively ethics of existence. They are linked to the application of techniques of the self for the shaping of the self. Foucault says "Liberation opens up new relationships of power, which have to be controlled by practices of liberty."[662]

In the Foucauldian world of thought examination of racism plays a central role, particularly within the scope of his concept of power. Foucault poses the question "How is racism rooted in occidental culture"?[663] He argues that racism is linked to the general occidental culture of knowledge and the subject. "Foucault takes this idea – that racism is a kind of interface between pre-modern and modern power systems – as his starting point."[664] When doing so, he refers to a historical[665] and a biological use of the term 'race' – race, on the one hand, is related to groups with differing origins, languages and religion and, in this context, to defeats, oppression, conquests, etc.; in other words, expresses historico-political divides, on the other it is based on the 'symbolism of blood' and has, since the mid-19th century, been understood in the biological-medical sense. The divide connected with it also runs right through the middle of society. Races become, on the one hand, the 'true' and, on the other, the 'other' race. It is this opinion which, as defined by Foucault, is racist. The concept of 'cleansing' is also linked to this. In this context Foucault writes about 'race in

---

661   Foucault 1987a: 113–114.

662   Foucault 1987a: 115.

663   Magiros, Angelika: *Foucaults Beitrag zur Rassismustheorie*. Hamburg (Argument), 1995, p. 10. The author refers to three texts by Foucault in connection with the racism problem: "The will to knowledge"; "From the light of war to the birth of history" and "To make live and to let die. The birth of racism".

664   Magiros 1995: 105. (Own translation)

665   Foucault argues that this type of historiography is directed against so-called 'Jupiter history', in which the unity and significance of the law is emphasised and justice is understood as a subjugating justice which manifests schism.

the singular'. The binary divide increasingly changes to an image of unity and parasite, becoming a 'state racism' with the state as the protector of the norm.

> "Modern racism results from a decision (albeit 'anonymous' since it is an operation of power) about who can die, either directly (the Holocaust and other ethnic cleansing practices) or indirectly (perhaps not as heinous, but definitely more common than the direct forms). These indirect forms of 'letting die' include decisions about whose crime and mortality rates can be higher, who needs medical insurance, and whose actions need more or less disciplinary control."[666]

A differentiation is made between 'state-supporting' and 'subversive' race. Foucault's linking of the racial discourse to bio-politics as a form of power integrates the dispositive of sexuality. In this context he also refers to a biologisation of war. "Once the State functions in the biopower mode, racism alone can justify the murderous function of the State."[667] Foucault writes as follows on this subject

> "What in fact is racism? It is primarily a way of introducing a break into the domain of life that is under power's control: the break between what must live and what must die ... It is a way of separating out the groups that exist within a population. It is, in short, a way of establishing a biological type caesura within a population that appears to be a biological domain. This will allow power to treat that population is a mixture of races, or to be more accurate, to treat the species, to subdivide the species it controls, into the subspecies known, precisely so, as races."[668]

The racism on which National Socialism was based is viewed as a combination of sovereign power and bio-politics. Foucault writes "How can one both make a biopower function and exercise the rights of war, the rights of murder, and the function of death, without becoming racist? That was the problem, and

---

666   Stone, Brad Elliott: "Power, Politics, Racism". In: Falzon, Christopher; O'Leary, Timothy; Sawicki, Jana (Eds.): *A Companion to Foucault*. Chichester (Blackwell Publishing), 2013, p. 364.
667   Foucault 2003a: 256.
668   Foucault in Stone 2013: 365. Stone comments on this "Racism is a necessary part of biopolitics because it allows society to take on the right to kill that once belonged to the sovereign." (Stone 2013: 366)

that, I think, is still the problem."[669] Foucault furthermore asserts that biology and medicine as sciences in general have contributed to the emergence of racism since they take terms such as 'normal' and 'pathological' as their starting points. These, argues Foucault, are the origins of contemporary racism. Parallel to this he clearly speaks out against a psychologisation of racism,[670] demanding the recognition of the otherness of the other.[671] In this context Foucault rejects universalist theories of the human being which result in the exclusion of the other, forgoing a general definition of the human being. He states "This is one of my deeply held beliefs, and it can be traced back to all the disservices, which this idea of the human being has done to us for many years."[672] Foucault in general takes historically different forms of racism and historical overlays as his starting point, undertaking a historiography of the term 'race'. It becomes clear that Foucault, even if he did not specifically take colonialism as the basis for his consideration of racism, identified key aspects of this topic such as, for example, the exclusion of the Oriental from colonial reason and developed the term 'biopolitics', which are appropriate tools for the analysis of the colonial and postcolonial situation. His differentiation between practices of liberation and practices of freedom indicates that the ensuring of freedom even following liberation from colonial power structures is a challenging task linked to the shaping of the self.

2.3.3.2 Bhabha's forms of resistance

Bhabha presents an examination of various forms of resistance in terms of the cultural theory of the *third space*, itself based on the historical and current analysis of colonial and postcolonial situations. He makes clear that mimetic forms of adaptation can also be understood as practices of resistance. Mimicry as a form of behaviour on the part of those who have been colonised provokes fear on the part of the colonial masters and is interpreted as derisive criticism. It affects both sameness and difference in equal measure – "as a subject of a dif-

---

669 Stone 2013: 366; Stone cites: Foucault 2003: 366. Stone localises the classical age as the beginning of a racism linked to biopolitics – "If biopower is necessary racist, we can say that the beginning of the Classical Age marks the start of racist age". (Stone 2013: 366)

670 Cf. Magiros 1995: 115.

671 Cf. Magiros 1995: 116.

672 Foucault, Michel: "Wer sind Sie, Professor Foucault?" In: Foucault, Michel: *Dits et Écrits: Schriften: Schriften in vier Bänden: Dits et Écrits I. 1954–1975*. Defert, Daniel; Ewald, François (Eds.), Frankfurt am Main (Suhrkamp), 2001c, p. 789. (Own translation)

ference that is almost the same, but not quite".[673] The colonial master is thus presented with a mirror, in which he recognises himself as a "democrat and despot"[674] and becomes conscious that he has left his ideals far behind him. Bhabha emphasises the opportunities available to the oppressed to resist.

"Now the question emerges of how one functions as an agent when one's own possibility to act is limited, for instance because one is excluded and oppressed. I think that even in this position of the underdog there are possibilities to turn around the imposed cultural authorities, to accept some of them, to reject others."[675]

He continues

"They could now also assert their own subaltern authority and negotiate space for themselves. In this context of not simply identitary but a complex notion of a collective, non-identical agency, they were able to constitute the agency of a subjectivity, whereby it was precisely the lack of subjectivity which could open up this Third Space."[676]

Within the scope of Bhabha's concept of the *third space*[677] migration is understood as a metaphor – "It insists – through the migrant metaphor – that cultural and political identity is constructed through a process of othering."[678] Hy-

---

673   Bhabha in Sieber, Cornelia: "Der 'dritte Raum des Aussprechens' – Hybridität – Minderheitendifferenz. Homi K. Bhabha: 'The Location of the Culture'". In: Reuter, Julia; Karentzos, Alexandra (Eds.): *Schlüsselwerke der Postcolonial Studies*. Wiesbaden (Springer VS), 2012, p. 105. Sieber cites Bhabha 1994: 86.

674   Sieber 2012: 106; Sieber cites Bhabha 1994: 97.

675   Bhabha, Homi K.: *Über kulturelle Hybridität: Tradition und Übersetzung*. Vienna, Berlin (Turia + Kant), 2012, p. 13. (Own translation)

676   Bhabha 2012: 65. (Own translation) Bhabha argues that the terms 'hybridity/hybridisation' should be understood in this context.

677   Bhabha, Homi K.: "The Third Space: Interview with Homi Bhabha". In: Rutherford, Jonathan (Ed.): *Identity, Community, Culture, Difference*. London (Lawrence and Wishart), 1990, p. 207. Elsewhere he writes "In this regard we should always be conscious that it is the 'inter' – the decisive factor in translation and action, in the space *between* – which bears the lion's share of cultural significance in it." In: Bhabha, Homi K.: *Die Verortung der Kultur*. Tübingen (Stauffenburg Verlag), 2011, unaltered reprint of the 1st edition 2000, p. 58. (Own translation)

678   Bhabha in Rutherford 1990: 219.

bridities[679] develop in the interspaces allowing the difference[680] to be experienced; a difference which should not be understood as a categorising adaption to hegemonic ideas and does not presuppose the forgoing of an own ethnic, cultural allegiance in the process of constructing identity. "Metaphor produces hybrid realities by yoking together unlikely traditions of thought."[681] Bhabha selects the metaphor of migration with regard to the literary context.[682] His concern is the construction of forms of solidarity. "The fragmentation of identity is often celebrated as a kind of pure anarchic liberalism or voluntarism, but I prefer to see it as a recognition of the importance of the alienation of the self in the construction of forms of solidarity."[683] Migration can thus be understood as a form of resistance which results in new forms of cooperation.[684]

---

679   Ha repeatedly points out that hybridity according to Bhabha should not be thought of in the sense of cultural or racist/ethnic blendings but rather as a political concept of the altering of knowledge and power in which cultural and ethnic difference should be located in particular in the self and a "*Displacement and/or relocation of a hegemonic narrative*" (Ha 2004: 164) should be carried out. Cf. Ha, Kien Nghi: *Ethnizität und Migration Reloaded: Kulturelle Identität, Differenz und Hybridität im postkolonialen Diskurs.* Berlin (Wissenschaftlicher Verlag Berlin), 2004, p. 158–160. Ha demonstrates that the term is often employed in postmodern and late capitalist discourses and has become a buzzword. Cf. in this context also: Ha, Kien Nghi: *Hype um Hybridität: Kultureller Differenzkonsum und postmoderne Verwertungstechniken im Spätkapitalismus.* Bielefeld (transcript), 2005.

680   Bhabha's term 'difference' is based on the work of Étienne Balibar. Cf. Balibar, Étienne: *Die Grenzen der Demokratie.* Hamburg (Argument), 1993, p. 119. Balibar develops the concept of an 'equality-in-difference'.

681   Bhabha in Rutherford 1990: 212.

682   Salman Rushdie in particular is his literary point of reference. "To think of migration as metaphor suggests that the very language of the novel, its form and rhetoric, must be open to meanings that are ambivalent, doubling and dissembling." (Bhabha in Rutherford 1990: 212)

683   Bhabha in Rutherford 1990: 213.

684   The metaphor of migration makes clear the contradiction between the Western ideals of *civitas* and 'civilisation'; the discourse on rights and the discriminatory legal and cultural status of migrants and refugees. (Cf. Bhabha in Rutherford 1990: 218–219)

Bhabha's starting point is the concept of the ambivalence[685] and hybridity of language. In the context of a specific situation and a specific counterpart, a space for interpretation, which must be negotiated within the scope of a performative, dialogical process, is created. It can be understood as a third area of discourse, a so-called *third space*, which spans one culture or bridges cultures, whereby it also encompasses a temporal dimension.[686] Culture[687] is thus not a homogenous or homogenizing space; it is, according to Bhabha, characterised by hybridity – as an area *between*; as an area between semiotic carriers and semiotic content within the scope of which hybrid subjects develop. "[A]ll forms of culture are continually in a process of hybridity. But for me the importance of hybridity is not to be able to trace two original moments from which the third emerges, rather hybridity to me is the 'third space' which enables other positions to emerge."[688] Hybridisation must, in this context, be understood as a process – "Hybridisation is therefore for me a process, a movement and does not revolve around multiple identities – a term, by the way, that I don't much care for."[689] In this performative cultural theory the *third space* proves itself to be a *space of translation*. Its objective should be to negotiate solutions. Bhabha argues that this also results in a new understanding of theory which should reference the examination of specific situations with regard to the constellation of

---

685 "At the end of my talk, I would like to point out that the lessons of ambivalence do not stop at steadfast endurance. The experience of ambivalence also includes the incentive to speak, the urge to speak out, a way of working through the unresolved and contradictory in order to preserve the right to narrate. The most extreme forms of ambivalence – 'There is never a document of culture without it simultaneously being one of barbarism.' [Bhabha quotes Walter Benjamin, *Illuminationen. Ausgewählte Schriften* 1, Frankfurt/M. 1961, p. 271–272 ('Es ist niemals ein Dokument der Kultur, ohne zugleich ein solches der Barbarei zu sein')] – are precisely those moments that drive steadfast endurance to claim the agency of address and conversation." (Bhabha 2012: 52; own translation)

686 Bhabha rejects an overvaluation of the spatial vis-à-vis the temporal as he identifies, for example, in the works of Foucault. (Cf. Bhabha 2012: 68)

687 "In Bhabha's work the cultural is not viewed as the 'source of conflict – in the sense of *different* cultures but rather as the *result* of discriminatory practices – in the sense of a production of cultural differentiation as a sign of authority'." (Bhabha 2012: 14; own translation) The authors of the preface, Anna Babka and Gerald Posselt, quote Bhabha 2000: 169.

688 Bhabha in Rutherford 1990: 211.

689 Bhabha 2012: 66. (Own translation)

subject positions and not be related to categorising and abstracting processes. Translation can, according to Bhabha, also take the form of resistance.

Parallel to this, Bhabha's theory also represents a proposal for the handling of contemporary problems in the global context. The subject model of hybridity favours a negotiation of differing models of the self; forms of living; values and goals of different cultures which must, already in themselves, be understood as hybrid constructions and which do not have a hierarchical relationship to one another. "The time for 'assimilating' minorities to holistic and organic notions of cultural value has passed – the very language of cultural community needs to be rethought from a postcolonial perspective."[690] There are thus no innately superior cultures. Cultures should enter into an exchange; these dialogical, dynamic processes are, as a matter of principle, never-ending. In contrast to multiculturalism, which assumes the special position of a specific culture and demands tolerance of differing cultures, Bhabha emphasises the necessity of fragmentary coexistence and community which allows plurality to co-exist – *pluriversality*. Cultural difference should not be understood as cultural diversity. He calls for a negotiation of the difference in the *in between* of the *third space*, which takes the fundamental thesis of cultural hybridity as its starting point, which is not perceived as a defect or threat. Hybrid subjects are distinguished both by identification as well as difference with regard to differing identity factors.[691] Bhabha's support of diversity is expressed in a strategy for a concept of "'critical and dialogical cosmopolitanism', wherein diversity itself might become a universal project."[692]

In Bhabha's work resistance must be understood in the sense of *negotiation*[693] – "we are always negotiating in any situation of political opposition or

---

690   Bhabha in Rutherford 1990: 219. Bhabha refers in this context to the linguistic changes in the field of *gender*.

691   Bhabha makes it clear that he does not understand hybridity in terms of identity logic, but in relation to the "constitution of the subject in the field of tension between power and authority". The authors of the foreword, Anna Babka and Gerald Posselt, quote here Bhabha 2012: 62. (Own translation) And Bhabha continues: "The concept of hybridisation refers to the constitution of the subject, but it is not about the constitution of subjectivity as such". (Bhabha 2012: 9; own translation)

692   Pollock, Sheldon; Bhabha, Homi K.; Breckenridge, Carol A.; Chakrabarty, D.: "Cosmopolitanism". In: Breckenridge, Carol A.; Pollock, Sheldon; Bhabha, Homi K.; Chakrabarty, Dipesh (Eds.): *Cosmopolitanism*. Durham, London (Duke University Press), 2002, p. 13.

693   "A negotiation which recognises that the levels of conflict or antagonism are very close, not simply polarised but rather much closer and more chaotic." (Bhabha 2012: 71–72;

antagonism. Subversion is negotiation; transgression is negotiation; negotiation is not just some kind of compromise or 'selling out' which people too easily understand it to be."[694] He also states

> "Similarly we need to reformulate what we mean by 'reformism': all forms of political activity involve reformations and reformulations. With some historical hindsight we may call it 'revolution', those critical moments, but what is actually happening if you slow them down are very fast reforms and reformulations."[695]

Bhabha attributes a 'transformational power' to the subject as a matter of principle.[696] The basis of his theory of resistance is the conviction that the simplified differentiation between the ruler and the ruled must be avoided – "then you avoid that very simplistic polarity between the ruler and the ruled: any monolithic description of authoritative power (such as 'Thatcherism'), based on that kind of binarism, is not going to be a very accurate reflection of what is actually happening in the world."[697] His theory of power and authority is concerned with the negotiating processes of authority in the context of questions of power; with moments of authorisation and de-authorisation. The starting point for this is his concept of the "ambivalent nature of that relationship".[698] He asserts that there is a connection between *negotiation* and *hybridity*: "So I think that political negotiation is a very important issue, and hybridity is precisely about the fact that when a new situation, a new alliance formulates itself, it may demand that you should translate your principles, rethink them, extend them."[699] He bemoans traditionalism and immobility in thinking, demanding a re-writing of the history of the West, into which the history of colonialism must be incorporated as a counter-history. For Bhabha there is a direct link

---

own translation) Bhabha argues that the only goal of the polarising perspective is to reverse power. (Cf. Bhabha 2012: 72)

694   Bhabha in Rutherford 1990: 216.
695   Ibid.
696   Bhabha, Homi K.: "DissemiNation: time, narrative, and the margins of the modern nation". In: Bhabha, Homi K.: *Nation and Narration*. London, New York (Routledge), 1990, p. 299.
697   Bhabha in Rutherford 1990: 220–221.
698   Bhabha in Rutherford 1990: 221.
699   Bhabha in Rutherford 1990: 216.

between the modernity of the West and colonialism.[700] "The other point I'm trying to make is not only that the history of colonialism is the history of the West but also that the history of colonialism is a *counter-history* to the normative, traditional history of the West."[701] This form of writing history can also be considered to be a form of resistance. To summarise it can be determined that

> "Bhabha's turning of the term 'hybridity' as well as also of the terms 'ambivalence' or 'mimicry', can, in summary and viewed in general terms, be interpreted as figures of thought and/or metaphors which allow the resistance and ability to act of the colonised vis-à-vis the claim of the colonisers to cul- . tural authority to be theorised and discoursed."[702]

Similar comments can be made with regard to the terms 'translation' and 'migration'. Bhabha's repertoire of practices of resistance refers in equal measure to colonial and postcolonial practices. In his work a concept of resistance which views the difference between reform and revolution as being only gradual becomes visible. His concept rejects violence – as a possible form of negotiation.[703]

---

700   "I think we need to draw attention to the fact that the advent of Western modernity, located as it generally is in the 18th and 19th centuries, was the moment when certain master narratives of the state, the citizen, cultural value, art, science, *the novel*, when these major cultural discourses and identities came to define the 'Enlightenment' of Western society and the critical rationality of Western personhood. The time at which these things were happening was the same time at which the West was producing another history of itself through its colonial possessions and relations. That ideological tension, visible in the history of the West as a despotic power, at the very moment of the birth of democracy and modernity, has not been adequately written in a contradictory and contrapuntal discourse of tradition. Unable to resolve that contradiction perhaps, the history of the West as a despotic power, a colonial power, has not been written side by side with its claims to democracy and solidarity." (Bhabha in Rutherford 1990: 218) He continues "The material legacy of this repressed history is inscribed in the return of post-colonial to the metropolis." (Ibid.)

701   Ibid.

702   Babka, Anna; Posselt, Gerald in Bhabha 2012: 13. (Own translation)

703   His attitude towards violence becomes clear in his foreword in: Fanon, Frantz: *The Wretched of the Earth*. New York (Grove Press), 2004.

2.3.3.3 Mignolo's concept of critique and resistance

In Mignolo's works resistance begins with breaking down colonial and post-colonial thought structures. Taking Mudimbe as his starting point, he references the term gnoseology, which does greater justice to the complexity of knowledge in its various forms than the term epistemology. In addition to alternative forms of knowledge gnosis includes both doxa and episteme. Mignolo calls for intellectual decolonisation and border thinking: "Border gnoseology is a critical reflection on knowledge production from both the interior borders of the modern/colonial world system [...] and the exterior borders".[704] Mignolo demands a 'political and epistemic de-linking' and 'decolonial knowledges' in order to change categories of consideration and evaluation and a geo- and body-politics of knowledge. He criticises the idea of a neutral subject of knowledge: "Once upon a time scholars assumed that the knowing subject in the disciplines is transparent, disincorporated from the known and untouched by geo-political configuration of the world in which people are racially ranked and regions are racially configured."[705] He argues that the subject of knowledge is not universal, as in Descartes' theory – referencing Castró-Gomez, Mignolo writes in this context of the *hubris of the zero point* – but rather integrated into geo- and body-political configurations. "By setting the scenario in terms of geo- and body-politics I am starting and departing from already familiar notions of 'situated knowledges'. Sure, all knowledges are situated and every knowledge is constructed. But that is just the beginning. The question is: who, when, why is constructing knowledges".[706] The starting point for this decolonial thought is, according to Mignolo, the *colonial wound*. "[T]he de-colonial path has one thing in common: the colonial wound, the fact that regions and people around the world have been classified as underdeveloped economically and mentally".[707] While Foucault may take an approach which is, in its basic principle, similar, examining the construction of knowledge, he does not, however, sufficiently take into

---

704 Mignolo, Walter D.: *Local Histories/Global Designs: Coloniality, Subaltern Knowledges, and Border Thinking*. Princeton, New Jersey (Princeton University Press), 2000, p. 11.

705 Walter D. Mignolo: "Epistemic Disobedience, Independent Thought and De-Colonial Freedom". In: *Theory, Culture & Society*, Vol. 26 (7–8): 1–23, Los Angeles, London, New Delhi, Singapore (Sage), 2009.

706 Mignolo 2009: 2.

707 Mignolo 2009: 3.

consideration the link between the history of modernity and that of colonialism; he lacks the colonial/postcolonial experience. "I would surmise, following Chatterjee's argument, that what Foucault did not have was the colonial experience and political interest propelled by the colonial wound that allowed Chatterjee to 'feel' and 'see' beyond both Kant and Foucault."[708] As a result Foucault's interpretation of Kant's essay 'What is Enlightenment' is deficient, since the former overlooks the latter's localisation in the European concept of the human being. At the heart of this secular version of the theological-cosmological framework of knowledge is Western philosophy's concept of reason, with its *ego/mind* views of reason in addition to the transcendental reason of its main proponents, Descartes and Kant. Their *ego-politics of knowledge* locate knowledge solely in the soul and factors such as the body, emotion, desire, humiliation, etc. remain excluded.

In addition to this, Michel Foucault's concept of biopolitics should be expanded to include the aspect of body-politics and greater attention should be paid to colonial techniques. "Body-politics is a fundamental component of de-colonial thinking, de-colonial doing and the de-colonial option."[709] Mignolo repeatedly references Fanon in this context, whose sociogenesis demonstrates classifications of the human being and the "formation of the modern/colonial world that placed Negros on the lower scale of the Renaissance idea of Man and Human Beings."[710] Fanon emphasises the shaping of a black identity through the eyes of the white. Mignolo argues "this consideration shifts the geography of reason and illuminates the fact that the colonies were not a secondary and marginal event in the history of Europe but, on the contrary, *colonial* history is the non-acknowledged center in the making of *modern* Europe".[711] Instead of Foucauldian historical a priori or the episteme Mignolo refers to *frames* and *super-frames*, which structure knowledge, and to the "transformation of the frame of mind and the organisation of knowledge, the disciplines and institutions".[712] The idea of framing indirectly references the Foucauldian Inside and Outside and his concept of the exclusion process,

---

708   Mignolo 2009: 12.

709   Ibid.

710   Mignolo 2009: 17.

711   Mignolo 2009: 16.

712   Mignolo 2009: 6. Mignolo thus shows a similarity to Judith Butler, who also refers to *framing* without, however, taking higher-ranking *super-frames* as her starting point. The latter are comparable to Foucault's epistemes. Foucault is also familiar with structuring principles operating at different levels and displaying differing degrees of impor-

his spatial theory of knowledge. Mignolo asserts "the first World had indeed the privilege of inventing the classification and being part of it."[713] In addition to this, he points out the link between identity and recognition – "you get the idea of the interrelations between the politics of identity and epistemology".[714] Mignolo emphasises that "there are many kinds of 'our modernity' around the globe – Ghanaian, Indian, Māori, Afro Caribbean, North African, Islamic in their extended diversity – while there is one 'their' modernity within the 'heterogeneity' of France, England, Germany and the United States".[715] Taking these considerations as his starting point Mignolo calls for *epistemic disobedience*, which should result in *civil disobedience* – "Epistemic disobedience is necessary to take on *civil disobedience* (Gandhi, Martin Luther King) to its point of non-return."[716] In this context, he calls on former colonies to develop new theories and to reflect on their own culture and history. His concept of *critical/decolonial cosmopolitanism* makes clear that Mignolo, despite all his criticism of Kant's cosmopolitanism,[717] nevertheless wishes to hold onto the cosmopolitan concept per se. Mignolo, however, warns against a cosmopolitan world order which has "all the features of global imperial designs"[718] at its disposal and must be felt to be "dictated from above".[719] He prefers communal

---

tance, dimension and dissemination. Cf. Butler, Judith: *Frames of war, when is life grievable?* London, New York (Verso), 2009, pp. 13–16.

713   Mignolo 2009: 8.
714   Mignolo 2009: 14.
715   Mignolo 2009: 15.
716   Ibid.
717   He views Kant's cosmopolitan project as being comparable to the project of Christianization – "Kant's cosmopolitanism was its secular version." In: Mignolo, Walter D.: "De-colonial cosmopolitanism and dialogues among civilizations". In: Delanty, Gerard (Ed.): *Routledge Handbook of Cosmopolitan Studies*. London, New York (Routledge), 2012, p. 87. The cosmopolitan project is neither "a natural course of history" nor a purely legal project. (Mignolo 2012: 87) The overcoming of the nation-state is also not desirable. In his critique of Kantian thought Mignolo, however, neglects the former's scepticism concerning a world state, the reason for Kant's opting for a voluntary federation of states, whereby he certainly presupposes the sovereignty of the nation-state. For Mignolo Kant's cosmopolitan must be seen in connection with the project of the modern, which must be viewed in the context of the West's post-/colonial intentions. Mignolo criticises hegemonic forms of knowledge, among which he includes Kant's theory, which he wishes to break down. By doing so, he reduces Kant's project to a specific form of knowledge.
718   Mignolo 2012: 85.
719   Ibid.

forms of organisation and grassroots change. *Border thinking* emphasises the plurality and heterogeneity of the global community as a counter-concept to globalisation[720] which, according to Mignolo, is in some parts based on cosmopolitan thought. Mignolo calls for a "reinscription of spirituality in socioeconomic organization".[721] He wishes to draw on categories of thought related to beliefs and forms of living, which presuppose respect for natural living conditions within the scope of his cosmopolitanism. He wants to explode the traditional Western frame of thought – "It is first and foremost to re-inscribe in the present and toward the future categories of thought, ways of living and believing, the human respect for life that Westerners labeled 'nature' and which became detached from the 'human and culture'".[722] Mignolo characterises his form of cosmopolitanism as transmodern: "De-colonial cosmopolitanism is, in a nutshell, transmodern cosmopolitanism".[723] Mignolo's concept of resistance consists above all in changing categories of thought, including other cultures of knowledge and rewriting history. Resistance originates in transformative thinking, leads to 'disobedience' and consequently to political change.

2.3.3.4   Foucault, Bhabha and Mignolo – A comparison

Foucault, Bhabha and Mignolo are all equally concerned with the breaking down of existing thought structures of an exclusive and normalising nature. All three employ spatial metaphors in this context. In his spatial theory of thought Foucault writes of the Inside and Outside and heterotopy; Bhabha of the *third space* and Mignolo of frames which construct exclusion. For all three philosophers, resistance and thought are closely connected. Bhabha emphasises the importance of hybrid thought, which represents thought on differences. "This inability to endure contradiction, ambivalence and alterity is the point at which, as I interpret it, the banality of evil comes in."[724] Taking the assertion "You always arrive too late to an appointment with your neighbour",[725] Bhabha calls for an ethics of closeness.[726] His forms of resistance such

---

720   The process of globalisation, "the project of homogenizing the world under the will and desires of Western civilization", should also be incorporated into critical analysis. (Mignolo 2012: 85)
721   Mignolo 2012: 87.
722   Ibid.
723   Mignolo 2012: 90.
724   Bhabha 2012: 76.
725   Bhabha 2012: 77.
726   Cf. Bhabha 2012: 76.

as, in particular, *mimesis, migration* and *translation* are examples of *negotiation* as, in most cases, reforming only in exceptions revolutionary activities. His concept of resistance gives preference to negotiation processes over practices of resistance by means of violence. Mignolo develops a post- and decolonially focused epistemology respectively gnoseology based on Foucauldian constructivism, which expands understanding of the modern decisively. Although Mignolo criticises Foucault on many issues, he does not wholly reject the latter's theoretical framework as, for example, demonstrated by the basing of the theory of cognition on the *frame* and *super-frame* categories. Mignolo, however, forgoes the application of Foucault's archaeological and genealogical processes, referencing the hermeneutic processes of text interpretation and socio-historical analysis, which are, however, executed with the same objective of identifying fundamental paradigms. Mignolo calls for a pluridimensional and multidimensional hermeneutics[727] and the critical reflection of scientific disciplines, within which the processes of understanding are located, in order to solve the dilemma of *colonial semiosis*.[728] He thus elaborates, on the one hand, the theological and, on the other, the secular cosmological basic principles, "theo-politically and ego-politically founded",[729] which have structured Western thinking since the Renaissance and which were at the root of the setting of goals; avenues of approach and legitimations of colonialisation processes. In contrast to Bhabha Mignolo does not take the era of *Enlightenment* and the 19th century as the starting point for his criticism of colonialism and the links which he argues exist between colonialism and modernity, but rather the Renaissance.

Referencing Fanon, Mignolo attributes racism in particular to the hierarchical perception and thought structures of hegemonic Western cultures and, in contrast to Foucault, interprets them psychologically. Foucault locates racism in the socio-historic and/or cultural context, illustrating its function as a "mechanism for the homogenization of society and the concealment of the contradictory interests of societal groups".[730] Racism is, according to both

---

727   Mignolo, Walter D.: "Colonial and Postcolonial Discourse: Cultural Critique or Academic Colonialism?" In: *Latin American Research Review*. Vol. 28, No. 3, 1993, p. 128.

728   Mignolo 1993: 126.

729   Mignolo 2009: 18. Mignolo writes of "Theo-and ego-politics of knowledge". (Mignolo 2009: 19)

730   Magiros 1995: 145.

authors, linked to the strategies of political power. In this context Mignolo references Foucault's concept of bio-power. The incorporation of a body-politics within the field of bio-power, which Mignolo calls for within the scope of his criticism of Foucault, already exists in Foucault's concept of the disciplining of the body in the context of his discussion of disciplinary power. It is, however, further expanded upon by Mignolo in conjunction with his reference to Fanon's ideas. Foucault also integrates body-politics into the field of bio-politics, however, in terms of a specific reference to the apparatus of sexuality. Foucault, however, always considers forms of power in combination and interlinking with one another. The particular focus of Foucault's examination of racism is on state racism, which must be transcended. He views racism primarily "as a discourse, function or structure [...] thus leaving unanswered the question of how the specific subjects come to support such a structure".[731] Magiros argues in this context that there is a gap in Foucault's theory, particularly with regard to racism among the classes and the racist subject. Stone in contrast asserts that, according to Foucault, racism is a general call to resistance.

> "In Foucault's account of racism, everyone is affected. Thus, it becomes everyone's problem, opening the possibility of resistance to anyone, regardless of whether they are the alleged victims of racism or not. Everyone is a victim of racism insofar as its operations go forth without critical reflection and resistance."[732]

He continues, "Foucault offers us important ways to rethink power and politics that help us not to be deceived by false understandings of power at play in experience, which in turn leads to more effective strategies of resistance".[733] In contrast to Foucault, Bhabha and Mignolo presuppose the transformation of epistemic considerations into practical action and do not enlarge any further on this. Foucault develops a theory of self-practices which includes the dimensions of the body and behaviour. He argues that a change in thought is, by itself, not sufficient for resistive behaviour.

While Foucault repeatedly sharply criticises the hegemonic thought of the Occidental cultural space with its epistemes, categories and values, presenting a theory of racism and, in particular, state racism, he does not succeed in doing

---

731   Cf. Magiros 1995: 145.
732   Stone 2013: 366.
733   Stone 2013: 366–367.

justice to the special requirements of an analysis of the colonial/postcolonial situation as a whole. In many areas he lacks, as Mignolo puts it, a *geopolitics of knowledge*, even if he possesses its fundamentals. It can, nevertheless, be established that the Foucauldian theoretical framework of thought is, partially, the basis for the ideas of both post/decolonial philosophers or can be considered as compatible with these ideas. Mignolo thus references Foucault's epistemic basic assumption of the constructed nature of knowledge in the contexts of power and the idea of the Inside and Outside and his concept of bio-politics. His emphasis on body-politics is also completely in line with Foucault. The expansion of epistemology towards gnoseology finds its counterpart in Foucault's work in the recognition of madness as a different form of cognisance and his criticism of the exclusion of madness since the era of Descartes. Both emphasise the necessity of criticism and resistance. With his call for *decolonial cosmopolitanism*[734] Mignolo, however, goes far beyond Foucault, as does Bhabha with his only partially developed concept of *dialogical-critical cosmopolitanism*.[735] Foucault fails to present any concrete political concepts to change the world in a global context. During his phase of developing the ethics and/or aesthetics of the self, Foucault took the path of emphasising the necessity of the self-shaping of the individual to achieve change towards a society in which liberty, friendship and responsibility should be of particular importance and in which the recognition of the other in his otherness should be possible. In this context Foucault believes that a pragmatic political approach, driven by criticism and resistance, makes sense.

Bhabha's postcolonial concept differs from Foucault in particular through its cultural understanding, which is oriented to the hypertext and asserts that culture has, as a matter of principle, a hybrid character, while Foucault questions the contradiction of nature and culture in particular, emphasising their differing socio-historical expressions, each of which are defined by discursive and dispositive structures formed in the contexts of power. Both, however, have a similar understanding of counterforce respectively resistance, which is, as a

---

734 Mignolo's *Critical* or *Decolonial Cosmopolitanism* is a cosmopolitanism which should not be initiated and supported from the top down by means of the creation of supra- or transnational institutions or the changing of human rights but rather should come from the bottom up. A more precise development of this concept would, however, be desirable.

735 Bhabha and his co-authors emphasise dialogue, criticism and diversity. The team of authors refers to the relevance of cosmopolitan practices. (Cf. Pollock/Bhabha/Breckenridge/Chakrabarty 2002)

matter of principle, always possible, also for those known as the powerless and the ruled. Both theoreticians base their concepts on a relational definition of power which includes renaming; re-evaluations and slight deviations in action as forms of resistance. Bhabha's concern is to consider the coexistence of different cultures in postcolonial contexts with regard to the contemporary requirements of getting on with each other, while Foucault focuses on the social enabling of living out different forms of living in the widest sense – e.g. with regard to the gender aspect – by means of criticism and resistance. Foucault, however, does not present any concrete analysis of the colonial/postcolonial situation, although he repeatedly sharply criticises Occidental thought. His concepts in this context can and should certainly be expanded – with him and beyond him. This expansion of thought would definitely be in the spirit of Foucault.

3. Conclusion

The Kantian roots of Foucault's philosophy are of great importance for his objectives, especially for the claim that philosophy can provide an analysis of the current social situation and also influence the shaping of the future through philosophical insights – in an emancipatory attitude related to the virtuality of a possible world. The recourse to Kant highlights the primary objective of Foucault's critical philosophising: liberation from power and domination and the partial regaining of the autonomy of the individual. In this context, Foucault speaks of de-subjectification and desubjugation. Latour wishes to replace this uncovering, unmasking, liberating and courageous form of critique, which Foucault genealogically derives in his analysis of parrhesia, with a new form of critique.[1] Starting from a realistic-material attitude, it should strive for a common movement towards relevant matters. An attitude of critique which addresses things; lets them speak; does not work destructively and has a caring tendency. Beginning with Foucault, the concern for relevant things can be seen as an extension of concern for oneself and others. For him, however, the starting point would be the rehearsal of practices integrated into a lifestyle which combines concern for relevant things with care of the self – in the context of concern for others. However, seen from Foucault's point of view, it could not be excluded from archaeological and genealogical analysis and a critical view of itself. For Foucault, criticism does not lead to relativism and arbitrariness, but to commitment and courageous effort. According to Foucault, the attitude of critique is fundamentally changeable, as shown in particular by parrhesia's genealogy, since historically new forms of critique continue to develop. This openness of critique has an experimental character

---

1   "I am aware that to get at the heart of this argument one would have to renew also what it means to be a constructivist, but I have said enough to indicate the direction of critique, not away but toward the gathering, the Thing." (Latour 2004: 246)

in its socio-cultural reference. A form of parrhesia which includes concern for relevant things is therefore conceivable in Foucault's work. Foucault does not pose the question of knowledge of a world independent of humans, although he wishes to overcome anthropomorphism. It becomes clear that Foucault adopts Kant's conception of the a priori, but not the distinction between things as we see them and things as they are. Foucault ignores a world which cannot be recognised by humans and is independent of them. In common with Kant, he asserts that things as we see them possess 'a priori' structured discourses, also in material terms of reality, and are not merely spiritual constructions. Foucault proceeds from a materiality of the cultural and thus espouses an ontologically oriented constructivism which proceeds equally from the materiality and reality of intellectual and social processes and products.[2] He states

> "It seemed to me that we had never attached much importance to the fact that, after all, speech exists. Speech isn't only a kind of transparent film through which we see things, not simply the mirror of what is and what we think. Speech has its own consistency, its own thickness and density, its way of functioning. The laws of speech exist the way economic laws exist. Speech exists the way a monument does, the way a technique does, the way a system of social relationships does, and so on."[3]

---

2   "The international discussion documented here is, of course, only an excerpt from a much more comprehensive debate, which is urgently needed because the humanities have for too long been dominated by exaggerated antirealism or the various varieties of postmodern constructivism. The concept of the mind and the concept of the human being were constantly 'under suspicion', which probably led to the fact that people today prefer to speak cautiously of 'culture' or 'cultures'. But this only conceals the fact that the question of realism is also and above all of utmost importance for the humanities, since it should have become clear that human civilisation, with its historical achievements and aesthetic manifestations, cannot simply be regarded as a biochemically induced collective hallucination which, moreover, only conceals a struggle for power or survival." In: Gabriel, Markus (Ed.): Der Neue Realismus. Berlin (Suhrkamp), 2015, p. 15. (Own translation) He continues "One should not be too hasty in underestimating the reality of our minds." (Gabriel 2015: 16; own translation)

3   Foucault 2013: 36–37. Foucault also says "But what I want to investigate is the mode of appearance of actual speech and how it functions, the things that are actually said. It involves an analysis of things said [...]." (Foucault 2013: 37–38)

And Foucault also states "It involves an analysis of things said to the extent that they are things."[4] However, analysis shows that Foucault's material constructivism ultimately welds natural phenomena and the material into the cultural. Thus, his theoretical movement can be regarded as a counterpart to new realism, inasmuch as the attempt to assign greater significance to materiality and materiality prevails in the new realism in other respects as well. In new realism, however, the radicalising reversal of constructivism leads away from the tendency for the dissolution of the cultural into nature or matter, although the attempt to abolish dualistic thinking strives for something similar in both theories. In both Foucault's constructivism and in the theories of new realism, the attempt to combine mind and matter; to abolish the opposites of culture and nature and to overcome humanism and anthropocentrism is equally evident. Thus, for example, Barad's post-humanist and performative approach demands the recognition of the "dynamic power of matter" and wishes to advance to an "enlightening conception of the cultural and the natural".[5]

> "What often appear as separate entities (and separate sets of concerns) with sharp edges, in fact implies no relation of absolute externality at all. [...] It is not a static relationality, but an activity – the enactment of boundaries – which always implies constitutive exclusions and therefore also indispensable questions of imputability."[6]

Barad develops a relational ontology, according to which "a relationality between specific material (re-)configurations of the world, through which boundaries, properties and meanings are set in effect in different ways (i.e. discourse practices in my post-humanist sense), and specific material phenomena (i.e. distinctive relevance patterns)".[7] The concept of intra-action is intended to characterise this type of intervening relation. "The boundaries and properties of the constituents of phenomena attain definiteness through specific agential intra-actions, and certain concepts (i.e. certain material structures of the world) attain their meaning through these interactions."[8]

---

4   Ibid.
5   Barad 2012: 11. (Own translation) "In fact, such practices constitute the different boundaries between humans and non-humans, between culture and nature, between science and society." (Barad 2012: 21; own translation)
6   Barad 2012: 12. (Own translation)
7   Barad 2012: 18. (Own translation)
8   Barad 2012: 19. (Own translation)

According to Barad, this leads to an agential intersection between 'subject' and 'object'.[9] She describes her approach as an "agential-realistic elaboration of performativity".[10] In doing so, Barad adopts the signals of the Foucauldian way of thinking,[11] but in contrast to him she emphasises the performativity of nature, which Foucault conceals in order to avoid dualism. With regard to an adequate representation of the relationship between discourse practice and material phenomena, it can be stated that Foucault considers the material character of the discourse itself, but not the materiality of what is constituted by the discourse, such as the body, or at least not to a sufficient degree. Barad's criticism that Foucault ignored the "nature of technical-scientific practices and their profound productive effects on human bodies and the way in which these practices are deeply involved in the constitution of being human and, more generally, in the functioning of power"[12] does not apply. However it becomes apparent that a further shift towards nature, towards material things – comparable to that towards the subject – would be necessary in Foucault's thinking in the sense of a reality of the object as the 'resistance' of nature. This is a shift which is inherent in Foucault's materialism but is not taken into account to the extent required. In this respect, Foucault's theorem of problematisation would be appropriate. He states

---

9   Cf. Barad 2012: 20.

10   Barad 2012: 13. (Own translation)

11   Foucault would certainly agree with the following assertion by Barad: "Phenomena are constitutive of reality. Reality does not consist of things-in-themselves or things-be-hind-the-phenomena, but of things-in-the-phenomena. The world is a dynamic process of interactivity and materialisation through the enactment of certain causal structures with certain boundaries, properties, meanings and patterns of markings on bodies." (Barad 2012: 21; own translation) She continues "the world is an open process of materialisation and relevance formation through the realisation of different possibilities of action acquiring meaning and form. Temporality and spatiality emerge in this processual historicity." (Ibid.; own translation) "Word and world" are also closely connected according to Foucault. (Cf. Barad 2012: 27) Barad references Foucault's conception of discourse practices; her understanding of apparatuses as material-discursive practices also basically corresponds to Foucault's idea. However, Foucault does not sufficiently emphasise the reconfiguration of world initiated with them in "space-time matter as part of the ongoing dynamic force of becoming". (Barad 2012: 24; own translation) He does not resolve the emphasis on the cultural. Another commonality in the thinking of Barad and Foucault lies in their preference for a natural-scientific terminology.

12   Barad 2012: 30. (Own translation)

"Given a certain problematization, you can only understand why this kind of answer appears as a reply to some concrete and specific aspect of the world. There is the relation of thought and reality in the process of problematization. And that is the reason why I think that it is possible to give an answer – the original, specific, and singular answer of thought – to a certain situation. And it is this kind of specific relation between truth and reality which I tried to analyze in the various problematizations of *parrhesia*."[13]

It is precisely in this methodological specification that possible access to nature and matter could also be rooted in Foucault. The problematisations associated with them and which arise, for example, from natural disasters or material obstacles in the human shaping of the world, within the scope of which, for example, natural, material, technical conditions oppose human planning and action, and implications emanating from constructed apparatuses, digital products, robots, etc., allow the reality of the world to be seen as connected to culture and, simultaneously, as an independent agential force. Foucault's approach, however, stops at the analysis of individual problematisations and makes little attempt to arrive at a general, comprehensible theory of a reality independent of humans. This only theory is only seen within the scope of the constantly shifting boundary. An expansion and differentiation of the theorem of problematisation could bring the agential of nature into focus and represent an expandable approach to a theoretical consideration based on Foucault. A comparison with the utopian historical views of Kant and Hegel shows that Foucault's pragmatic orientation towards an ad hoc change in society corresponds to the model of a heterotopic conception of history – in keeping with Foucault's concept of heterotopia. His philosophy implies a social vision in which the freedom of each individual is guaranteed, thus ensuring that different individual lifestyles remain feasible. It is a model of negotiation and balancing in communicative situations. His model of friendship presupposes mutual acceptance, mutual respect, mutual goodwill and mutual support. Furthermore, the other or the others are indispensable as critical counterparts in the dialogical or relational situation of parrhesia. However, Foucault does not make any concrete proposals from a real political point of view, neither on the institutional and/or state political level in a national sense nor on the inter- and supranational level.

---

13   Foucault, Michel: *Fearless Speech*. Joseph Pearson (Ed.), Los Angeles (Semiotext(e)), 2001d, p. 173.

In this context, Kant, Bloch and the postcolonial and decolonial thinkers discussed in this book each exceed Foucault in various respects – mostly with regard to their provision of cosmopolitan concepts. Foucault strongly emphasises the importance of the individual constitution in ethical/aesthetic terms and the quality of human interaction with one another, which are required to make political changes sustainable in the first place. According to him, without this, the liberating transformations which political movements strive for cannot actually be implemented or be permanently successful. It is therefore possible to speak of a specific significance of Foucault's philosophical reflections on the subject. They are linked to human hope in his project of the possible future, which, as becomes clear in the comparison with Kant and Hegel, reveals a pragmatic ad hoc character in an emancipatory orientation and is related to his interest in Bloch. The use of an archaeological and genealogical approach in the analysis of the present reveals the dimensions of the possible, the *not-yet*, the virtuality. Foucault wishes to tread this path by using his philosophy of critique as a call to shift and cross the boundary and for permanent transformation. This is a path which requires experience, practical endeavours and experimentation with the combination of theory and practice.

The ontology of the present requires genealogical analysis of the becoming of the present in its eventfulness and, parallel to this, diagnosis of future possibilities – of another knowledge, of other ways of governing and being governed and of other self-relations. The level of *no more* and *not yet*, which is generally already visible, opens the horizon of freedom in its openness to the subject and is a guarantor of their possible autonomy as continuous work also, and especially, on themselves in the process of knowing and acting. The dimension of virtuality in Foucault's work is already provided by the assumption and historicization of the Kantian concept of the a priori as a disposition and its conception of a critical attitude as a philosophical ethos – an exercise of freedom in the sense of a border posture. It acquires a visionary dimension through the referencing of Kant's figurative expression of identifying contemporary signs for human morality and thus for the possibility of progress[14] from his historical-philosophical writings. This can also be found in the sense of Bloch's prelude to Foucault, e.g. in his analysis of the Iranian Revolution, which equally reveals dis-

---

14   Specifically, Kant's interpretation of the French Revolution is referred to in this context as a symbol of the "moral disposition within the human race". (Kant, SF, AA 07: 85) In: Kant, Immanuel: "The Contest of Faculties". In: Reiss, Hans (Ed.): *Kant: Political Writings*. Cambridge (Cambridge University Press), 1991b, p. 182.

positions and dimensions of future otherness. However, Foucault's thinking differs markedly from Kant's and Bloch's insofar as it has been demonstrated that he fails to provide a concrete vision of the future and a fixed path for the realisation of the virtually possible. In Foucault's work, the virtual[15] always remains suspended, moving between boundary and transgression, focusing on the possibility of liberating the subject.[16] Critique as experimental critique is always perpetually in motion in the sense of permanent self-criticism.

The subject-theoretical element of this analysis illustrates the argumentative position of ethics and aesthetics in the overall context of Foucault's theory. The focus of the analysis allows both an understanding of the specificity of Foucault's ethics in its aesthetic dimension, in which its socio-political orientation becomes clear, and – by means of the theorem of the empty form of salvation – its relation to the concept of the historical a priori, which makes it possible to embed ethical-aesthetic thought in the archaeological-genealogical process of historicising analysis. It is therefore also evident at this point that the subject-theoretical phase of Foucault's work does not represent a fundamental fracture, but rather a methodological and thematic reappraisal of a theoretical gap in the field of discourse and power analysis and thus a further development of his thinking. The analysis of the significance of the constitution of affects within the framework of Foucault's philosophy makes it clear that Foucault considers the emotional constitution of the individual and their bodily experiences as decisive for any change of the subject, for their liberation from power constellations, in a specific way. It is precisely the feelings and the corporeality of the human being which bring about arrest in subject modes. The emancipation of the subject must therefore go hand in hand with changes in the field of affect in the context of bodily experiences. In many ways Butler's critique of Foucault can be interpreted as a continuation of Foucault's concept, for example with regard to the aspect of mediality. The theorem of invocation

---

15   "The virtual is thus not designed to realise the potential which would allow it to become the current; rather, virtuality should be understood as a constant actualisation through which the virtual is never completely suspended in the current, but always disposes it". (Raffnsøe/Gudmand-Høyer/Thaning 2011: 354; own translation)

16   Foucault writes on this "I shall thus characterize the philosophical ethos appropriate to the critical ontology of ourselves as a historico-practical test of the limits we may go beyond, and thus as work carried out by ourselves upon ourselves as free beings." (Foucault 1997: 316) He continues "The historical analysis of the limits imposed on us and an experiment with the possibility of going beyond them." (Foucault 1997: 319)

and the vulnerability of the individual associated with it provide a concrete way to understand the ethical dimension of subject formation processes.

The contrasting juxtaposition with the power and resistance concepts of postcolonial and decolonial thinkers such as Mbembe, Mignolo and Bhabha and with Han's contemporary theory of power, which primarily emanates from Hegel, and the manner in which Mbembe focuses on the elaboration and investigation of new power strategies such as the digital form of power, reveals both the strength and the weakness of Foucault's concept of power. Han proves to be Foucault's most severe critic, completely rejecting Foucault's theory of power. However, he also references Foucault critically and incorporates his reflections on microphysical forms of power – from the starting point of a revised theoretical basis – into his concept of power. Furthermore, Han expands the spectrum of current forms of power in many respects, citing, for example, viral power and the power of transparency as critical to analysis of current socio-political conditions.

The application of Foucault's power-theoretical concept to colonial and postcolonial socio-political peculiarities also constitutes a touchstone for the question of the current relevance of Foucault's thinking. Postcolonial and decolonial thinkers still believe that other forms of power are essential today. Mignolo stresses in particular the power forms of body- and geopolitics, while Mbembe concentrates on digital as well as necropower as pivotal for analysis of current power. It becomes apparent that although, when modelling and expanding Foucault's theory, postcolonial and decolonial thinkers are critical, they do not abandon it altogether. They continue to proceed from Foucault in particular with regard to the aspects of subject, knowledge, power and resistance and in methodological terms. This nexus is of decisive importance in postcolonial situations and contexts for the analysis and resolution of impending problems, although Foucault has not developed and applied his theoretical tools and procedures in this field. He often serves as a point of reference for a critical differentiation, so that his theorems are not completely superfluous. The postcolonial context in particular requires a critical examination of the complex of subject, knowledge and power, however this must be carried out in a manner which models and transcends it. Foucault thus remains an important source of inspiration for the development of questions, procedures and problem-solving approaches. It becomes apparent that Foucault's thinking is still of paramount importance for the development of approaches to solving contemporary problems – also in a global context.

4. Bibliography

Appadurai, Arjun: *Fear of small numbers*. Durham (Duke), 2006.

Arabatzis, Stavros: "Zur Aktualität Ernst Blochs". In: Zeilinger, Doris (Ed.): *Grenzen der Utopie? Krieg der Hoffnung?: Ernst Bloch zum 25. Todestag*. Berlin, Vienna (Philo & Philo Fine Arts), 2004, VorSchein: Almanac of the Ernst-Bloch-Assoziation. No. 24/2003, pp. 102-119.

Avanessian, Armen (Ed.): *Realismus Jetzt: Spekulative Philosophie und Metaphysik für das 21. Jahrhundert*. Berlin (Merve), 2013.

Baberowski, Jörg: *Der Sinn der Geschichte: Geschichtstheorien von Hegel bis Foucault*. Munich (C. H. Beck), 2013.

Babka, Anna; Posselt, Gerald: "Vorwort". In: Bhabha, Homi K.: *Über kulturelle Hybridität: Tradition und Übersetzung*. Vienna, Berlin (Turia + Kant), 2012.

Balibar, Étienne: *Die Grenzen der Demokratie*. Hamburg (Argument), 1993.

Barad, Karen: *Meeting the Universe Halfway: Quantum Physics and the Entanglement of Matter and Meaning*. Durham, London (Duke University Press), 2007.

Barad, Karen: *Agentieller Realismus*. Berlin (Suhrkamp), 2012.

Baudrillard, Jean: *Der Geist des Terrorismus*. Peter Engelmann (Ed.), Vienna (Passagen Verlag), [2]2003.

Baudrillard, Jean: *Oublier Foucault*. Paris (Édition Galilée), Réédition de 2004 [1977].

Baudrillard, Jean: *Forget Foucault*. Los Angeles (Semiotext(e)), 2007.

Baudrillard, Jean: *The Spirit of Terrorism and Other Essays*. London, New York (Verso), 2012.

Baumann, Zygmunt; Lyon, David: *Daten, Drohnen, Disziplin: Ein Gespräch über flüchtige Überwachung*. Berlin (Suhrkamp), 2014.

Beck, Lewis W.: "Kant and the Right of Revolution". In: Beck, Lewis W. (Ed.): *Essays on Kant and Hume*. New Haven, London (Yale University Press), 1978, pp. 171–187.

Beckenridge, Carol A.; Pollock, Sheldon; Bhabha, Homi K.; Chakrabarty, Dipesh (Eds.): *Cosmopolitanism*. Durham, London (Duke University Press), 2002.

Benhabib, Seyla: *Selbst im Kontext: Kommunikative Ethik im Spannungsfeld von Feminismus, Kommunitarismus und Postmoderne*. Frankfurt a. M. (Suhrkamp), 1995.

Benjamin, Walter: *Illuminationen. Ausgewählte Schriften 1*. Frankfurt a. M. (Suhrkamp), 1961.

Ben-Ze'ev, Aaron: *The Subtlety of Emotions*. Cambridge, London (MIT Press), 2001.

Bhabha, Homi K.: "DissemiNation: time, narrative, and the margins of the modern nation". In: Bhabha, Homi K.: *Nation and Narration*. London, New York (Routledge), 1990, pp. 291–322.

Bhabha, Homi K.: *The Location of Culture*. London, New York (Routledge), 1994.

Bhabha, Homi K.: *The Location of Culture*. London, New York (Routledge), 2004.

Bhabha, Homi K.: "Foreword: Framing Fanon by Homi K. Bhabha". In: Fanon, Frantz: *The Wretched of the Earth*. New York (Grove Press), 2004, pp. VII-XLI.

Bhabha, Homi K.: *Über kulturelle Hybridität: Tradition und Übersetzung*. Vienna, Berlin (Turia + Kant), 2012.

Binkley, Sam; Capetillo, Jorge (Eds.): *A Foucault for the 21st Century: Governmentality, Biopolitics and Discipline in a New Millennium*. Newcastle (Cambridge Scholars Publishing), 2009.

Bloch, Ernst: *Das Prinzip Hoffnung*. Vol. 1. Frankfurt a. M. (Suhrkamp), 1978.

Bloch, Ernst: *Das Prinzip Hoffnung*. Vol. 2. Frankfurt a. M. (Suhrkamp), 1978.

Bloch, Ernst: *Das Prinzip Hoffnung*. Vol. 3. Frankfurt a. M. (Suhrkamp), 1978.

Bloch, Ernst: *Philosophische Aufsätze zur objektiven Phantasie*. Complete Edition, Vol. 10. Frankfurt a. M. (Suhrkamp), 1985.

Blumenberg, Hans: *Paradigms for a Metaphorology*. Ithaca (Cornell University Press and Cornell University Library), 2016.

Braun, Eberhard: "Ernst Bloch – der philosophische Schriftsteller des Exils". In: Zeilinger, Doris (Ed.): *Grenzen der Utopie? Krieg der Hoffnung? Ernst Bloch zum 25. Todestag*. Berlin, Vienna (Philo & Philo Fine Arts), 2004, VorSchein: Almanac of the Ernst-Bloch-Assoziation. No. 24/2003, pp. 187–197.

Brieler, Ulrich: "Foucault und 1968: Widerspenstige Subjektivitäten". In: Hechler, Daniel; Philipps, Axel (Eds.): *Widerstand denken: Michel Foucault und die Grenzen der Macht*. Bielefeld (transcript), 2008, pp. 19–37.

Brocker, Manfred: *Kants Besitzlehre. Zur Problematik einer transzendentalphilosophischen Eigentumslehre*. Würzburg (Königshausen und Neumann), 1997.

Bröckling, Ulrich; Krasmann, Susanne; Lemke, Thomas (Eds.): *Governmentality: Current Issues and Future Challenges*. London, New York (Routledge), 2010.

Butler, Judith: *Excitable Speech: A Politics of the Performative*. New York, London (Routledge), 1997.

Butler, Judith: *Antigone's Claim: Kinship Between Life and Death*. New York (Columbia University Press), 2002.

Butler, Judith: *Giving an Account of Oneself*. New York (Fordham University Press), 2005.

Butler, Judith: *Precarious Life: The Powers of Mourning and Violence*. London, New York (Verso), 2006.

Butler, Judith: *Frames of War: When Is Life Grievable?* London, New York (Verso), 2010.

Carver, Terrell; Chambers, Samuel A. (Eds.): *Judith Butler's Precarious Politics: Critical encounters*. London, New York (Routledge), 2008.

Chambers, Samuel A.; Carver, Terrell: *Judith Butler and Political Theory. Troubling Politics*. London, New York (Routledge), 2008.

Cummiskey, David: "Justice and Revolution in Kant's Political Philosophy". In: Muchnik, Pablo (Ed.): *Rethinking Kant, Volume I*. Newcastle upon Tyne (Cambridge Scholars Publishing), 2009, pp. 217–240.

Davidson, Arnold I.: "Archaeology, Genealogy, Ethics". In: Hoy, David Couzens (Ed.): *Foucault: A Critical Reader*. Oxford, Cambridge (Blackwell), 1996, pp. 221–233.

Deleuze, Gilles: *Foucault*. Frankfurt a. M. (Suhrkamp), 1987.

Detel, Wolfgang: *Foucault and Classical Antiquity. Power, Ethics and Knowledge*. Cambridge (Cambridge University Press), 2005.

Dreyfus, Herbert L.; Rabinow, Paul (Eds.): *Michel Foucault: Beyond Structuralism and Hermeneutics*. Chicago (University of Chicago Press), 1983.

Dussel, Enrique: *Philosophy of Liberation*. Eugene (Wipf & Stock Publishers), 2003.

Falzon, Christopher; O'Leary, Timothy; Sawicki, Jana (Eds.): *A Companion to Foucault*. Chichester (Wiley-Blackwell), 2013.

Fanon, Frantz: *Peau noire, masques blancs*. Paris (Éditions Points), 1971.

Faubion, James D. (Ed.): *Foucault Now: Current Perspectives in Foucault Studies*. Cambridge (polity), 2014.

Foucault, Michel: *The lost interview*. Paris, 1971. Retrieved August 28, 2024, from: https://www.youtube.com/watch?v=qzoOhhh4aJg.

Foucault, Michel: "The Discourse on Language". In: Foucault, Michel: *Archaeology of Knowledge*. New York (Pantheon), 1972, pp. 215–237.

Foucault, Michel: "A Preface to Transgression". In: *Language, Counter-memory, Practice. Selected Essays and Interviews.* Bouchard, Donald F. (Ed.), Ithaca, New York (Cornell University Press), 1977, pp. 29–52.

Foucault, Michel: *The History of Sexuality. Vol. I: An Introduction.* New York (Pantheon Books), 1978.

Foucault, Michel: *I, Pierre Riviére, Having Slaughtered my Mother, my Sister, and my Brother: A Case of Parricide in the 19th Century.* Lincoln (University of Nebraska Press), 1982.

Foucault, Michel: *Von der Subversion des Wissens.* Frankfurt a.M. (Fischer), 1983.

Foucault, Michel: "What is Enlightenment?" In: Rabinow, Paul (Ed.), *The Foucault Reader.* New York (Pantheon Books), 1984, pp. 32–50.

Foucault, Michel: „On the Genealogy of Ethics: An Owerview of Work in Progress". In: Rabinow, Paul (Ed.): *The Foucault Reader.* New York (Pantheon Books), 1984, pp. 340–359.

Foucault, Michel: *The History of Sexuality. Vol. III: The Care of the Self.* New York (Pantheon Books), 1986.

Foucault, Michel: "The ethic of care of the self as a practice of freedom". An interview conducted with Fornet-Betancourt, Raúl; Becker, Helmut; Gomez-Müller, Alfredo with Michel Foucault on January 20, 1984, transl. by Gauthier J. D. In: *Philosophy & Social Criticism.* 12(2-3), 1987a, pp. 112–131.

Foucault, Michel: *Mental Illness and Psychology.* Dreyfus, Hubert L.; Sheridan, Alan (Eds.), Berkeley (University of California Press), 1987b.

Foucault, Michel: "An Aesthetics of Existence (An Interview with Alessandro Fontana, 1984)". In: Foucault, Michel: *Politics, Philosophy, Culture: Interviews and Other Writings 1977–1984.* Kritzman, Lawrence D. (Ed.), London, New York (Routledge), 1988a, pp. 47–53.

Foucault, Michel: *Madness and Civilization. A History of Insanity in the Age of Reason.* New York, Toronto (Vintage Books), 1988b.

Foucault, Michel: *The History of Sexuality. Vol. II: The Use of Pleasure.* New York (Vintage Books), 1990.

Foucault, Michel: *Remarks on Marx. Conversations with Duccio Trombadori.* New York (Semiotext(e)), 1991.

Foucault, Michel: *Discipline and Punish: the Birth of the Prison.* New York (Vintage Books), 1995.

Foucault, Michel: "Candidacy Presentation: Collège de France, 1969". In: Foucault, Michel: *Ethics: Subjectivity and Truth (Essential Works of Foucault, 1954–1984, Vol. 1).* Rabinow, Paul (Ed.), New York (The New Press), 1997, pp. 5–10.

Foucault, Michel: "Friendship as a Way of Life". In: Foucault, Michel: *Ethics: Subjectivity and Truth (Essential Works of Foucault, 1954–1984, Vol. 1)*. Rabinow, Paul (Ed.), New York (The New Press), 1997, pp. 135–140.

Foucault, Michel: "On the Genealogy of Ethics". In: Foucault, Michel: *Ethics: Subjectivity and Truth (Essential Works of Foucault, 1954–1984, Vol. 1)*. Rabinow, Paul (Ed.), New York (The New Press), 1997, pp. 253–269.

Foucault, Michel: "The Ethics of the Concern for Self as a Practice of Freedom". In: Foucault, Michel: *Ethics: Subjectivity and Truth (Essential Works of Foucault, 1954–1984, Vol. 1)*. Rabinow, Paul (Ed.), New York (The New Press), 1997, pp. 281–301.

Foucault, Michel: "What is Enlightenment?" In: Foucault, Michel: *Ethics: Subjectivity and Truth (Essential Works of Foucault, 1954–1984, Vol. 1)*. Rabinow, Paul (Ed.), New York (The New Press), 1997, pp. 303–319.

Foucault, Michel: "The Masked Philosopher". In: Foucault, Michel: *Ethics: Subjectivity and Truth (Essential Works of Foucault, 1954–1984, Vol. 1)*. Rabinow, Paul (Ed.), New York (The New Press), 1997, pp. 321–328.

Foucault, Michel: *Ethics: Subjectivity and Truth (Essential Works of Foucault, 1954–1984, Vol. 1)*. Rabinow, Paul (Ed.), New York (The New Press), 1997.

Foucault, Michel: "What is an Author?". In: Foucault, Michel: *Aesthetics, Method, and Epistemology (Essential Works of Foucault, 1954–1984, Vol. 2)*. Rabinow, Paul (Ed.), New York (The New Press), 1998, pp. 205–222.

Foucault, Michel: *Aesthetics, Method, and Epistemology (Essential Works of Foucault, 1954–1984, Vol. 2)*. Faubion, James D. (Ed.), New York (The New Press), 1998.

Foucault, Michel: *Discourse and Truth: The Problematization of Parrhesia. (six lectures given by Michel Foucault at Berkeley, Oct-Nov. 1983)*. Joseph Pearson (Ed.), 1985. Reedited and adapted for the Internet in 1999 by foucault.info (info foucault.info/downloads/discourseandtruth.doc). Online: https://foucault.info/parrhesia/ (Retrieved September 10, 2024).

Foucault, Michel: "Foucault". In: Foucault, Michel: *Aesthetics, Method, and Epistemology (Essential Works of Foucault, 1954–1984, Vol. 2)*. Faubion, James D. (Ed.), London, New York et al. (Penguin Books), 2000, pp. 459–463.

Foucault, Michel: "La recherche scientifique et la psychologie". In: Foucault, Michel: *Dits et Écrits I. 1954–1975*. Paris (Gallimard), 2001a, pp. 137–158.

Foucault, Michel: "La naissance d'un monde". In: Foucault, Michel: *Dits et Écrits I. 1954–1975*. Paris (Gallimard). 2001a, pp. 814–817.

Foucault, Michel: "Pouvoir et corps". In: Foucault, Michel: *Dits et Écrits I. 1954–1975*. Paris (Gallimard), 2001a, pp. 1622–1628.

Foucault, Michel: *Dits et Écrits I. 1954–1975*. Paris (Gallimard). 2001a.

Foucault, Michel: "La grande colère des faits". In: Michel Foucault: *Dits et Écrits II. 1976–1988*. Paris (Gallimard), 2001b, pp. 277–281.

Foucault, Michel: "Entretien avec Michel Foucault". In: Foucault, Michel: *Dits et Écrits II. 1976–1988*. Paris (Gallimard), 2001b, pp. 860–914.

Foucault, Michel: "Le style de l'histoire". In: Foucault, Michel: *Dits et Écrits II. 1976–1988*. Paris (Gallimard), 2001b, pp. 1468–1474.

Foucault, Michel: "Le souci de la vérité'". In: Foucault, Michel: *Dits et Écrits II. 1976–1988*. Paris (Gallimard), 2001b, p. 1487–1497.

Foucault, Michel: *Dits et Écrits II. 1976–1988*. Paris (Gallimard), 2001b.

Foucault, Michel: "Wer sind Sie, Professor Foucault?" In: Foucault, Michel: *Dits et Écrits: Schriften: Schriften in vier Bänden: Dits et Écrits I. 1954–1975*. Defert, Daniel; Ewald, François (Eds.), Frankfurt am Main (Suhrkamp), 2001c, pp. 770–793.

Foucault, Michel: "Die Geburt einer Welt". In: Foucault, Michel: *Dits et écrits: Schriften: Schriften in vier Bänden: Dits et écrits: Band I: 1954-1969*. Defert, Daniel; Ewald, François (Eds.), Frankfurt am Main (Suhrkamp), 2001c, pp. 999–1002.

Foucault, Michel: *Fearless Speech*. Joseph Pearson (Ed.), Los Angeles (Semiotext(e)), 2001d.

Foucault, Michel: *Archaeology of Knowledge*. London, New York (Routledge Classics), 2002a.

Foucault, Michel: "The Subject and Power". In: Foucault, Michel: *Power (Essential Works of Foucault 1954–1984. Vol. 3)*. Faubion, James D. (Ed.), London (Penguin Books), 2002b, pp. 326–348.

Foucault, Michel: "Useless to Revolt?" In: *Michel Foucault: Power (Essential works of Foucault 1954–1984. Vol. 3)*. Faubion, James D. (Ed.), London (Penguin Books), 2002b, pp. 449–455.

Foucault, Michel: *Society Must Be Defended. Lectures at the Collège de France, 1975–1976*. Davidson, Arnold I. (Ed.), New York (Picador), 2003a.

Foucault, Michel: *The Birth of the Clinic. An Archaeology of Medical Perception*. London, New York (Routledge), 2003b.

Foucault, Michel: "Die Rückkehr des Pierre Rivière". In: Foucault, Michel: *Dits et Écrits: Schriften in vier Bänden: Dits et Écrits III: 1976–1979*. Defert, Daniel; Ewald, François (Eds.), Frankfurt a.M. (Suhrkamp), 2003c, pp. 152–164.

Foucault, Michel: *Death and the Labyrinth. The World of Raymond Roussel*. London, New York (Continuum), 2004.

Foucault, Michel: *The Order of Things. An Archaeology of the Human Sciences*. London, New York (Routledge), 2005a.

Foucault, Michel: *The Hermeneutics of the Subject. Lectures at the Collège de France, 1981–1982*. New York (Palgrave Macmillan), 2005b.

Foucault, Michel: *Die Heterotopien: Les hétérotopies: Der utopische Körper: Le corps utopique: Zwei Radiovorträge*. Frankfurt am Main (Suhrkamp), 2005c.

Foucault, Michel: "Denken, Fühlen". In: Foucault, Michel: *Dits et Écrits: Schriften in vier Bänden: Dits et Écrits IV: 1980–1988*. Defert, Daniel; Ewald, François (Eds.), Frankfurt a.M. (Suhrkamp), 2005d, pp. 294–302.

Foucault, Michel: *Psychiatric Power: Lectures at the Collège de France, 1973–1974*. New York (Palgrave Macmillan), 2006.

Foucault, Michel: "The Meshes of Power". In: Crampton, Jeremy W.; Elden, Stuart (Eds.): *Space, Knowledge and Power. Foucault and Geography*. London (Routledge), 2007a, pp. 153–162.

Foucault, Michel: "What is Critique". In: Foucault, Michel: *The Politics of Truth*. Los Angeles (Semiotext(e)), 2007b, pp. 41–81.

Foucault, Michel: *The Birth of Biopolitics. Lectures at the Collège de France, 1978–79*. London, New York (Palgrave Macmillan), 2008a.

Foucault, Michel: *Introduction to Kant's Anthropology*. Nigro, Roberto (Ed.), Los Angeles (Semiotext(e)), 2008b.

Foucault, Michel: *Security, Territory, Population. Lectures at the Collège de France, 1977–78*. London, New York (Palgrave Macmillan), 2009.

Foucault, Michel: *The Government of Self and Others. Lectures at the Collège de France, 1982–1983*. Burchell, Graham; Davidson, Arnold (Eds.), London (Palgrave Macmillan), 2010a.

Foucault, Michel: *Herculine Barbin. Being the Recently Discovered Memoirs of a Nineteenth Century French Hermaphrodite*. New York (Vintage Books), 2010b.

Foucault, Michel: *Einführung in Kants Anthropologie*. Berlin (Suhrkamp), 2010c.

Foucault, Michel: *The Courage of the Truth (The Government of Self and Others II). Lectures at the Collège de France, 1983–1984*. London, New York (Palgrave Macmillan), 2011.

Foucault, Michel: *Speech Begins after Death. In Conversation with Claude Bonnefoy*. Artières, Philippe (Ed.), Minneapolis, London (University of Minnesota Press), 2013.

Foucault, Michel: "Interview with Christian Panier and Pierre Watté". In: Foucault, Michel: *Wrong-Doing, Thruth Telling: The Function of Avowal in Justice*. Brion, Fabienne; Harcourt, Bernard E. (Eds.), Chicago (The University of Chicago Press), 2014, pp. 247–252.

Foucault, Michel: *The Punitive Society. Lectures at the Collège de France, 1972–1973*. London (Palgrave Macmillan), 2015.

Foucault, Michel; Sassine, Farès: "Foucault en l'entretien". [1979] 2014. Retrieved August 30, 2024, from: http://fares-sassine.blogspot.de/2014/08/e ntretien-inedit-avec-michel-foucault.html.

Friedman, Michael: "Transcendental Philosophy and A Priori Knowledge: A Neo-Kantian Perspective". In: Boghossian, Paul; Peacocke, Christopher (Eds.): *New Essays on the A Priori*. Oxford, New York (Oxford University Press), reprinted 2008, pp. 367–383.

Frommann, Anne: "Augenblick – dreifach". In: Zeilinger, Doris (Ed.): *Grenzen der Utopie? Krieg der Hoffnung? Ernst Bloch zum 25. Todestag.* Berlin, Vienna (Philo & Philo Fine Arts GmbH), 2004, VorSchein: Almanac of the Ernst-Bloch-Assoziation. No. 24/2003, pp. 156–166.

Früchtl, Josef: *Ästhetische Erfahrung und moralisches Urteil: Eine Rehabilitierung.* Frankfurt a. M. (Suhrkamp), 1996.

Gabriel, Markus: "Analytik der Wahrheit und Ontologie der Gegenwart? Der späte Foucault über Freiheit, Wahrheit und Kontingenz". In: Gehring, Petra; Gelhard, Andreas (Eds.): *Parrhesia: Foucault und der Mut zur Wahrheit.* Zürich (diaphanes), 2012, pp. 33–47.

Gabriel, Markus (Ed.): *Der Neue Realismus.* Berlin (Suhrkamp), 2015.

Gallagher, Shaun: "Hegel, Foucault, and Critical Hermeneutics". In: Gallagher, Shaun (Ed.): *Hegel, History and Interpretation.* Albany (State University of New York Press), 1997, pp. 145–166.

Gamm, Gerhard; Kimmerle, Gerd (Eds.): *Ethik und Ästhetik: Nachmetaphysische Perspektiven.* Tübingen (edition discord), 1990.

Gehring, Petra: "Foucault'sche Freiheitsszenen". In: Gehring, Petra; Gelhard, Andreas (Eds.): *Parrhesia: Foucault und der Mut zur Wahrheit.* Zürich (diaphanes), 2012, pp. 13–31.

Gehring, Petra; Gelhard, Andreas (Eds.): *Parrhesia: Foucault und der Mut zur Wahrheit.* Zürich (diaphanes), 2012.

Gethmann-Siefert, Annemarie: "Danto und Hegel zum Ende der Kunst – Ein Wettstreit um die Modernität der Kunst und Kunsttheorie". In: Gethmann-Siefert, Annemarie; Nagl-Docekal, Herta; Rózsa, Erzébet; Weisser-Lohmann, Elisabeth (Eds.): *Hegels Ästhetik als Theorie der Moderne.* Berlin (Akademie), 2013, pp. 17–37.

Goldie, Peter (Ed.): *The Oxford Handbook of Emotion.* Oxford, New York (Oxford University Press), 2002.

Ha, Kien Nghi: *Ethnizität und Migration Reloaded: Kulturelle Identität, Differenz und Hybridität im postkolonialen Diskurs.* Berlin (Wissenschaftlicher Verlag), 2004.

Ha, Kien Nghi: *Hype um Hybridität: Kultureller Differenzkonsum und postmoderne Verwertungstechniken im Spätkapitalismus*. Bielefeld (transcript), 2005.

Habermas, Jürgen: "The New Obscurity: The Crisis of the Welfare State and the Exhaustion of Utopian Energies." In: *Philosophy & Social Criticism*, Vol. 11, Issue 2, 1986, pp. 1–18.

Haggerty, Kevin: "Tear down the walls. On demolishing the panopticon". In: Lyon, David (Ed.): *Theorizing Surveillance. The panopticon and beyond*. Cullompton (Willan), 2006, pp. 23–45.

Han, Byung-Chul: *Hegel und die Macht: Ein Versuch über die Freundlichkeit*. Munich (Wilhelm Fink), 2005.

Han, Byung-Chul: *Topology of Violence*. Cambridge (The MIT Press), 2018.

Han, Byung-Chul: *What is power?* Cambridge (Polity Press), 2019.

Hatzimoysis, Anthony (Ed.): *Philosophy and Emotions*. Cambridge, New York, Melbourne et al. (Cambridge University Press), 2003.

Hauskeller, Christine: *Das paradoxe Subjekt: Unterwerfung und Widerstand bei Judith Butler und Michel Foucault*. Tübingen (Perspektiven), 2000.

Haverkamp, Anselm (Ed.): *Theorie der Metapher*. Darmstadt (Wissenschaftliche Buchgesellschaft), 1996.

Hebel, Kirsten. "Dezentrierung des Subjekts in der Selbstsorge: Zum ästhetischen Aspekt einer nicht-normativen Ethik bei Foucault". In: Gamm, Gerhard; Kimmerle, Gerd (Eds.): *Ethik und Ästhetik: Nachmetaphysische Perspektiven*. Tübingen (edition discord), 1990, pp. 226–241.

Hechler, Daniel; Philipps, Axel: "Einleitung". In: Hechler, Daniel; Philipps, Axel (Eds.): *Widerstand denken: Michel Foucault und die Grenzen der Macht*. Bielefeld (transcript), 2008, pp. 7–16.

Hechler, Daniel; Philipps, Axel (Eds.): *Widerstand denken: Michel Foucault und die Grenzen der Macht*. Bielefeld (transcript Verlag), 2008.

Hegel, Georg Wilhelm Friedrich: *Aesthetics: Lectures on Fine Art. Vol. I*, translated by T. M. Knox, Oxford (Oxford University Press), 1975.

Hegel, Georg Wilhelm Friedrich: *Difference Between Fichte's & Schelling's Philosophy*. New York (State University of New York Press), 1977.

Hegel, Georg Wilhelm Friedrich: *The Philosophy of History*. Kitchener (Batoche Books), 2001.

Hegel, Georg Wilhelm Friedrich: *Hegel's Philosophy of Mind*. Translated by W. Wallace & A. V. Miller, Introduction by M. J. Inwood, Oxford (Oxford University Press), 2007.

Hegel, Georg Wilhelm Friedrich: *Outlines of the Philosophy of Right*. Oxford, New York (Oxford University Press), 2008.

Hegel, Georg Wilhelm Friedrich: *Science of Logic*. Di Giovanni, George (Ed.), Cambridge, New York (Cambridge University Press), 2010.

Hegel, Georg Wilhelm Friedrich: *Encyclopedia of the Philosophical Sciences in Basic Outline*. Brinkmann, Klaus; Dahlstrom, Daniel O. (Eds.), Cambridge, New York (Cambridge University Press), 2010.

Heidbrink, Ludger: "Autonomie und Lebenskunst: Über die Grenzen der Selbstbestimmung". In: Kersting, Wolfgang; Langbehn, Claus (Eds.): *Kritik der Lebenskunst*. Frankfurt a. M. (Suhrkamp), 2007, pp. 261–286.

Hemminger, Andrea: *Kritik und Geschichte – Foucault ein Erbe Kants?* Berlin (Philo Verlagsgesellschaft), 2003.

Hemminger, Andrea: "Nachwort". In: Foucault, Michel: *Einführung in Kants Anthropologie*. Berlin (Suhrkamp), 2010c, pp. 119–141.

Henckmann, Wolfhart: "Über das Verstehen von Gefühlen." In: Herding, Klaus; Stumpfhaus, Bernhard (Eds.): *Pathos, affect, feeling*. Berlin, New York (De Gruyter), 2004, pp. 51–79.

Hesse, Heidrun: "'Ästhetik der Existenz': Foucaults Entdeckung des ethischen Selbstverhältnisses". In: Honneth, Axel; Saar, Martin (Eds.): *Zwischenbilanz einer Rezeption: Frankfurter Foucault-Konferenz 2001*. Frankfurt a. M. (Suhrkamp), 2003, pp. 300–308.

Hinske, Norbert: *Kants Weg zur Transzendentalphilosophie: Der dreißigjährge Kant*. Stuttgart (Kohlhammer), 1982.

Hübner, Dietmar: *Die Geschichtsphilosophie des deutschen Idealismus: Kant – Fichte – Schelling – Hegel*. Stuttgart (Kohlhammer), 2011.

Hübsch, Stefan: "Vom Affekt zum Gefühl." In: Hübsch, Stefan; Kaegi, Dominic (Eds.): *Philosophische Beiträge zur Theorie der Emotionen*. Heidelberg (Universitätsverlag C. Winter), 1999, pp. 137–150.

Jambet, Christian: "The constitution of the subject and spiritual practice". In: Armstrong, Timothy J. (Ed.): *Michel Foucault, Philosopher. Essays translated from the French and German*. New York, London (Harvester Wheatsheaf), 1992, pp. 233–247.

Kammerer, Dietmar: *Bilder der Überwachung*. Frankfurt a. M. (Suhrkamp), 2008.

Kant, Immanuel: *Gesammelte Schriften*. Vol. 1–22 edited by the Preußische Akademie der Wissenschaften; vol. 23 Deutsche Akademie der Wissenschaften zu Berlin; vol. 24–27 Akademie der Wissenschaften zu Göttingen. Berlin (De Gruyter), 1900 et seq.

Kant, Immanuel: *"The Conflict of the Faculties (Der Streit der Fakultäten)"*. Translation and introduction by Mary J. Gregor, New York (Abaris Books), 1979. (Cited as "SF")

Kant, Immanuel: *The Metaphysics of Morals*. Introduction, translation and notes by Mary Gregor, Cambridge (Cambridge University Press), 1991a. (Cited as "MS")

Kant, Immanuel: "The Contest of Faculties". In: Reiss, Hans (Ed.): *Kant: Political Writings*. Cambridge (Cambridge University Press), 1991b. (Cited as "SF")

Kant, Immanuel: *Opus Postumum*. Förster, Eckart (Ed.), Cambridge (Cambridge University Press), 1995. (Cited as "OP")

Kant, Immanuel: *Practical Philosophy (The Cambridge Edition of the Works of Immanuel Kant)*. Translator and editor Gregor, Mary J., Cambridge et al. (Cambridge University Press), 1996. (Texts cited as "KpV"; "GMS"; "MS"; "ZeF"; "TP")

Kant, Immanuel: *Critique of Pure Reason*. Guyer, Paul; Wood, Allen W. (Eds.), Cambridge (Cambridge University Press), 1998. (Cited as "KrV")

Kant, Immanuel: *Religion within the Boundaries of Mere Reason*. In: Wood, Allen; di Giovanni, George (Eds.): *Religion within the Boundaries of Mere Reason. And Other Writings*. Cambridge (Cambridge University Press), 1998. (Cited as "RGV")

Kant, Immanuel: *Critique of the Power of Judgment*. Guyer, Paul (Ed.), Cambridge (Cambridge University Press), 2000. (Cited as "KU")

Kant, Immanuel: *Notes and Fragments*. Guyer, Paul (Ed.), Cambridge (Cambridge University Press). 2005.

Kant, Immanuel: *Toward Perpetual Peace and Other Writings on Politics, Peace, and History*. Doyle, Michael W.; Wood, Allen W. (Eds.), New Haven, London (Yale University Press), 2006. (Cited as "ZeF")

Kant, Immanuel: *Critique of Judgement*. Walker, Nicholas (Ed.), Oxford (Oxford University Press), 2007a. (Cited as "KU")

Kant, Immanuel: *Anthropology, History, and Education. The Cambridge Edition of the Works of Immanuel Kant*. Zöller, Günter; Louden, Robert B. (Eds.), Cambridge, New York (Cambridge University Press), 2007b. (Cited as "Anth"; "ZeF"; "IaG")

Kant, Immanuel: *Groundwork of the Metaphysics of Morals (A German-English Edition)*. Gregor, Mary; Timmermann, Jens (Eds.), Cambridge (Cambridge University Press), 2011. (Cited as "GMS")

Kant, Immanuel: *Critique of Practical Reason.* (*Cambridge Texts in the History of Philosophy*). Gregor, Mary; Reath, Andrews (Eds.), Cambridge (Cambridge University Press), 2015. (Cited as "KpV")

Kastner, Jens: "(Was heißt) Gegen-Verhalten im Neoliberalismus". In: Hechler, Daniel; Philipps, Axel (Eds.): *Widerstand denken: Michel Foucault und die Grenzen der Macht.* Bielefeld (transcript), 2008, pp. 75–91.

Kersten, Jens: *Das Anthropozän-Konzept: Kontrakt – Komposition – Konflikt.* Baden-Baden (Nomos), 2014.

Kersting, Wolfgang: "Einleitung: Die Gegenwart der Lebenskunst". In: Kersting, Wolfgang; Langbehn, Claus (Eds.): *Kritik der Lebenskunst.* Frankfurt a. M. (Suhrkamp), 2007a, pp. 10–88.

Kersting, Wolfgang: *Wohlgeordnete Freiheit: Immanuel Kants Rechts- und Staatsphilosophie.* Paderborn (mentis), 2007b.

Kertscher, Jens: "Vorurteilslosigkeit oder Wahrhaftigkeit: Kant und Foucault über Aufklärung". In: Gehring, Petra; Gelhard, Andreas (Eds.): *Parrhesia: Foucault und der Mut zur Wahrheit.* Zürich (diaphanes), 2012, pp. 143–159.

Klass, Tobias N.: "Foucault und der Widerstand: Anmerkungen zu einem Missverständnis". In: Hechler, Daniel; Philipps, Axel (Eds.): *Widerstand denken: Michel Foucault und die Grenzen der Macht.* Bielefeld (transcript), 2008, pp. 149–168.

Konersmann, Ralf (Ed.): *Wörterbuch der philosophischen Metaphern.* Darmstadt (Wissenschaftliche Buchgesellschaft), 2011.

Korsgaard, Christine M.: "Taking the Law in Our Own Hands: Kant on the Right to Revolution". In: Reath, Andrews; Herman, Barbara; Korsgaard, Christine (Eds.): *Reclaiming the History of Ethics: Essays for John Rawls.* Cambridge, New York, Melbourne etc. (Cambridge University Press), 1997, pp. 297–328.

Krämer, Thomas: *Die Ökonomie der Macht: Zum Ökonomiebegriff in Michel Foucaults Spätwerk (1975–1979).* Marburg (Tectum), 2011.

Künzel, Werner: *Foucault liest Hegel: Versuch einer polemischen Dekonstruktion dialektischen Denkens.* Frankfurt a. M. (Haag + Herchen), 1985.

Kuhn, Thomas: "Afterwards". In: Horwich, Paul (Ed.): *World changes: Thomas Kuhn and the Nature of Science.* Cambridge, Mass. (MIT Press), 1993.

Kuhn, Thomas: *The Structure of Scientific Revolutions*, Chicago (University of Chicago Press), 2012.

Kupke, Christian: "Widerstand und Widerstandsrecht. Ein politik-philosophischer Versuch im Ausgang von Foucault". In: Hechler, Daniel; Philipps, Axel (Eds.): *Widerstand denken: Michel Foucault und die Grenzen der Macht.* Bielefeld (transcript), 2008, pp. 75–91.

Labarrière, Pierre-Jean: *L'utopie logique*. Paris (L'Harmattan), 1992.

Landweer, Hilge: "Normativität, Moral und Gefühle." In: Landweer, Hilge (Ed.): *Gefühle – Struktur und Funktion*. Berlin (Akademie), 2007, Deutsche Zeitschrift für Philosophie, Special Edition 14, pp. 237–254.

Latour, Bruno: "Why Has Critique Run Out of Steam? From Matters of Fact to Matters of Concern Application". In: *Critical Inquiry – Special Issue on the Future of Critique*, 30(2), 2004, pp. 225–248.

Löwith, Karl: *From Hegel to Nietzsche. The Revolution in Nineteenth-Century Thought*. New York (Columbia University Press), 1991.

Lloyd, Moya: "Towards a cultural politics of vulnerability: Precarious lives and ungrievable deaths". In: Carver, Terrell; Chambers, Samuel A. (Eds.): *Judith Butler's Precarious Politics: Critical Encounters*. London, New York (Routledge), 2008, pp. 92–105.

Lomar, Achim: *Anthropologie und Vernunftkritik: Hegels Philosophie der menschlichen Welt*. Paderborn, Munich, Vienna, Zürich (Schöningh), 1997.

Lyon, David: *Surveillance Society. Monitoring Everyday Life*. Buckingham (Open University Press), 2001.

Lyon, David: *Theorizing Surveillance. The Panopticon and Beyond*. Cullompton (Willan), 2006.

Magiros, Angelika: *Foucaults Beitrag zur Rassismustheorie*. Hamburg (Argument), 1995.

Marcuse, Herbert: "Das Ende der Utopie". In: Marcuse, Herbert: *Psychoanalyse und Politik*. Frankfurt a. M. (Suhrkamp), 1968, pp. 69–78.

Mares, Edwin: *A Priori*. Durham (Acumen Publishing), 2011.

Martin Alcoff, Linda: "Enrique Dussel's Transmodernism". In: *Transmodernity: Journal of Peripheral Cultural Production of the Luso-Hispanic World*, 1(3), 2012, pp. 60–68.

Mbembe, Achille: *On the Postcolony*. Berkeley, Los Angeles, London (University of California Press), 2001.

Mbembe, Achille: "Necropolitics". In: *Public Culture*, 15(1), 2003, pp. 11–40. Retrieved August 4, 2024, from: https://warwick.ac.uk/fac/arts/english/c urrentstudents/postgraduate/masters/modules/postcol_theory/mbembe _22necropolitics22.pdf.

Mbembe, Achille: "What is postcolonial thinking? An interview with Achille Mbembe". In: *Eurozine*. 2008, pp. 1–13. Retrieved August 28, 2024, from: w ww.eurozine.com/pdf/ 2008-01-09-mbembe-en.pdf.

Mbembe, Achille: "Africa and the Future: An Interview with Achille Mbembe". In: *Swissfuture* 03/2013a, pp. 1–6. Retrieved August 28, 2024, from: http:

//africasacountry.com/2013/11/ africa-and-the-future-an-interview-with-achille-mbembe/.

Mbembe, Achille: *Critique de la raison nègre*. Paris (La Découverte), 2013b.

Mbembe, Achille: "Was bleibt von Immanuel Kant?" ZEIT ONLINE, 2015, p. 1; retrieved August 28, 2024, from: www.zeit.de/2015/49/philosophie-imma nuel-kant-vermaechtnis-philosophen.

Mbembe, Achille: *Critique of Black Reason*. Durham (Duke University Press), 2017.

McGushin, Edward: "Foucault's theory and practice of subjectivity". In: Taylor, Dianna (Ed.): *Michel Foucault: Key Concepts*. Durham (Acumen), reprinted 2013, pp. 127–142.

Menke, Christoph: "Two Kinds of Practice: On the Relation between Social Discipline and the Aesthetics of Existence". In: *Constellations*, 10 (2), pp. 199–210.

Meillassoux, Quentin: "Metaphysik, Spekulation, Korrelation". In: Avanessian, Armen (Ed.): *Realismus Jetzt: Spekulative Philosophie und Metaphysik für das 21. Jahrhundert*. Berlin (Merve), 2013, pp. 23–56.

Michalitsch, Gabriele: *Die neoliberale Domestizierung des Subjekts: Von den Leidenschaften zum Kalkül*. Frankfurt, New York (Campus), 2006.

Mignolo, Walter D.: "Colonial and Postcolonial Discourse: Cultural Critique or Academic Colonialism?" In: *Latin American Research Review*, 28/3, 1993, pp. 120–134.

Mignolo, Walter D.: *Local Histories/Global Designs: Coloniality, Subaltern Knowledges, and Border Thinking*. Princeton, New Jersey (Princeton University Press), 2000.

Mignolo, Walter: "The Many Faces of Cosmopolis: Border Thinking and Critical Cosmopolitanism". In: Beckenridge, Carol A.; Pollock, Sheldon; Bhabha, Homi K.; Chakrabarty, Dipesh (Eds.): *Cosmopolitanism*. Durham, London (Duke University Press), 2002, pp. 157–187.

Mignolo, Walter D.: "Epistemic Disobedience, Independent Thought and Decolonial Freedom". In: *Theory, Culture & Society*. Vol. 26, Los Angeles, London, New Delhi, Singapore (SAGE), 2009, pp. 1–23.

Mignolo, Walter D.: "Delinking the Rhetoric of Modernity, the Logic of Coloniality and the Grammar of De-coloniality". In: Mignolo, Walter D.; Escobar, Arturo (Eds.): *Globalization and the Decolonial Option*. London, New York (Routledge), 2010, pp. 303–368.

Mignolo, Walter D.: "Border Thinking, Decolonial Cosmopolitanism and Dialogues Among Civilizations". In: Rovisco, Maria; Nowicka, Magdalena (Eds.): *The Ashgate Research Companion to Cosmopolitanism*. Farnham, Burlington (Ashgate), 2011, pp. 329–365.

Mignolo, Walter D.: "De-colonial cosmopolitanism and dialogues among civilizations". In: Delanty, Gerard (Ed.): *Routledge Handbook of Cosmopolitan Studies*. London, New York (Routledge), 2012, pp. 85–100.

Nagl-Docekal, Herta; Vetter, Helmuth (Eds.): *Tod des Subjekts?* Vienna, Munich (Oldenbourg), 1987.

Nehamas, Alexander: *The Art of Living: Socratic Reflections from Plato to Foucault*. Berkeley (University of California Press), 1998.

Nietzsche, Friedrich: "On the Genealogy of Morality". In: Ansell-Pearson, Keith (Ed.): *'On the Genealogy of Morality' and Other Writings: Revised Student Edition (Cambridge Texts in the History of Political Thought)*. Cambridge (Cambridge University Press), 2006.

Oberhausen, Michael: *Das neue Apriori: Kants Lehre von einer ‚ursprünglichen Erwerbung' apriorischer Vorstellungen*. Stuttgart, Bad Cannstatt (frommann-holzboog), 1997.

Oksala, Johanna: *Foucault on Freedom*. Cambridge, New York (Cambridge University Press), 2005.

Oksala, Johanna: "Freedom and Bodies". In: Taylor, Dianna (Ed.): *Michel Foucault: Key Concepts*. Durham (Acumen), reprinted 2013, pp. 85–97.

Oksenberg Rorty, Amélie; Schmidt, James (Eds.): *Kant's Idea for a Universal History with a Cosmopolitan Aim: A Critical Guide*. Cambridge, New York (Cambridge University Press), 2009.

Ortega, Francisco: *Michel Foucault: Rekonstruktion der Freundschaft*. Munich (Fink), 1997.

Pickett, Brent: *On the Use and Abuse of Foucault for Politics*. London, Boulder, New York (Lexington Books), 2006.

Pietsch, Lutz-Henning: *Topik der Kritik: Die Auseinandersetzung um die Kantische Philosophie (1781–1788) und ihre Metaphern*. Berlin, New York (De Gruyter), 2010.

Pippin, Robert: *After the Beautiful. Hegel and the Philosophy of Pictorial Modernism*. Chicago, London (University of Chicago Press), 2014.

Pollock, Sheldon; Bhabha, Homi K.; Breckenridge, Carol A.; Chakrabarty, Dipesh: "Cosmopolitanism". In: Breckenridge, Carol A.; Pollock, Sheldon; Bhabha, Homi K.; Chakrabarty, Dipesh (Eds.): *Cosmopolitanism*. Durham, London (Duke University Press), 2002, pp. 1–14.

Rabinow, Paul (Ed.): *Foucault Reader*. London (Pantheon Books), 1984.

Rabinow, Paul (Ed.): *Foucault Reader*. London (Penguin Books), 1991.

Raffnsøe, Sverre; Gudmand-Høyer, Marius; Thaning, Morten S. (Eds.): *Foucault: Studienhandbuch*. Munich (Fink), 2011.

Recki, Birgit: "Wie fühlt man sich als vernünftiges Wesen? Immanuel Kant über ästhetische und moralische Gefühle". In: Herding, Klaus; Stumpf-haus, Bernhard (Eds.): *Pathos, Affekt, Gefühl: Die Emotionen in den Künsten*. Berlin, New York (De Gruyter), 2004, pp. 274–294.

Recki, Birgit: *Die Vernunft, ihre Natur, ihr Gefühl und der Fortschritt*. Paderborn (mentis), 2005.

Ricœur, Paul: *The Rule of Metaphor: Multi-Disciplinary Studies of the Creation of Meaning in Language*. London, New York (Routledge), 2003 [1975].

Rorty, Richard: *Philosophy and Social Hope*. London (Penguin Books), 1999.

Rutherford, Jonathan: "The Third Space: Interview with Homi Bhabha". In: Rutherford, Jonathan (Ed.): *Identity, Community, Culture, Difference*. London (Lawrence and Wishart), 1990, pp. 207–221.

Saar, Martin: *Genealogie als Kritik: Geschichte und Theorie des Subjekts nach Nietzsche und Foucault*. Frankfurt, New York (Campus), 2007.

Said, Edward W.: *Orientalism*. London (Penguin Classics), 2003 [1978].

Santos, Leonel Ribeiro dos: *Metafóras da razão ou economia poética do pensar kantiano*. Lisbon (Fundação Calouste Gulbenkian), 1994.

Sarasin, Philipp: *Darwin und Foucault. Genealogie und Geschichte im Zeitalter der Biologie*. Frankfurt a. M. (Suhrkamp), 2009.

Sarasin, Philipp: *Foucault zur Einführung*. Hamburg (Junius), 2016a.

Sarasin, Philipp: *Wie weiter mit Michel Foucault? ("Wie weiter mit ... ?")*. Hamburg (Hamburger Edition HIS), 2016b.

Schmidt, Christian: "Kritik als Lebensform: Foucaults Studien zu Kant und revolutionärer Subjektivität." In: Schmidt, Christian (Ed.): *Können wir der Geschichte entkommen? Geschichtsphilosophie am Beginn des 21. Jahrhunderts*. Frankfurt, New York (Campus), 2013, pp. 106–130.

Schönherr-Mann, Hans-Martin: *Der Übermensch als Lebenskünstlerin: Nietzsche, Foucault und die Ethik*. Berlin (Matthes & Seitz), 2009.

Seel, Martin: *Ethisch-ästhetische Studien*. Frankfurt a. M. (Suhrkamp), 1996.

Seel, Martin: *Versuch über die Form des Glücks*. Frankfurt a. M. (Suhrkamp), 1999.

Seitter, Walter: "Michel Foucault – von der Subversion des Wissens". In: Foucault, Michel: *Von der Subversion des Wissens*. Frankfurt a. M. (Fischer), 1993, pp. 116–139.

Sieber, Cornelia: "Der 'dritte Raum des Aussprechens' – Hybridität – Minderheitendifferenz. Homi K. Bhabha: 'The Location of the Culture'". In: Reuter, Julia; Karentzos, Alexandra (Eds.): *Schlüsselwerke der Postcolonial Studies*. Wiesbaden (Springer VS), 2012, pp. 97–108.

Simons, Jon: "Power, Resistance, and Freedom". In: Falzon, Christopher; O'Leary, Timothy; Sawicki, Jana (Eds.): *A Companion to Foucault*. Chichester (Wiley-Blackwell), 2013, pp. 301–319.

Sonderegger, Ruth: *Für die Ästhetik des Spiels: Hermeneutik, Dekonstruktion und der Eigensinn der Kunst*. Frankfurt a. M. (Suhrkamp), 2000.

Stone, Brad Elliott: "Power, Politics, Racism". In: Falzon, Christopher; O'Leary, Timothy; Sawicki, Jana (Eds.): *A Companion to Foucault*. Chichester (Blackwell Publishing), 2013, pp. 353–367.

Suárez Müller, Fernando: *Skepsis und Geschichte: Das Werk Michel Foucaults im Lichte des absoluten Idealismus*. Würzburg (Königshausen & Neumann), 2004.

Taureck, Bernhard H. F.: *Metaphern und Gleichnisse in der Philosophie*. Frankfurt a. M. (Suhrkamp), 2004.

Taylor, Dianna: "Introduction: Power, Freedom and Subjectivity". In: Taylor, Dianna (Ed.): *Michel Foucault: Key Concepts*. Durham (Routledge), 2011, pp. 1–9.

Taylor, Dianna (Ed.): *Michel Foucault: Key Concepts*. Durham (Acumen), 2011.

Taylor, Dianna: "Practices of the self". In: Taylor, Dianna (Ed.): *Michel Foucault: Key Concepts*. Durham (Acumen), reprinted 2013, pp. 173–186.

Timmermann, Jens: *Sittengesetz und Freiheit. Untersuchungen zu Immanuel Kants Theorie des freien Willens*. Berlin, New York (De Gruyter), 2003.

Traub, Rainer; Wieser, Harald (Eds.): *Gespräche mit Ernst Bloch*. Frankfurt a. M. (Suhrkamp), 1975.

Walzer, Michael: "The Politics of Michel Foucault". In: Hoy, David Couzens (Ed.): *Foucault: A Critical Reader*. Oxford UK, Cambridge USA (Blackwell), 1996, pp. 51–68.

Weber, Max: *Economy and Society. An Outline of Interpretive Sociology*. Berkeley (University of California Press), 1978.

Welsch, Wolfgang: "Ästhet/hik: Ethische Implikationen und Konsequenzen der Ästhetik". In: Wulf, Christoph; Kamper, Dietmar; Gumbrecht, Hans Ulrich (Eds.): *Ethik der Ästhetik*. Berlin (Akademie), 1994, pp. 3–22.

Wils, Jean-Pierre: "Emotionen in ethischen Begründungsverfahren". In: Landweer, Hilge (Ed.): *Gefühle – Struktur und Funktion*. Berlin (Akademie), 2007, pp. 221–235.

Winnubst, Shannon: "The missing link: homo economicus (reading Foucault and Bataille together)". In: Falzon, Christopher; O'Leary, Timothy; Sawicki, Jana (Eds.): *A Companion to Foucault*. Chichester (Blackwell Publishing), 2013, pp. 454–469.

Index

GPSR Authorized Representative: Easy Access System Europe, Mustamäe tee
50, 10621 Tallinn, Estonia, gpsr.requests@easproject.com

www.ingramcontent.com/pod-product-compliance
Lightning Source LLC
Chambersburg PA
CBHW061726120626
46550CB00005B/1721